Entrepreneurship, Community, and Community Development

While entrepreneurship is widely cited as playing a key role in economic development, job creation, and advances in well-being in capitalist nations, there has been an overwhelming focus on the firm, firm founders, and founders' strategies and decision-making processes. Only more recently, the important link between communities and entrepreneurs has emerged as a new frontier in entrepreneurship research.

This book brings the emerging nexus between community and entrepreneur to light by exploring the mutual impact that communities and entrepreneurs have on one another. It focuses on how entrepreneurship development can push beyond the traditional emphasis on economic growth: from enriching the local lifestyle to building self-sufficiency; from attracting new markets to rediscovering traditional work; and from the highest tech enterprises to the most ancient crafts and trades. The authors cover a wide range of topics including rural community entrepreneurship development and culture, innovation and regional development, community-based enterprise learning, and urban revitalization strategies.

This book was originally published as a special issue of the journal *Community Development*.

Michael W.-P. Fortunato is a founding partner of Creative Insight Community Development (CICD), co-founder of the North Bay Music Foundry (California, USA), an instructor in Community and Economic Development at Penn State University (Pennsylvania, USA), and former Assistant Professor of Sociology, Engaged Scholar, and Director of the Center for Rural Studies at Sam Houston State University, USA. His professional interests include finding ways to infuse community development practice with high levels of creativity, enthusiasm, and compassion. His research focuses on how local culture and institutional structure shape local innovation, entrepreneurship, and well-being in communities both domestically and internationally; and how to enable transformation from legacy social systems into newer, flexible, more democratic, and entrepreneurial local systems that serve the public good.

Theodore R. Alter is Professor of Agricultural, Environmental and Regional Economics, and Co-Director of the Center for Economic and Community Development, at Pennsylvania State University, USA. He also serves as an Adjunct Research Fellow in the School of Law at the University of New England in Australia. His research and teaching focus on community and rural development, resource and environmental economics, public sector economics and policy, institutional and behavioral economics, and public scholarship and civic engagement in higher education.

Entrepreneurship, Community, and Community Development

Edited by
Michael W.-P. Fortunato and Theodore R. Alter

Routledge
Taylor & Francis Group
LONDON AND NEW YORK

First published 2018 by Routledge

2 Park Square, Milton Park, Abingdon, Oxfordshire OX14 4RN
52 Vanderbilt Avenue, New York, NY 10017

Routledge is an imprint of the Taylor & Francis Group, an informa business

First issued in paperback 2020

British Library Cataloguing in Publication Data
A catalogue record for this book is available from the British Library

ISBN 13: 978-1-138-08118-5 (hbk)
ISBN 13: 978-0-367-59475-6 (pbk)

Typeset in TimesNewRomanPS
by diacriTech, Chennai

Publisher's Note
The publisher accepts responsibility for any inconsistencies that may have arisen during the conversion of this book from journal articles to book chapters, namely the possible inclusion of journal terminology.

Disclaimer
Every effort has been made to contact copyright holders for their permission to reprint material in this book. The publishers would be grateful to hear from any copyright holder who is not here acknowledged and will undertake to rectify any errors or omissions in future editions of this book.

Contents

Citation Information

The chapters in this book were originally published in *Community Development*, volume 46, issue 5 (2015). When citing this material, please use the original page numbering for each article, as follows:

Chapter 1
Community entrepreneurship development: an introduction
Michael W-P Fortunato and Theodore Alter
Community Development, volume 46, issue 5 (2015) pp. 444–455

Chapter 2
Entrepreneurship and community development: what matters and why?
Thomas S. Lyons
Community Development, volume 46, issue 5 (2015) pp. 456–460

Chapter 3
Rural economic development under devolution: A test of local strategies
Jessica A. Crowe, Ryan Ceresola, Tony Silva and Nicholas Recker
Community Development, volume 46, issue 5 (2015) pp. 461–478

Chapter 4
Complex transactions: Community development financial institutions lending to ethnic entrepreneurs in Los Angeles
R. Varisa Patraporn
Community Development, volume 46, issue 5 (2015) pp. 479–498

Chapter 5
Invisible struggles: the representation of ethnic entrepreneurship in US newspapers
Leona Achtenhagen and Cindy J. Price Schultz
Community Development, volume 46, issue 5 (2015) pp. 499–515

Chapter 6
Constructing a multi-dimensional measure of local entrepreneurial culture
Nicole Breazeale, Michael W.-P. Fortunato, James E. Allen IV, Ronald J. Hustedde and Helen Pushkarskaya
Community Development, volume 46, issue 5 (2015) pp. 516–540

Chapter 7
Government and the entrepreneurial ecology: The case of Halifax, Nova Scotia
Bruce Dye and Theodore R. Alter
Community Development, volume 46, issue 5 (2015) pp. 541–558

Chapter 8
Creating and sustaining a model of community-based enterprise learning: a participatory case study of ready hubs
Tim Vorley and Nick Williams
Community Development, volume 46, issue 5 (2015) pp. 559–579

Chapter 9
Creating entrepreneurial communities: building community capacity for ecosystem development
Deborah M. Markley, Thomas S. Lyons and Donald W. Macke
Community Development, volume 46, issue 5 (2015) pp. 580–598

Notes on Contributors

Leona Achtenhagen is Professor in Entrepreneurship and Business Development, Jönköping International Business School, Media Management and Transformation Centre, Jönköping University, Sweden.

James E. Allen IV is Research Director at the Community and Economic Development Initiative of Kentucky, University of Kentucky, USA.

Theodore R. Alter is Professor of Agricultural, Environmental and Regional Economics, and Co-Director of the Center for Economic and Community Development, Pennsylvania State University, USA.

Nicole Breazeale is Assistant Professor of Sociology at the Department of Sociology, Western Kentucky University, USA.

Ryan Ceresola is Assistant Professor at Hartwick College in Oneonta, New York, USA.

Jessica A. Crowe is Assistant Professor at the Department of Sociology, Southern Illinois University Carbondale, USA.

Bruce Dye is studying for a Doctorate of Social Science in Human Resource Development at the School of Management, University of Leicester, UK.

Michael W.-P. Fortunato is a founding partner of Creative Insight Community Development (CICD), co-founder of the North Bay Music Foundry (California, USA), and instructor in Community and Economic Development at Penn State University (Pennsylvania, USA).

Ronald J. Hustedde is Extension Professor at the Department of Community and Leadership Development, University of Kentucky, USA.

Thomas S. Lyons is Field Family Chair in Entrepreneurship and Professor of Management at Baruch College, The City University of New York, USA.

Donald W. Macke is Community Innovation Fellow at the Center for Rural Entrepreneurship, Lincoln, Nebraska, USA.

Deborah M. Markley is co-founder and managing director of the Center for Rural Entrepreneurship, Lincoln, Nebraska, USA.

R. Varisa Patraporn is Assistant Professor in Sociology at California State University, USA.

Cindy J. Price Schultz is Associate Professor of Communication and Journalism, University of Wyoming, USA.

Helen Pushkarskaya is Associate Research Scientist in Comparative Medicine at Yale School of Medicine, USA.

Nicholas Recker is a Professor in the Department of Sociology, Metropolitan State University of Denver, USA.

Tony Silva is a doctoral student at the Department of Sociology, Southern Illinois University Carbondale, USA.

Tim Vorley is Professor of Entrepreneurship at the Centre for Regional Economic and Enterprise Development, University of Sheffield, UK.

Nick Williams is Associate Professor of Enterprise and and Entrepreneurship Studies at Leeds University Business School, UK.

Community entrepreneurship development: an introduction

Michael W-P Fortunato and Theodore Alter

An emerging area of scholarship can be found at the nexus between entrepreneurship and community development. Beyond a mere focus on firms and their contributions, this growing nexus in the literature seeks to understand the complex ways that entrepreneurs benefit their communities, and that communities enhance or inhibit entrepreneurship. This exploration is fundamentally economic, sociological, psychological, strategic, behavioral, and cultural; it should incorporate many contributions of scholars across a wide range of disciplines. This introductory article examines the current state of research at the nexus of community and entrepreneurship, and conceptually positions entrepreneurship as deeply embedded in – and inseparable from – community, social, and economic structures. The article presents community entrepreneurship development as a multidimensional and challenging strategy economically speaking, but one that produces many benefits beyond economic growth. The article discusses both the challenges and benefits of promoting entrepreneurship in the community, presents the articles comprising the special issue, and ends with a call to action and scholarship in this exciting conceptual space.

Introduction to community entrepreneurship development

It is a privilege to present this special issue of *Community Development* on a topic that, the guest editors believe, deserves ongoing attention in the academic literature: community entrepreneurship development. Entrepreneurship continues to be a popular topic in the academic literature due to a growing fascination with many contributions of entrepreneurs to the broader community and economy. Entrepreneurs are widely considered to be an economic growth engine, catalysts of change and innovation, and often times powerful contributors to the local society (Baumol, Litan, & Schramm, 2007; Schumpeter, 1934). Naturally, community developers are paying increased attention to entrepreneurship because it is widely cited as playing a key role in economic development, job creation, and advances in well-being in capitalist nations (Baumol et al., 2007). Seventy-nine percent of Americans say that entrepreneurs are more important to job creation and the economy than big business, scientists, and the government (Kauffman Foundation, 2009a), and between 1980 and 2005, all net job growth in the United States was due to firms less than five years old (Kauffman Foundation, 2009b). Viewed through this lens, not much has changed since Schumpeter (1934) declared that the entrepreneur is the central player driving economic development.

Research on entrepreneurship fills many academic journals, some of which are dedicated exclusively to entrepreneurship (and more are appearing every few years). A large portion of this literature focuses tightly on the traditional locus of entrepreneurial control: the firm, firm founders, and founders' strategies and decision-making processes. This focus likely exists for two reasons. One is cultural: the highly individualistic culture of the industrialized West mythicizes, even glorifies, the heroic attempts of entrepreneurs who create value for others using their creativity, resourcefulness, and managerial prowess (Drakopoulou Dodd & Anderson, 2007; Nijkamp, 2003; Schumpeter, 1934). The other is historical: entrepreneurship, as a field of study, never really had a home. Its roots can be found in economics, management, social and behavioral psychology, marketing, and even bits of sociology (Low & MacMillan, 1988). In each field, the entrepreneur is viewed as somewhat of a productive deviant, whose counter-intuitive actions break from established cultural pathways to produce immense value for others. Think of an entrepreneur who leaves a perfectly good job and gets a second mortgage on the family home to produce and market a new carpet cleaning tool. To many, this shirking of stability sounds like frivolous madness, but certainly not to any entrepreneur committed to an idea about which they are passionate. Studies from many fields have been committed to understanding why a few brave individuals take on enormous risks to chase a dream, and why some succeed while others flounder. The failure of each field of study to completely and adequately describe the entrepreneur is well recognized (Davidsson, 2009; Low & MacMillan, 1988), which may be why research on this elusive, diverse economic actor continues to coalesce into a rather confusing, complex pastiche of creative, risk-bearing, venture-launching behaviors.

Only more recently, the link between *communities* and *entrepreneurs* has also emerged as a new frontier in entrepreneurship research (Lyons, Alter, Audretsch, & Augustine, 2012). This perspective builds on the scholarship of social scientists observing that culture, local and state policy, social and physical infrastructure, and even the level of social interaction deeply influence entrepreneurial behavior. In fact, the social structure of communities may be a critical antecedent to entrepreneurial action by producing culturally supported relationships for sharing opportunistic information, collaborating for the benefit of the community or region, and creating an ecosystem that supports small businesses (Fortunato & Alter, 2011; Julien, 2007). The idea that economic action is deeply influenced by both society and policy is not a new one (Baumol, 1968; Granovetter, 1985), and there is a wealth of knowledge on the impact of both culture and policy on entrepreneurship rates and entrepreneurial attitudes (see the Global Entrepreneurship Monitor, Amorós & Bosma, 2014, for a major longitudinal example). The idea that culture may have just as profound an impact at the sub-national level – or even at the local level – is an idea that is likely to resonate deeply with scholars of community. The community is where we as humans get our first introduction to human society beyond our own family (Wilkinson, 1991). The impacts of culture within that society can therefore fundamentally shape our perception of reality, what is valued, and what is honorable (Berger & Luckmann, 1966; Dana, 1995; Dana & Dana, 2005). It begs an important question: Can the culture, structure, and institutions of community profoundly impact whether or not entrepreneurship is valued? Can entrepreneurs conversely shape and impact the communities around them, for better or for worse? Perhaps the community is not only the next frontier for entrepreneurship research, as Lyons et al. (2012) suggest. Perhaps entrepreneurship is also an emerging and growing new frontier for community research as well.

If the community is indeed the next frontier of entrepreneurship research (or vice versa), and if entrepreneurs are an important key to healthy and vibrant local communities, then this brings the complicated nexus between the entrepreneur and the community into full view. Complicated, because both the terms "entrepreneur" and "community" have discordant, messy, evolving, and multifaceted definitions across the literature – and even across different academic fields. The link between entrepreneurship and community development is not, therefore, straight forward and linear. Entrepreneurs are a widely diverse group – perhaps as diverse as the businesses that they launch (Davidsson, 2009; Gartner, 1989). One could even say that entrepreneurs are as diverse as communities, and for readers of this journal, the diversity of perspectives on community represented in these pages over the years has been wonderfully immense. For this same reason, it is nearly impossible to isolate entrepreneurs as a type of individual or a set of specific traits found in a person (Davidsson, 2009; Gartner, 1989). If anything, entrepreneurship is a series of *behaviors* that are bounded, guided, enhanced, and restricted by the social, economic, and environmental context in which entrepreneurs find themselves (Julien, 2007; Shane, 2003).

This brings us to a special nexus in the literature that inspired this special issue: community entrepreneurship development. It is the study of how communities shape entrepreneurial action at the local and regional level through culture, leadership, institutions, policies, histories and narratives, and beliefs about what is possible. It is conversely the study of how entrepreneurs impact their communities – not just by creating jobs and increasing revenue, but by meeting unmet needs, solving local problems inclusively and holistically, resolving uncertainty, reviving the spirit of the past and/or future, giving back to the community: any impact, really, that entrepreneurs can make in order to make life better. This special issue is a call to research and action in entrepreneurship that, we hope, captures the nexus between entrepreneurship and the community in all its glorious messiness. It is an important opportunity to revisit the complex interaction between communities and entrepreneurs in the literature by presenting some of the latest scholarship available in this conceptual space. Most importantly, the guest editors hope that this issue sparks an ongoing discussion that pushes the boundaries of traditional entrepreneurship scholarship, leading to new theories grounded in understandings that span the Community Development Society family. The special issue thus embraces research from a wide variety of conceptual backgrounds, and also varied methodological traditions, including qualitative, quantitative, mixed method, and robust case study approaches.

This introductory article next attempts to illuminate the conceptual nexus between the entrepreneur and the community in the literature. Two important questions will be explored. Do communities catalyze growth, development, or both? Are communities supporting or leading players in cultivating entrepreneurial action? The examination of these two questions provides insights into the complex relationship between entrepreneurs and their surrounding community – with clues about how entrepreneurship can be supported more effectively at the local and regional level. The article ends by examining several of the benefits of entrepreneurship development beyond economic development, and focusing on how entrepreneurship can be a catalyst for improving overall community well-being. Finally, the outline of the special issue is presented, and the guest editors call readers of this special issue to action and scholarship following this important and multidimensional discussion.

Entrepreneurs and the community

Before delving into the contents of the special issue, a bit of background is warranted. Entrepreneurship can be a deceptively simple topic. A favorite community engagement exercise of the guest editors is to ask a room of community members to raise their hand if they know what the term "entrepreneurship" means. Nearly every hand shoots up. Then, participants are asked to write down their definition of entrepreneurship, and pass it to the front to be read aloud. Naturally, the answers are wonderfully – even hilariously – diverse, and of course they would be! Entrepreneurship is a concept that most people grasp viscerally, but who is an entrepreneur, really? Is entrepreneurship about Silicon Valley-style, high-growth tech businesses? Is it about mom and pop boutique stores? Do entrepreneurs have to be in the community to have an impact? What about someone who launches a "non-business," like a new club or program that serves the public good? How about entrepreneurial thinkers in existing organizations, or people in governments and nonprofits that launch new projects? All of these ideas are likely to appear, sometimes putting famous entrepreneurs like Mark Zuckerberg of Facebook at the same entrepreneur's cocktail party as Cynthia from Cynthia's Lawn Care in rural Missouri. How can we talk about entrepreneurship development when so many people have a different idea of what the target of that development should be? This can lead to some interesting discussion and even conflict, as some community members may value some types of entrepreneurship over others ("we should be focusing on high growth business, not little dinky mom and pops"). Or conversely, what some community members consider entrepreneurial may not seem very innovative at all ("what we really need in this town are healthier school lunches").

Behind this diversity are different social and cultural values about who entrepreneurs are and how they are supposed to behave. If one sees entrepreneurs as a critical engine for economic growth above all other things, a focus on supporting small, existing businesses might seem like a waste of time and money. To others, if simply expanding the entrepreneurial mindset of current residents is an important goal, empowering local residents with knowledge about how to solve local problems and "launch new stuff," then education and mentorship should be central. A focus on growth-oriented entrepreneurship may even seem completely out of line. The financial and institutional supports necessary for supporting an emerging biotech sector (skilled labor, high-tech facilities, links to research institutions) are vastly different from those supporting a new community supported agriculture initiative (latent demand, available land, organic agriculture knowledge) or a new river walk district (available real estate with frontage, shoreline improvements, retail consulting, a river). Merely supporting entrepreneurship as an economic development tool can lead to a great deal of local conflict, as the varied expectations of the underlying term can lead to confusion and disappointment about who gets supported, and what the outcome should be.

In our observations, there are two common narratives that appear regularly in both the practitioner and academic literature about the link between entrepreneurship and economic development. Each presents an opportunity to examine the nexus between entrepreneurs and communities through a different lens.

Are entrepreneurs catalysts of growth, development, or both?

One common narrative found in the economic development literature is the idea that entrepreneurship is being rediscovered as a way to catalyze economic and employment growth and wealth creation (Acs, 2006; Baumol et al., 2007; Wennekers & Thurik, 1999).

This narrative has emerged as industrial recruitment is increasingly viewed as a lackluster strategy – one that is unlikely for many rural and economically troubled communities (Mayer & Knox, 2006; Turner, 2003). It is easy to view entrepreneurs as economic heroes who can create massive value, even in the depths of a recession (Fairlie, 2013; Shane, 2011). In an economic climate where industrial recruitment is increasingly viewed as a failing strategy, who would not want to capture the creative growth potential of entrepreneurs within their own community? It is a promising narrative, but as we will argue shortly, it is an incomplete one.

In times of high economic uncertainty, and with the continued influx of capital, resources, and talent into high growth areas, many communities struggle to reinvent themselves. There is high pressure to attract new strategies for job creation that do not rely on outdated methods of industrial recruitment. Simultaneously, much of the literature focuses on what makes *firms* successful, rather than what makes *communities* successful. And, it is increasingly clear that high-tech, high-growth strategies that work in Silicon Valley, CA are not appropriate for many communities, with the exception of a few knowledge- and capital-intensive metropolitan areas (see Fortunato, 2014 for a fuller argument of this point). There continues to be a need to explore what entrepreneurship development can really do for communities beyond the traditional focus on economic growth: from enriching the local lifestyle to building self-sufficiency; from attracting new markets to rediscovering traditional work; from the highest tech enterprises to the most ancient crafts and trades.

Entrepreneurship as a development strategy is neither as easy nor as successful as it appears on the surface – and the biggest and best returns on this strategy often have nothing to do with traditional growth. Entrepreneurs are largely responsible for job growth in the aggregate (Kauffman Foundation, 2009b), but this does not mean that all entrepreneurs are equally successful, or have an equivalent impact on local society. Research has concluded that most high-growth entrepreneurship tends to be clustered around urban areas (Acs & Armington, 2006) or around major research institutions (Audretsch & Lehmann, 2005). Growth-oriented firms are not only spatially concentrated in some places (and virtually absent from others) (Acs & Mueller, 2008), overall, only a very small percentage of firms create enough jobs to have a major impact on economic development that could rival industrial recruitment (Henrekson & Johansson, 2010). "Gazelles," or high-growth startups, typically start growing quickly when they have between 50 and 200 employees (Acs & Mueller, 2008): a high bar for some smaller communities to meet. Put simply, supporting entrepreneurs exclusively for their growth potential is similar to supporting race horses based solely on their winning potential. Not every horse is going to win every time, some horses never win, and it may take years for some horses to develop into true champions. It is a strategy that requires incredible patience over time, and the results are far from certain. It misclassifies many horses as failures just because they are not born to race, irrespective of their other talents and contributions. Such an economic development strategy may be wholly inappropriate given the culture, history, and values of the surrounding community.

In communities as in organizations, culture impacts strategy (Hustedde, 2007). If economic and community development policy uses traditional business strategies and means to support entrepreneurs, entrepreneurship, and entrepreneurial development while ignoring culture, that strategy will likely fail or at best achieve sub-optimal performance. Residents understand the history of their community, the narratives that shape their sense of place, the nature of their relationships with each other, their ability to participate in collective decisions affecting the community, the interpersonal and collective dynamics of power, and other such matters. How these understandings affect perspectives on future opportunities and thus impact strategy and its implementation in all domains goes beyond economic development strategy. Entrepreneurship as an economic development strategy needs to focus on relationship and community development as much as it concentrates on technology innovation, business plans, management fads, marketing strategies, and jobs and income. The point is not to focus on one or the other but to take a more holistic and pluralistic approach than is reflected typically in local and regional economic development policy. The result is a broadening view of the contributions of entrepreneurs beyond mere economic growth, opening the field to the myriad ways that entrepreneurs contribute to human well-being.

Are communities supporting or leading players?

A second common narrative has to do with how entrepreneurship is supposed to work, and the roles played by entrepreneurs and by the community. In a more traditional view of the firm, entrepreneurs are individuals who are capable of reallocating existing resources to find more efficient outcomes (the Marshallian view, or "doing more with less") (Marshall, 1997). Or, entrepreneurs might make step-wise, incremental innovations that advance upon other existing technologies (the Kirznerian view, or "building a better mousetrap") (Kirzner, 1978). Or, in some cases, entrepreneurs might discover something so revolutionary that they create a rift in the current market space, causing old firms to become obsolete and new markets to appear (the Schumpeterian view, or "creative destruction") (Schumpeter, 1934; also see van Praag, 1999 for a discussion of the contributions of these and other entrepreneurial theorists in context). In any of these cases, the centerpiece of the entrepreneurial equation is the entrepreneur, or more broadly, the entrepreneurial firm, where profit is a primary motivator for innovating competitively and taking on risk (Casson, 2005). Several scholars, including Shane (2003), have noted the importance of the entrepreneur's environment in structuring opportunistic action (i.e. having good access to information, resources, suppliers, buyers, and so on). An entrepreneur's networks, made available through a supportive environment rich with weak ties, can produce information critical to recognizing and exploiting opportunities (Aldrich & Zimmer, 1986; Granovetter, 1973; Shane, 2003). Although the entrepreneur's environment plays a crucial role in firm creation and growth in the traditional view, the entrepreneur is still, undoubtedly, the actor in the spotlight. That makes sense: entrepreneurs are the ones starting the business after all, not their friends and neighbors. This view does not say much about the role the community plays in an entrepreneur's life. There is a clear recognition that culture is more than just context, but this relegates the community (and community developers) to more of a supportive role, when in reality, entire communities are capable of supporting entrepreneurship.

New research is emerging each year challenging traditional conventions about entrepreneurs, who they are, how they create value, and the kinds of impacts they are having on communities. A more community-oriented view of entrepreneurship sees the process of venturing not uniquely as a strategic behavior, but as holistic and humanistic – just like community life itself. This idea has deep roots in behavioral economics (Schmid, 2008) and institutional sociology (Granovetter, 1985), whereby too narrow a focus on individual, rational action produces an undersocialized view of society. The reality is far messier. Entrepreneurs are real people with real problems, real life circumstances, and real ideas – favoring a complex view of the interactions between firm and society over a profit-oriented, individualistic view of *homo œconomicus*. Communities may likewise support or discourage entrepreneurship in very subtle, often conflicting ways. A simple example might be a city council that prefers to invest in tax abatements to attract large businesses and national chains to a community, or the failure to include small business owners effectively at the Chamber of Commerce, or the cultural habit of referring to would-be entrepreneurs as "crazies" whose ideas will never work. Alternatively, communities could start a buy local campaign, feature local entrepreneurs prominently in local news, or step out on a limb and launch a co-working incubator space. These forces are acting upon local societies all the time, opening doors to entrepreneurship for some, closing doors for others.

Entrepreneurs are, as with all of us, immersed in a web of human relationships, interdependencies, and power that can be observed at the community level. Entrepreneurs both shape and are shaped by this web. The nature of those interdependencies creates different types of opportunities that are a function of particular situations in particular places. In fact, these opportunities are culturally situated, and change from place to place, even shaping whether or not entrepreneurship is valued, or whether people become entrepreneurs in the first place (Dana, 1995; Fortunato & Alter, in press).

Additionally, socially constructed formal and informal cultural "rules" (i.e. anything from cultural norms through formal, written policy) existing in those particular places at points in time and over time (Schmid, 2008) are critical to understanding entrepreneurial behavior and performance. Entrepreneurship does not occur in a vacuum, and it is certainly not just about the individual. Entrepreneurs are embedded in this dynamic web of relationships, and must be understood in this context (Granovetter, 1985). A focus on the heroic qualities of the entrepreneur, and his/her behaviors and strategies alone without a deep understanding of the society that helped to produce and support that entrepreneur, is insufficient. The field of entrepreneurship continues to witness a deep transition from thinking about entrepreneurship as an individualistic effort, supported by community actors – toward one that sees entrepreneurship as a socially embedded, community-wide effort where many actors can contribute. The business literature calls this an entrepreneurial ecosystem, which has little to do with individuals, and everything to do with the shared culture among them (Feld, 2012). Put simply, to have an innovative, entrepreneurial community requires having an innovative, entrepreneurial society that is willing to value and support entrepreneurial action (Julien, 2007).

Communities (or ecosystems) support entrepreneurs and entrepreneurship not just on a functional level (e.g. access to capital via banks, local tax and land use policy, availability of reasonable financing options), but also on a relational level. Relationships (the nature of the community field as noted by Wilkinson (1991)) matter to the extent they do or do not foster an enabling setting supporting entrepreneurs and entrepreneurship. Entrepreneurs need each other, and they need other people from other sectors of the economy and society (Fortunato & Alter, 2011). All are a source of differing views, ideas, and approaches. At this intersection of difference is opportunity for learning, creativity, innovation, and entrepreneurship. Competition is important, but it is not the necessary condition for economic growth and development. Collaboration, a byproduct of community, is the key: to fuel growth and development, to unlock entrepreneurial opportunity and success, and to understanding and taking advantage of collaboration. In fact, at the individual and community level, creativity, innovation, growth, and development can be energized through collaboration because of the intersection of differing ideas that such boundary spanning entails. Collaboration holds the promise of positive sum outcomes for all individuals and communities, and is different from a narrow competition mindset, which connotes tradeoffs within an unchanged resource endowment, and thus negative or at best zero sum outcomes for some interests, individuals, and/or communities. Interaction among entrepreneurs may matter even more to stimulating entrepreneurship locally than their interactions with local leaders (Fortunato & McLaughlin, 2012), demonstrating a unique sense of community among entrepreneurs even within the broader community. In this view, it is hard to relegate the importance of the community to a supporting role when both individual and collective imagination and creativity matter in supporting innovation and entrepreneurship!

A call to create many creative paths forward

In the spirit of imagination and creativity, this special issue also serves as a formal call to action and publicly engaged scholarship about community entrepreneurship development. This area of inquiry goes well beyond a reductionist focus on economic growth, seeking to explore the broad range of the unsung benefits of entrepreneurship to communities everywhere. A comprehensive list of these benefits does not, and cannot, exist – innovative entrepreneurs and scholars will only find more. The following brief list is submitted by the guest editors as a starting point for scholarly discussion.

(1) Entrepreneurship does not only improve local economies, it influences local well-being as well (Tolbert, Irwin, Lyson, & Nucci, 2002).
(2) Entrepreneurship, particularly social entrepreneurship, provides a pathway to local problem solving (Alvord, Brown, & Letts, 2004).
(3) Over time, entrepreneurship can provide some sustainable job creation and retention, even if small in scale (Henrekson & Johansson, 2010; Thurik & Wennekers, 2004).
(4) Entrepreneurs have the power to diversify away from older industries, and therefore can diversify the local economic base (Clark, 2009; Nickerson, Black, & McCool, 2001).
(5) Entrepreneurship can empower local citizens with greater control of their financial future, especially among marginalized groups (Oviawe, 2010).
(6) Entrepreneurship has a deep basis in local culture (Dana & Dana, 2005), and may have greater attachment and applicability to the local community (Malecki, 1997).
(7) Entrepreneurship can create positive disruptions in local economies that are economically stuck or recovering from the loss of industry, providing opportunities, and resources for economic renewal (Pe'er & Vertinsky, 2008).
(8) As long as a supportive community exists, community-based enterprise can transform the lives of poor and economically distressed residents by providing an outlet for earning and economic self-expression (Peredo & Chrisman, 2006).

This special issue presents seven outstanding articles that capture a wide range of approaches and ideas for supporting entrepreneurship, and embracing the diversity of benefits entrepreneurs bring to their community. Because a diversity of approaches is likely to come from a diversity of people, this special issue pays special attention to issues of equity, accessibility, and social justice in cultivating an entrepreneurial mindset across a wide variety of populations for the enrichment of the entire community. The special issue begins with an invited essay by Thomas S. Lyons that discusses the role that entrepreneurship plays in community development. Far from a simple economic development strategy, Lyons argues that entrepreneurship, if it is equitable and inclusive in its intent, has the revolutionary potential to build upon local assets, culture, imagination, and skills in ways that other strategies cannot.

Such strategies often face very real constraints and challenges, as elaborated in the first article by Crowe, Ceresola, Silva, and Recker, who demonstrate that real barriers exist across many minority communities in the face of devolution. While appeals to cultivate the creative class in many historically African-American communities have failed, these authors show that formal education and economic development strategy is a successful way to engage the local population. One bright spot is the presence of community development financial institutions (CDFIs), providing essential startup capital to many disadvantaged entrepreneurs who otherwise would have little access to capital. An article by Patraporn examines the complex role of CDFIs in stimulating entrepreneurial activity among ethnic minorities in the United States, and through qualitative inquiry, shows how the unique interactions between CDFI staff and emerging entrepreneurs allows CDFIs to take on greater risks and help underserved populations.

Much of the power of community entrepreneurship development stems from its ability to build wealth from cultural assets that are unique to the community. The role of culture is not only a building block, but can also fundamentally inspire or inhibit entrepreneurship. Importantly, it is not only culture that matters to inspiring entrepreneurship, but how entrepreneurial action is perceived in that culture, creating very real supports and constraints in the minds of current and would-be entrepreneurs. Continuing with a focus on minority entrepreneurship as an example, Achtenhagen and Price Schultz demonstrate how the portrayal of entrepreneurship in American media can have a profound effect on the entrepreneurial aspirations of ethnic minorities. Examining the role of culture through a different lens, the fourth article, by Breazeale, Fortunato, Allen, Hustedde, and Pushkarskaya, examines the divergent role of rural and urban culture in supporting entrepreneurship, using survey data from Kentucky. These authors produce a scale for assessing the Entrepreneurial Community Culture of a place, and discuss the very different roles that local culture plays in supporting entrepreneurship in rural and urban areas.

Finally, the last three articles focus on applied strategies for supporting entrepreneurship locally by creating an entrepreneurial "ecosystem" – a whole system of diverse players with a common intent of working together to innovate, collaborating to solve problems, forming partnerships and friendly rivalries, and competing together as a team. Dye and Alter, authors of the fifth article in the special issue, offer a case study from Halifax, Nova Scotia (Canada) demonstrating how governments can improve their efforts to support entrepreneurial ecologies, become more helpful, and overcome troublesome reputations when it comes to supporting entrepreneurship. In a similar vein, the sixth article by Vorley and Williams examines a community-based enterprise learning initiative in Rotherham (UK). These authors share the benefits of this approach, and provide constructive strategies for improving community-based learning efforts in other communities. Finally, Markley, Lyons, and Macke author our seventh article, providing strategies for improving entrepreneurial capacity locally by blending two compelling entrepreneurship frameworks to put entrepreneurs front and center in economic development efforts. For those readers who are keen to get to work supporting entrepreneurs in their own community, the guest editors are confident that this section of the special issue will be especially appealing.

As the fields of entrepreneurship and community development continue to evolve in positive and productive ways, we as guest editors of the special issue sincerely hope to encourage an evocative, evolutionary exploration at the nexus of these two fields.

Entrepreneurship and community development are messy, complex topics. For scholars of either (or both), this is great news! It means that there is no "one right way" to do entrepreneurship development, no magic bullet or panacea. There are, however, a multitude of effective approaches that can work in a variety of different local and regional contexts, and for a multitude of reasons. Thank goodness for that, because a diversity of entrepreneurs and development approaches means that communities can evolve to become as unique as the local businesses they help to support. Entrepreneurship in these communities may be viewed as a route to economic growth, or toward development and well-being. It may be a destination to raise the visibility of a place, or a journey toward resilience and a new vision. With many ways to convene entrepreneurs and support different types of entrepreneurship, even neighboring communities can collaborate without competing for the same set of opportunities. It is the goal of this special issue to underscore the diversity of approaches and outcomes that can help communities to transform into spaces of creative and opportunistic exploration.

Diversity is healthy for any local economy, but so is a call to creativity, imagination, and trying new things. Likewise, community entrepreneurship development can promote this idea by helping to build entrepreneurial ecosystems and safe spaces that promote the potential and possibility of citizens as a foil to everyday conflict, divisiveness, and narratives of defeat and pessimism. Best of all, entrepreneurs *and their supporters* can be active participants in this important journey. Absolutely anyone can take part in the action, and absolutely anyone can think like an entrepreneur. Entrepreneurial thinking is a skill that can be learned across the community (Lichtenstein & Lyons, 2010), and its scope can include the creation of highly profitable enterprises – or better – the broader pursuit of working with others to effectively launch new ideas that improve the community in a manner that makes sense for local citizens. For those who study entrepreneurship, community development, or those who are simply intrigued by the idea of empowering communities through these means of organizing, it is hoped that this special issue will inspire your own creative and entrepreneurial thinking in this important conceptual space. In the spirit of co-creating new knowledge and insight, and thus the spirit of both entrepreneurship and community, we enthusiastically welcome you to this discussion and hope this special issue fosters and feeds your curiosity, scholarship, and action.

Acknowledgments

This special issue represents a collaboration between the Center for Rural Studies housed in the Department of Sociology at Sam Houston State University, the Center for Economic and Community Development (CECD) housed in the Department of Agricultural Economics, Sociology, and Education at Penn State University, and the Community Development Society. The guest editors would like to thank *Community Development* Editor in Chief Dr. John J. Green and Editorial Assistants Molly Phillips and Amy Greer for their expert guidance and incredible patience in putting this special issue together. We are deeply indebted to you for this tremendous honor and opportunity, and for your flexibility, creativity, professionalism, and ability to get things done. We thank you so much for your foresight and support of entrepreneurship in communities everywhere. Additionally, we would like to thank the anonymous peer reviewers of this article for their prompt and helpful review of our work.

Disclosure statement

No potential conflict of interest was reported by the authors.

References

Acs, Z. (2006). How is entrepreneurship good for economic growth? *Innovations: Technology, Governance, Globalization, 1*, 97–107.

Acs, Z. J., & Armington, C. (2006). *Entrepreneurship, geography, and American economic growth*. Cambridge, MA: Cambridge University Press.

Acs, Z. J., & Mueller, P. (2008). Employment effects of business dynamics: Mice, gazelles, and elephants. *Small Business Economics, 30*, 85–100.

Aldrich, H. E., & Zimmer, C. (1986). Entrepreneurship through social networks. In D. L. Sexton & R. W. Smilor (Eds.), *The art and science of entrepreneurship* (pp. 2–23). Cambridge, MA: Ballinger Publishing.

Alvord, S. H., Brown, L. D., & Letts, C. W. (2004). Social entrepreneurship and societal transformation: An exploratory study. *Journal of Applied Behavioral Science, 40*, 260–282.

Amorós, J. E., & Bosma, N. (2014). *Global entrepreneurship monitor 2013 global report.* Recovered on February 28, 2014. Retrieved from http://www.gemconsortium.org/report

Audretsch, D. B., & Lehmann, E. E. (2005). Does the Knowledge Spillover Theory of Entrepreneurship hold for regions? *Research Policy, 34*, 1191–1202.

Baumol, W. J. (1968). Entrepreneurship in economic theory. *The American Economic Review, 58*, 64–71.

Baumol, W. J., Litan, R. E., & Schramm, C. J. (2007). *Good capitalism, bad capitalism, and the economics of growth and prosperity.* New Haven, CT: Yale University Press.

Berger, P., & Luckmann, T. (1966). *The social construction of knowledge: A treatise in the sociology of knowledge.* New York, NY: Open Road Media.

Casson, M. (2005). Entrepreneurship and the theory of the firm. *Journal of Economic Behavior & Organization, 58*, 327–348.

Clark, J. (2009). Entrepreneurship and diversification on English farms: Identifying business enterprise characteristics and change processes. *Entrepreneurship and Regional Development, 21*, 213–236.

Dana, L. P. (1995). Entrepreneurship in a remote sub-Arctic community. *Entrepreneurship Theory and Practice, 20*, 57–72.

Dana, L. P., & Dana, T. E. (2005). Expanding the scope of methodologies used in entrepreneurship research. *International Journal of Entrepreneurship and Small Business, 2*, 79–88.

Davidsson, P. (2009). *The entrepreneurship research challenge.* Cheltenham: Edward Elgar.

Drakopoulou Dodd, S., & Anderson, A. R. (2007). Mumpsimus and the mything of the individualistic entrepreneur. *International Small Business Journal, 25*, 341–360.

Fairlie, R. W. (2013). Entrepreneurship, economic conditions, and the great recession. *Journal of Economics & Management Strategy, 22*, 207–231.

Feld, B. (2012). *Startup communities: Building an entrepreneurial ecosystem in your city.* Hoboken, NJ: Wiley.

Fortunato, M. W. P. (2014). Supporting rural entrepreneurship: A review of conceptual developments from research to practice. *Community Development, 45*, 387–408.

Fortunato, M. W. P., & Alter, T. R. (2011). The individual-institutional-opportunity nexus: An integrated framework for analyzing entrepreneurship development. *Entrepreneurship Research Journal, 1*, 1–34, Article 6.

Fortunato, M. W. P., & Alter, T. R. (in press). Culture and entrepreneurial opportunity in high- and low-entrepreneurship rural communities: Challenging the discovery/creation divide. *Journal of Enterprising Communities: People and Places in the Global Economy.*

Fortunato, M. W. P., & McLaughlin, D. K. (2012). Interaction and purpose in highly entrepreneurial communities. *Entrepreneurship Research Journal, 2*, 1–34, Article 5.

Gartner, W. (1989, Summer). "Who is an entrepreneur" is the wrong question. *Entrepreneurship Theory & Practice*, 47–67.

Granovetter, M. (1985). Economic action and social structure: The problem of embeddedness. *American Journal of Sociology, 91*, 481–510.

Granovetter, M. S. (1973). The strength of weak ties. *American Journal of Sociology, 78*, 1360–1380.

Henrekson, M., & Johansson, D. (2010). Gazelles as job creators: A survey and interpretation of the evidence. *Small Business Economics, 35*, 227–244.

Hustedde, R. (2007). What's culture got to do with it? Strategies for strengthening an entrepreneurial culture. In N. Walzer (Ed.), *Entrepreneurship and local economic development* (pp. 39–58). Lanham, MD: Lexington Books.

Julien, P. A. (2007). *A theory of local entrepreneurship in the knowledge economy*. Cheltenham: Edward Elgar.

Kauffman Foundation. (2009a). *Kauffman Poll: Entrepreneurship and economic recovery – America's views on the best ways to stimulate growth*. Kansas City, MO: Author.

Kauffman Foundation. (2009b). *Business dynamics statistics briefing: Jobs created from business startups in the United States*. Kansas City, MO: Author.

Kirzner, I. M. (1978). *Competition and entrepreneurship*. Chicago, IL: University of Chicago Press.

Lichtenstein, G. A., & Lyons, T. S. (2010). *Investing in entrepreneurs: A strategic approach for strengthening your regional and community economy*. Santa Barbara, CA: Praeger.

Low, M. B., & MacMillan, I. C. (1988). Entrepreneurship: Past research and future challenges. *Journal of Management, 14*, 139–161.

Lyons, T. S., Alter, T. R., Audretsch, D., & Augustine, D. (2012). Entrepreneurship and community: The next frontier of entrepreneurship inquiry. *Entrepreneurship Research Journal, 2*(1), 1–24.

Malecki, E. J. (1997). Entrepreneurs, networks, and economic development: A review of recent research. *Advances in Entrepreneurship, Firm Emergence and Growth, 3*, 57–118.

Marshall, A. (1997). *Principles of economics* (Great minds series ed.). Amherst, NY: Prometheus Books.

Mayer, H., & Knox, P. L. (2006). Slow cities: Sustainable places in a fast world. *Journal of Urban Affairs, 28*, 321–334.

Nickerson, N. P., Black, R. J., & McCool, S. F. (2001). Agritourism: Motivations behind farm/ranch business diversification. *Journal of Travel Research, 40*, 19–26.

Nijkamp, P. (2003). Entrepreneurship in a modern network economy. *Regional Studies, 37*, 395–405.

Oviawe, J. I. (2010). Repositioning Nigerian youths for economic empowerment through entrepreneurship education. *European Journal of Educational Studies, 2*, 113–118.

Pe'er, A., & Vertinsky, I. (2008). Firm exits as a determinant of new entry: Is there evidence of local creative destruction? *Journal of Business Venturing, 23*, 280–306.

Peredo, A. M., & Chrisman, J. J. (2006). Toward a theory of community-based enterprise. *Academy of Management Review, 31*, 309–328.

Schmid, A. A. (2008). *Conflict and cooperation: Institutional and behavioral economics*. Hoboken, NJ: Wiley.

Schumpeter, J. A. (1934). *The theory of economic development: An inquiry into profits, capital, credit, interest, and the business cycle*. New York, NY: Transaction Publishers.

Shane, S. (2003). *A general theory of entrepreneurship*. Cheltenham: Edward Elgar.

Shane, S. (2011). *The great recession's effect on entrepreneurship*. Economic Commentary. Cleveland, OH: Federal Reserve Bank of Cleveland. Retrieved from https://www.clevelandfed.org/en/Newsroom%20and%20Events/Publications/Economic%20Commentary/2011/ec%202011104%20the%20great%20recessions%20effect%20on%20entrepreneurship.aspx

Thurik, R., & Wennekers, S. (2004). Entrepreneurship, small business and economic growth. *Journal of Small Business and Enterprise Development, 11*, 140–149.

Tolbert, C. M., Irwin, M. D., Lyson, T. A., & Nucci, A. R. (2002). Civic community in small-town America: How civic welfare is influence by local capitalism and civic engagement. *Rural Sociology, 67*, 90–113.

Turner, R. C. (2003). The political economy of gubernatorial smokestack chasing: Bad policy and bad politics? *State Politics & Policy Quarterly, 3*, 270–293.

van Praag, C. M. (1999). Some classic views on entrepreneurship. *De Economist, 147*, 311–335.

Wennekers, S., & Thurik, R. (1999). Linking entrepreneurship and economic growth. *Small Business Economics, 13*, 27–56.

Wilkinson, K. P. (1991). *The community in rural America*. Appleton, WI: Social Ecology Press.

INVITED ESSAY

Entrepreneurship and community development: what matters and why?

Shortly before writing this essay, I had the opportunity to participate in a gathering of social entrepreneurship educators in New York City, sponsored by the Moxie Foundation. We were there to meet each other, many for the first time, and to explore avenues of collaboration. As an icebreaker, the organizers facilitated an opening exercise in which we were divided into groups of three. In round-robin fashion, we asked each other "What matters to you?" When that question was posed to each of us, we had two minutes to answer. It is a simple question; yet, it has the power to open a self-reflective door on one's values that allows a flood of complex thoughts to rush in. Concurrently, the time constraint imposed forces a concise, focused response. My attempt at answering this question as it relates to entrepreneurship and community development follows.

I have long been an advocate of entrepreneurship as a mindset, process, skill set, and tool kit that can help us solve the economic, environmental, and social challenges that our communities face. I believe in the power of the passion, determination, and resiliency displayed by entrepreneurs. I embrace the concept of using markets to accomplish social good. I ascribe to the entrepreneurial principle that one should not be limited by the resources one currently possesses in the pursuit of one's goals (Stevenson, 1983) but should strive to attract the resources of others to one's cause through the power of a shared vision for a better future. I accept as true that we all can benefit from the entrepreneur's restless and creative search for opportunities to add value to the lives of others and the innovation that brings new ideas to their intended markets (Drucker, 1985; Schumpeter, 1991). I believe that entrepreneurship in pursuit of community development matters.

Yet, answering the question "What matters to you?" carries with it a corollary question: "Why does it matter?" It is within the answer to this latter question that one's core values lie as well as one's motivation to act. If entrepreneurship-driven community development matters, why is it important? I believe that the answer can be found in one of the most pressing challenges our society currently faces: economic inequality.

It has been well documented that the gap between the wealthy and the poor is growing and that the middle class has been eroded significantly in the United States. This continues to perpetuate, and in some cases worsen, our social problems. Despite this, we remain mired in inaction. Government lacks the political will to address the problem. Many in the private sector resist action for fear that intervention in economic markets will kill the goose that laid the golden egg. Meanwhile, this situation is hurting us all.

The late Paul Newman, founder of Newman's Own, Inc., a social enterprise that gives all its after-tax profits to charity, stated the impact of economic inequality succinctly when explaining why he pursued his venture:

> The thing that makes the United States such an enviable place to invest in and to be in is that it's so stable. The more the gap starts to increase between the haves and have-nots, the rich and the poor, the employable and the unemployable, the less stability you're going to

> have, and the very great strength of the nation erodes. (Wei-Skillern, Austin, Leonard, & Stevenson, 2007, p. 190)

Looking at Newman's observation from the perspective of economic development theory, there are six prerequisites to any economy's development and its capacity to continue to develop: surplus, savings, investment, efficiency, equity, and stability (Hamlin & Lyons, 1996). Surplus permits money to be saved, which, in turn, can be invested in the infrastructure necessary for development. If this is done with efficiency, surplus will be maximized and the process perpetuated. However, if there is no equity, stability will ultimately be eroded and development slowed or stopped. By allowing economic inequality to grow, we are jeopardizing everything we have worked so hard to build over the past two and a half centuries. Economic equality matters.

This brings me to my thesis: entrepreneurship as a mechanism for fostering community development matters because it can help us address economic inequality in our communities and in our nation. Of course, like anything else, this requires intentional focus and a strategic approach. I will dedicate the remainder of this essay to my thoughts about how this can be achieved.

First, I believe, we need to broaden our definition of "entrepreneurship" and who is considered to be an "entrepreneur." In my opinion, too much attention has been, and continues to be, paid to individuals who launch high-growth, technology-focused, venture capital-backed enterprises. In some quarters, these individuals are considered to be the only "true" entrepreneurs. Research has shown that these so-called "high impact" entrepreneurs are leading job creators (Ernst & Young & Kauffman Foundation, 2013), which has made them the darlings of local economic developers. However, this thinking has led to a certain entrepreneurial exceptionalism that tends to, in effect, discourage and exclude some individuals who have great potential from participating.

What this perspective fails to recognize is that the appropriate focus of entrepreneurship is the entrepreneur, not the business. By placing emphasis on the business, we get distracted by issues of secondary importance, such as the industry in which the business operates, the life cycle stage of the business and its source of financing. I suspect that this confusion is caused, in part, by our society's obsession with growth and our tendency to conflate growth and development. We assume that the wise investment is in *businesses* that operate in "growth" industries, that are second stage or later, and that have the capacity to attract capital sufficient for scaling the enterprise. None of this takes into account the capability of the entrepreneur to successfully start, grow, and sustain the business. This is either assumed or largely ignored. However, the investment should be made in the entrepreneur, not the business (Lichtenstein & Lyons, 2010). Properly skilled individuals or teams drive thriving businesses. Entrepreneurs who are ultimately successful may start out operating a business that is in an industry or of a size that is not favored by economic developers; however, as they build their skills that can change. Today's bodega owner may become tomorrow's grocery chain mogul.

We in community development understand the difference between growth and development. We know growth emphasizes quantity, while development features quality. We strive to develop first, and then grow, so that we are expanding quality, not merely expanding. This is no less true for fostering entrepreneurship in our communities. If we begin by creating an environment for developing the skills of our entrepreneurs so that they can develop their businesses, we will get what we want – a diverse and growing community of high-quality entrepreneurs and enterprises that creates wealth for us all. I will revisit the concept of wealth creation later in this essay.

Focusing on developing entrepreneurs, regardless of their industry, accomplishes something else. It allows us to think beyond business to civic entrepreneurship (public officials and policy-makers thinking and acting entrepreneurially) and social entrepreneurship (entrepreneurs who operate nonprofit, for-profit, or hybrid organizations that are mission driven). Facilitating all three kinds of entrepreneurship is crucial to creating a fully entrepreneurial community (Lyons, 2004).

If we are genuinely committed to developing and growing entrepreneurs and enterprises (business, civic, and social) in our communities, we need to be strategic, systemic, and systematic in our approach. That is, we need to think about the whole, its parts, and the connections between those parts that yield synergy: a whole that is greater than the sum of its parts. Synergy is vital to community transformation – deep, lasting, positive change. A popular framing of these elements and their inter-relationships is as an "entrepreneurial ecosystem." While this characterization is not perfect, in a broad sense the metaphor is appropriate.

An entrepreneurial ecosystem that fosters community development by creating and innovating solutions to the community's problems through leveraging its assets must include government, the education subsystem, nonprofit social services, entrepreneurship support organizations (e.g. incubators, one-stop shops, microenterprise programs), private business support entities (e.g. banks, law offices, accounting services), religious and cultural institutions, and service clubs, among others. It must include forums for networking and social capital building among these players – in the parlance of entrepreneurship, "co-working spaces" – that permit their physical coming together in order to share challenges, solutions, and resources and to find common values, while building trust in the process. The ecosystem must also take full advantage of social media tools in this effort to foster interaction.

Such an entrepreneurial ecosystem must be accessible to anyone who is motivated to participate, not just a select few. It should not attempt to predict in advance who will be a successful entrepreneur or which ideas are workable, as so many of our current approaches try to do. I have lost count of how many times people whose success at entrepreneurship I would not have predicted have proven me wrong. My fieldwork has taught me that people who get help building their entrepreneurship skills develop self-efficacy, and that self-efficacy empowers them to think bigger about their enterprises and to manage the necessary risks required for success. It is not true that people are either entrepreneurs or they are not. There is a continuum of entrepreneurship skill along which individuals can move. The ecosystem must support all entrepreneurs and prospective entrepreneurs on this journey.

Over the years, I have met numerous people – counselors in entrepreneurship support organizations, entrepreneurship educators, and others – who sincerely believe that it is their duty to tell prospective entrepreneurs when their ideas are "bad" and should not be pursued. Some of these would-be gatekeepers of entrepreneurship maintain that to not disabuse prospective entrepreneurs of these "bad" ideas is irresponsible and amounts to coddling. I have learned that this approach is not only unfairly subjective, but it also has a chilling effect on creativity and innovation. Lean start-up thinking holds that an entrepreneur's initial idea is nothing more than a hypothesis about what customers need. Through a series of tests and resulting adjustments, the idea can be refined to become a better fit with what the customer truly needs (Blank, 2013). A well-functioning entrepreneurial ecosystem will support the community's entrepreneurs in the hypothesis testing necessary to move an idea from "bad" to viable.

In sum, communities can successfully leverage the power of entrepreneurship to help them address their economic, environmental, and social challenges. Specifying and maintaining a healthy ecosystem for fostering business, civic, and social entrepreneurship can best accomplish this. Such an ecosystem must be focused on the entrepreneur and her/his individual development, open to all entrepreneurs and prospective entrepreneurs, committed to supporting the development of new ideas and new ways of bringing these ideas to the "market" that needs them (including tolerance of failed hypotheses), and facilitative of the interactions necessary to idea generation, resource sharing, and risk pooling. In addition, the ecosystem must have a coordinator or facilitator that holds the mission, vision, and values of that ecosystem and guides their pursuit (Lyons & Wyckoff, 2014).

All of this addresses the "what" and the "how." I now want to bring this discussion back to the "why." If the ultimate goal of creating an entrepreneurial ecosystem is fostering economic equality, what is the direct connection between that goal and entrepreneurship? The answer is wealth creation. The purpose of entrepreneurship is to create wealth. For the business entrepreneur, this is financial wealth for the entrepreneur and her/his family. When the wealth-building efforts of all the community's business entrepreneurs are considered together, it becomes *community* financial wealth building. For social and civic entrepreneurs, it may be one, or more, of the eight types of wealth identified by the Ford Foundation: built, cultural, financial, individual, intellectual, natural, political, and social (Ratner & Markley, 2014). I would argue that all of these forms of wealth are interrelated, and they all contribute to the overall economic (considered broadly) wealth of individuals, families, and communities. By "economic," I refer here to the entire societal value chain of which we are all a part, as producers, distributors, consumers, and citizens on multiple levels – our community wealth-creating ecosystem.

The building blocks of wealth are assets. The beauty of assets is that they can be intergenerationally transferred. That is, they can be sustained over time. Business entrepreneurs build business assets that contribute to financial and individual wealth. Social entrepreneurs build assets that can provide cultural, natural, and social wealth, while civic entrepreneurs can generate assets that contribute to built, cultural, intellectual, and political wealth. The division of labor here is a bit artificial, but the point is that each of these collections of entrepreneurs has a role to play in building the economic wealth of the community. When this is done in an inclusive, integrative, and systemic manner, as in an ecosystem, wealth is not concentrated in pockets but is diffused. This can foster economic equality and ensure the stability necessary to permit further development.

This approach does not require the overthrow of the capitalist system or violent revolution. It is not facilitated by massive protests. These are but symptoms of societal instability. Instead, it makes use of markets in a responsible and sustainable way by fostering the efforts of entrepreneurial thinkers and actors, who are, and always have been, the agents of economic and social change in our society. In this way, entrepreneurship-driven community development truly matters.

References

Blank, S. (2013, May). Why the lean start-up changes everything. *Harvard Business Review*, pp. 65–72.

Drucker, P. F. (1985). *Innovation and entrepreneurship: Practice and principles*. New York, NY: Harper & Row.

Ernst & Young & Kauffman Foundation. (2013). *The vital entrepreneur: High impact at its best.* London: Ernst & Young Global.

Hamlin, R. E., & Lyons, T. S. (1996). *Economy without walls: Managing local development in a restructuring world.* Westport, CT: Praeger.

Lichtenstein, G. A., & Lyons, T. S. (2010). *Investing in entrepreneurs: A strategic approach for strengthening your regional and community economy.* Santa Barbara, CA: Praeger/ABC-CLIO.

Lyons, T. S. (2004). Creating a complete entrepreneurial community. *Rural Research Report, 15*, 1–8.

Lyons, T. S., & Wyckoff, B. (2014). Facilitating community wealth building: Understanding the roles played and capacities needed by coordinating institutions. *Community Development, 45*, 443–457.

Ratner, S., & Markley, D. (2014). Linking rural assets to market demand: Wealth creation value chains in rural America. *Local Economy, 29*, 1–9.

Schumpeter, J. (1991). Comments on a plan for the study of entrepreneurship. In R. Swedberg (Ed.), *Joseph A. Schumpter: The economics and sociology of Capitalism* (pp. 406–428). Princeton, NJ: Princeton University Press.

Stevenson, H. H. (1983). *A perspective on entrepreneurship* (Harvard Business School Working Paper 9-384-131). Cambridge, MA: Harvard Business School.

Wei-Skillern, J., Austin, J. E., Leonard, H., & Stevenson, H. (2007). *Entrepreneurship in the social sector.* Los Angeles, CA: Sage.

Thomas S. Lyons
Loomba Department of Management
Zicklin School of Business, Baruch College
City University of New York, New York, USA

Rural economic development under devolution: A test of local strategies

Jessica A. Crowe, Ryan Ceresola, Tony Silva and Nicholas Recker

During the past 30 years, the federal government has transferred more responsibility for the control, development, and support of public policy to states and local communities in a process known as devolution. In this context, economic hardships that have hit many rural communities often lead to increased tension over economic development strategies, which is further influenced by a community's racial composition and racial history. Using devolution as a framework, we quantitatively explore the relationship between general economic development strategies, including two concepts that are linked to entrepreneurship, the creative class and bridging social capital, on several measures of economic development. Analysis includes rural communities that have historically excluded African-Americans from living within city limits, as well as rural communities that did not. Using data from 217 rural communities in the American Midwest and nontraditional South, we find no support for the creative class, the importance of tolerance, the importance of technology, or bridging social capital on increasing economic development, but we do find that formal education and incorporating economic development strategies are significantly related.

Introduction

During the last decades of the twentieth century and continuing into the twenty-first, the federal government has transferred more responsibility for the control, development, and support of public policy to states and local communities (Sharp & Parisi, 2003). This shift, referred to as "devolution," is intended to increase the efficiency and flexibility of public policy in hopes of better serving local populations, with the idea that local communities are better able to manage local problems. However, while communities may better know the needs of residents, they are fiscally, administratively, and technically limited to meet those needs (Warner, 2003). Nevertheless, local governments invest in a wide range of economic development strategies that are intended to promote development, build the tax base, and entice employers.

There may be, however, different ways to facilitate economic development; newer theories of economic development emphasize the creative class, social tolerance, and bridging social capital as features that positively influence a community's entrepreneurial spirit. For instance, Richard Florida's concept of the "creative class" suggests that increasing the density of innovative people in occupations that produce new knowledge and ideas boosts economic development (Florida, 2002). Members of the creative class are attracted to communities that have high levels of talent and technology, and are tolerant towards diverse groups of individuals (Florida, 2002). Bridging social capital connects different groups within a community, and it also connects the community to other communities as well as state and federal agencies. Finally, advocates of social capital suggest that communities with higher levels of such capital are "better able to create networks of governance that support cooperative competition and promote development" (Warner, 2003, p. 256).

We seek to quantitatively explore the relationship between economic development strategies, the creative class, and bridging social capital on economic development in rural communities during a time of devolution. We do not test the effects of devolution directly, but rather test the aforementioned relationships to determine the characteristics of rural communities that have been most economically successful during devolution. Essentially, we are applying some theoretical ideas in the literature on devolution, measures of entrepreneurship in terms of the creative class and social capital, and economic development to a very specific data-set in order to make inferences about how devolution likely plays out in rural areas.

Furthermore, we examine these indicators in rural communities that have historically excluded African-Americans from living in the community and compare them to rural communities that did not historically exclude them from living within city limits. We hope to better understand how racial history affects the economic performance of rural communities, which in turn adds to the literature about characteristics, including tolerance, that are theoretically assumed to attract the creative class (which in turn increases economic development). Providing insight on decentralization and rural economies, this study examines survey data and secondary data on 217 rural communities throughout the Midwest and nontraditional South.[1]

Patterns of economic development for rural communities

We begin with a brief overview of devolution, with an emphasis on its racial characteristics, to contextualize how these economic strategies are employed. Next, we discuss several ways communities attempt to facilitate economic development, specifically through conventional economic development strategies; efforts to acquire a creative class through investment in human capital, technology, and tolerance; and bridging social capital. Finally, we emphasize the importance of understanding devolution and social capital through the lens of race.

Devolution and economic development

From the 1930s through the 1960s, the U.S. federal government played a large role in providing economic and social welfare. As part of the New Deal, the national government developed social security, provided unemployment assistance, and took leadership in economic planning and regulation. The role of the national government further increased in the decades following World War II, with the national government developing social programs directed at eradicating poverty, and increasing environmental and health standards (Sharp & Parisi, 2003). However, concerns about a large federal government coupled with a preference for greater local control led toward devolution of governmental functions and responsibilities. During the 1970s and 1980s, responsibilities shifted among national, state, and local governments, which led to a substantial decrease in resources available to local governments to provide for the programs they now administered. Devolution continued in the 1990s as federal programs were merged and local governments were provided greater discretion to use limited resources to meet local needs (Conlan, 1998; Sharp & Parisi, 2003).

Now well into the twenty-first century, devolution continues to create struggles for state and local governments tasked with developing, administering, and funding local social and economic policies. For instance, in 1996, the provision of welfare benefits was changed whereby assistance was given to individuals for only a limited time, and only so long as the person receiving the benefit was working or in the process of finding work (Harvey, 2011). This federal mandate was enforced by states generally, and communities specifically, and led to increased hardships for those living in areas of the state that were economically underdeveloped, as they came to rely on informal labor, charitable organizations, and social support networks to make ends meet (Harvey, 2011; Parisi, McLaughlin, Grice, Taquino, & Gill, 2003). This, in turn, put strain on families which might alternatively have been a source of social capital and potential community development (Duncan, 2001). Simply put, small communities – especially those in rural areas – often do not have the ability to provide much for their least fortunate, as they control limited resources (Sharp & Parisi, 2003).

Economic development strategies

The shift to greater local responsibility has encouraged local officials to attempt a variety of economic development strategies, especially in rural areas. Economic development strategies include tax and land incentives, loans to businesses, as well as efforts to increase entrepreneurship in terms of increasing the human capital of residents, increasing a community's social capital, and attracting the "creative class" to an area.

One strategy that communities use to promote economic development is industrial recruitment. This involves efforts to attract outside firms and industries to locate to the town (Crowe, 2008). One attractive feature of industrial recruitment is its ability to generate a large number of jobs in a relatively short time period. In contrast, a second type of activity, self-development, involves fostering local businesses and other entrepreneurial activities (Emery & Flora, 2006). Examples of self-development activities include revitalizing downtown businesses, promoting local tourism, and retaining or expanding locally owned businesses. A third type of activity, providing incentives, can be directed toward industrial recruitment and self-development. These efforts include tax abatements and tax increment financing, low-interest loans, assistance with physical infrastructure such as water hookups, sewer connections, or access roads, and land incentives, such as help acquiring and clearing land.

The prospect of creating jobs for residents in their communities drives cities to pursue and implement multiple economic development strategies. However, the benefits that communities can offer differ based on the unique context of each (Gittell & Thompson, 2002; Majee & Hoyt, 2011). For instance, Bartik (1991) argues that when policies are aimed at directly assisting businesses, the effects of state and local economic development activities are beneficial to the local workforce and the unemployed, but cautions that the effects of economic development strategies may depend on the context of the state or city. In his study of over 600 cities, Robichau (2010) found that cities with a written business attraction plan had a significantly *higher* unemployment rate than cities without such a plan, the opposite of the intended effect. Furthermore, providing incentives for businesses and having a business retention plan did not significantly affect unemployment rates.

Because many rural communities use multiple economic development strategies with the intent of increasing jobs and lowering residential unemployment, in this paper, we test the effects of implementing economic development strategies on measures of businesses, jobs, unemployment, and income. We expect an increase in economic development strategies to positively affect the number of businesses, jobs, and income and negatively affect unemployment.

The creative class and economic development

A second approach that local communities can use is to make their community more attractive to employers and entrepreneurs by improving their communities' resources, broadly speaking, so that job creators will want to live there and bring their businesses with them, and so entrepreneurs will choose their communities to start their own businesses. The creative class theory suggests that local officials should make their communities desirable so that people employed in "creative occupations" will want to live there. Creative occupations are found in sectors such as arts and entertainment, architecture and engineering, computer technology and math, and management and business operations. People in these occupations produce new knowledge and ideas, and understand their use (Florida, 2002). Employees of such occupations are collectively known as the "creative class", the modern-day driver of economic development, as businesses and industry move to where it is located and its members create new businesses as well (Florida, 2002).

Most studies focus on the role the creative class plays on economic development in urban areas, and the few studies that examine the relationship between the creative class and economic development in rural areas have produced mixed results. McGranahan and Wojan (2007) find a positive association between the presence of the creative class and economic development in rural areas between 1990 and 2004. Herslund (2012) conducted a qualitative study of creative class residents who moved to a rural area from Copenhagen, Denmark, and shows that despite forming new businesses in the rural area, none of those in her sample of 30 created new jobs other than their own. Rather than impacting the economy through job creation, the new creative class entrepreneurs added "organizational energy" to the area by extending the networks of local businesses. Thus, while findings are indeed limited, like McGranahan and Wojan (2007), we expect that the creative class will positively affect economic development in rural communities.

Human capital

The association between human capital and economic development originates from the early work of Schultz (1961), who argues that economic development is largely the result of investing in human capital. He suggests that investments in human knowledge and skill are the major determinants of economic development. Indeed, Glaeser (2000) shows a correlation between human capital and regional economic development, claiming that firms locate in areas with a high concentration of human capital to gain competitive advantages. As for rural areas, Gordon (2000) suggests that education and training are crucial in an increasingly high-technology global economy in determining which communities will economically flourish and which will fall behind.

The conventional measure of human capital is educational attainment. When it comes to economic development in rural communities, Rainey, Robinson, Allen, and Christy (2003) argue that the level of formal education of a community's residents is an increasingly important asset of a community. Businesses and industries that are currently growing are computer-oriented and thus require more highly educated workers. Thus, we expect an increase in educational attainment to have a positive effect on the number of businesses, jobs, and income, and a negative effect on unemployment.

Technology

Florida (2003) defines technology as a function of both innovation and high-technology concentrations in a region. High-technology firms are highly concentrated in urban areas, especially those in the U.S. Northeast, West, and in Florida. Their locations are highly correlated with population. Thus, rural communities face a significant disadvantage when attempting to attract high-technology firms (Goetz & Rupasingha, 2002). Instead of focusing on high-technology concentrations, researchers, and community leaders emphasize high-quality physical infrastructure, such as roads, sewer treatment, water lines, and telecommunications as key elements to economic development in rural areas (Crowe, 2008; Harrison, 1992). Further, Rainey et al. (2003) suggest that in an increasingly global economy, communities with deficient infrastructure will be at a considerable disadvantage for attracting and maintaining industry. Accordingly, we expect an increase in the quality of infrastructural technology to have a positive effect on the number of businesses, jobs, and income, and a negative effect on unemployment.

Tolerance

Tolerance is an important factor in drawing the creative class to an area. According to Florida (2002, 2005), cities that attract the creative class are characterized by high levels of tolerance for people of different races and ethnicities, various sexual preferences, and, in general, "openness to diversity of all kinds" (2005, p. 36). Florida emphasizes the role that tolerance plays in attracting creative class individuals, concluding that "members of this class strongly favor organizations and environments in which they feel that anyone can fit in and can get ahead" (2002, p. 79). While Florida (2002) provides evidence that cities that have a higher prevalence of gays, foreign-born residents, and bohemians rate high on the creative class index and subsequently have higher levels of economic development, he acknowledges that racial diversity does not appear to be associated with a rise of the creative class. To examine this, Sharp and Joslyn (2008) look at the relationship between the creative class and racial attitudes, and find that individuals who live in cities and score high on the creative class index have more progressive racial attitudes than those living in more conventional cities. Thus, while racial diversity does not seem to be positively associated with the creative class index, racial tolerance does appear to be.

Bridging social capital

Early studies of social capital were tied to individual outcomes, such as educational attainment (Coleman, 1988) and wealth (Bourdieu, 1979). However, later studies, led by Putnam (1993), began to associate social capital with larger units such as communities. Under this conceptualization, communities could possess a "stock" of social capital. Accordingly, communities that built a "stock" of social capital would have higher levels of community development, as communities with high levels of this capital "often also have many social assets and internal capabilities to develop additional assets" (Gittell &

Thompson, 2002, p. 122). Relatedly, the ability to build social capital in rural areas is tied to historical social relations – especially those involving class and race – and how those relations affect the distribution of resources (Duncan, 2001, p. 75).

Social capital is composed of both bonding capital and bridging capital. Bonding social capital consists of strong ties among a homogenous group of people, whereas bridging social capital involves ties that link dissimilar social groups. Several studies (Crowe, 2008; Flora, Sharp, Flora, & Newlon, 1997) find a link between high levels of bridging capital and economic development. However, Hoyman and Faricy (2009), using religious pluralism as a measure of bridging social capital, find mixed support.

While debates exist about the robustness of social capital as a positive tool communities can use to better themselves (e.g. see Letki, 2008 and Putnam, 2007), others note that the presence of social capital increases various measures of community well-being, and provides a basis for further development (Gittell & Thompson, 2002). The concept of social capital and the argument that its presence leads to an increase in community well-being coincides with the neoliberal narrative that devolution succeeds by allowing local civic actors to flourish. Under this narrative, increasing bridging social capital is a tool that rural communities can use to increase local economic development.

Race in rural America

Finally, as mentioned above, oftentimes poor rural communities are divided along both class and racial lines (Duncan, 2001), depending on the history of a particular region. In addition to claiming that devolution places an unfair burden on the rural poor, critics argue that devolution has racialized effects. For instance, with respect to government assistance to the poor, welfare was originally intended for white mothers; as more African-American mothers entered the welfare rolls, states lowered welfare payments (Moller, 2002). Additionally, Soss, Fording, and Schram (2008) found that American states with higher African-American population rates had more stringent and locally controlled Temporary Assistance for Needy Families regimes and higher levels of investment in incarceration, and argue that welfare devolution is colored, with racial differences in states and communities shaping policy choices.

Additional studies have explored the link between racial tolerance and economic development. In Tupelo, Mississippi, the second community in Mississippi to sign a school antidiscrimination agreement and desegregate its schools without confrontation, African-American residents are active in community development organizations, are prominent on the city payroll, and are business entrepreneurs (Grisham & Gurwitt, 1999), suggesting tolerance can lead to economic benefits for African-Americans. Crowe (2012) finds that rural communities with a historical legacy of inclusiveness of African-Americans had higher levels of economic development activities than communities that had historical patterns of exclusiveness of racial minorities. Contrarily, Crowe and Ceresola (2014) found that rural communities with a history of racial intolerance limited development strategies to those activities they thought would maintain an all-white community. In sum, it seems that rural communities that are more racially inclusive engage in more economic development activities. Thus, we expect that increased racial tolerance and diversity positively affect the number of businesses, jobs, and income, and negatively affect unemployment.

Hypotheses

Consistent with previous research on the effect of the creative class, talent, technology, and tolerance on economic development, we expect an increase in the creative class, in educational attainment, the quality of infrastructural technology, and racial tolerance and diversity to positively affect the number of businesses, jobs, and income, and to negatively affect unemployment. Additionally, we expect that an increase in the number of economic development strategies a community has implemented along with an increase in a community's bridging social capital will have a positive effect on the number of businesses, jobs, and income, and a negative effect on unemployment.

Data and methods

Sample

Data for these analyses come from a survey of economic development leaders in small to mid-sized rural communities in eight Midwestern and nontraditional Southern states conducted during the fall of 2009, in addition to secondary data from the U.S. Census Bureau, the American Community Survey, U.S. Census Business Patterns, and the Economic Research Service. Because we test the role of historical racial tolerance on rural economic development, we sample communities in the Midwest and nontraditional South; these are the regions of the USA with the largest number of communities that were intolerant of racial minorities (Loewen, 2005). The sampling frame consisted of all incorporated towns with a population between 1500 and 17,000[2] in the states of Illinois, Indiana, Iowa, Kentucky, Michigan, Missouri, Ohio, and Wisconsin. This yielded a sampling population of 2214 towns.[3]

From the 2214 towns in the sampling population, towns were selected based on their level of racial inclusion. First, census data from 1880, 1930, and 2000[4] were compared to determine whether a town had always had African-American residents. In seven of the eight sampled states (all except for Kentucky), every town with a consistent African-American population was included in the sample. A random sample was taken from towns in Kentucky that consistently had a significant African-American population.[5] African-Americans that were labeled as prisoners or servants were excluded from consideration. For example, if a town had 50 African-Americans in 1880, but all or nearly all were servants, the town would not be included as one that consistently had African-American residents. In total, 182 towns that consistently had African-American residents – at least five African-Americans in 1880 and 1930 and more than 1% in 2000[6] – were included in the sample.

Census data from 1880, 1930, and 2000 were then compared to determine whether a town was most likely purposefully exclusive of racial minorities.[7] A random sample of towns that never had a considerable African-American population – fewer than five African-American individuals in 1880 and 1930 and less than 1% of the town's population in 2000 – was taken from Illinois, Indiana, Ohio, Michigan, Wisconsin, and Iowa. Every town that never had a significant African-American population in Missouri and Kentucky was included in the sample.[8] This yielded an additional 418 towns. In total, 600 towns were sampled.

For each of the 600 towns, surveys were mailed to a person knowledgeable about economic development in the town as well as other general aspects of the community. Community leaders had the position of mayor, city manager, chamber of commerce director, or economic development director. City clerks and local websites helped identify participants.

A mail survey was conducted using a modified tailor design method (Dillman, Smyth, & Christianson, 2008). Five contacts were made; however, the second contact was by e-mail rather than mail. Since nearly all participants had access to e-mail, attaching the survey to an e-mail led to fast responses. Furthermore, several selected individuals replied that another person was better suited to answer the questionnaire and subsequently forwarded the survey to that individual. Completed surveys totaled 439, resulting in a 73% response rate. Only those towns located in nonmetropolitan counties are used for the current study, yielding a final *N* of 217.

Variables

Descriptive statistics for all variables are provided in Table 1.

Outcome variables

Local economic development is measured by the change in the number of establishments per 1000 population (U.S. Census Business Patterns, 2000, 2010), change in the number of paid employees (U.S. Census Business Patterns, 2000, 2010), and change in the percent of unemployed (U.S. Census Bureau, 2000, 2010) for the years 2000 and 2010 for each community.[9] While these measures capture the growth or decline of jobs and businesses in a particular community, they do not capture the quality of jobs, as

Table 1. Descriptive characteristics of sample communities ($N = 217$).

	M or %	SD	Minimum	Maximum
Creative class occupations	.17	.05	.11	.36
Bohemian occupations	.01	.00	0	.02
Current racial tolerance	1.94	.64	1	3
Historical racial tolerance (exclusive)	78		0	1
Historical racial tolerance (inclusive)	22		0	1
African-American (%)	1.11	3.88	0	61.70
Human capital (% Bachelor's degree and above)	16.93	9.80	4	70
Technology	2.66	1.06	1	4
Economic development strategies	2.50	1.11	1	4
Bridging social capital (within)	2.53	1.14	1	4
Bridging social capital (outside)	2.66	1.07	1	4
Poverty rate (%)	10.31	5.42	1	34
Population	6079.67	3013.57	1805	1662
Farming	1		0	1
Mining	1		0	1
Manufacturing	61		0	1
Government	5		0	1
Service	8		0	1
Unspecialized	24		0	1
Change in establishments	−2.57	12.96	−63	120
Change in paid employees	−373.34	966.89	−6424	2864
Change in percent unemployed	5.21	3.23	−4	18
Change in median household income	6264.85	4853.20	−32001	23572

measured by pay. Thus, we use a measure of change in median household income (U.S. Census Bureau, 2000, 2010) to measure a community's overall income.

Independent variables

The creative class. This entrepreneurial class is measured at the county level using the percentage of residents employed in creative occupations (U.S. Census Bureau, 2000) and bohemian occupations (U.S. Census Bureau, 2000).

Historical racial tolerance[10]. A variety of sources were used to identify whether a town was purposefully exclusive of African-Americans, including Ancestry.com (Ancestry, 2015)[11] the U.S. Census,[12] and Loewen's (2005) database of sundown towns.[13] The following types of towns were identified: (1) those that had at one point in history purposely excluded African-Americans from residing within city limits (i.e. went sundown)[14] and whose current population is less than 1% African-American, and (2) towns that have consistently had a significant African-American population.

Current racial tolerance. Survey respondents were provided with a scenario of an employer locating to the community that would employ a large number of local residents at a living wage or higher. Respondents were asked how receptive community residents would be to the employer locating to the community if they thought the employer would attract a large number of African-Americans and/or Latinos to the community. Response categories included: 3 = very receptive, 2 = somewhat receptive, and 1 = not very receptive.

Technology. Respondents were asked to indicate the quality of physical infrastructure in the town related to water, sewer, roads, natural gas, high-speed internet, and rail. Response categories included: 1 = not available, 2 = terrible, 3 = poor, 4 = fair, 5 = good, 6 = very good. A summative index was created by summing the responses to the six items. Following the creation of the index, a variable was created based on the frequency variable.

Bridging social capital (within community). Respondents were asked to indicate how often different groups in the community cooperated for community betterment in the past five years. Groups included: (1) men and women, (2) younger and older residents, (3) different racial/ethnic groups, (4) rural residents and townsfolk, (5) newcomers and longtime residents, and (6) different religious groups. Response categories included: 1 = never, 2 = rarely, 3 = sometimes, 4 = often. A summative index was created by summing the responses to the six items (Cronbach's $\alpha = .839$). Following the index's creation, a variable was created based on the frequency variable.

Bridging social capital (outside community). Respondents were asked if in the past three years a group from the community: (1) visited another town to learn about its community development efforts, (2) went outside the community to seek financial or technical assistance, or (3) went outside the community to lobby or to protest a decision affecting the community. Response categories included: 0 = no, 1 = yes. Bridging social capital outside the community is measured by the number of affirmative responses.

Economic development strategies. Respondents were asked to indicate the level of frequency an individual or organization representing the community had engaged in each economic development strategy over the past three years. Response categories included: 0 = never, 1 = once, 2 = more than once. A summative index was created by summing the responses to the 15 items.[15] Following creation of the index, a variable was created based on the frequency variable.

Control variables

A total of three control variables were used, including town population size (U.S. Census Bureau, 2000), truncated into four categories; the poverty rate as the percent of individuals below the poverty line in each town (U.S. Census Bureau, 2000); and county economic typology, measuring each town's dominant economic sector (Economic Research Service, 2004).[16]

Analytic strategy

We use ordinary least squares (OLS) regression to test the major independent variables of economic development strategies, bridging social capital, creative class, human capital, tolerance, and technology, while controlling for demographic and economic characteristics, against four measures of economic development: business growth, job growth, change in unemployment, and change in median household income. Variance inflation factor scores for all of the independent variables were under 3.0, suggesting little multicollinearity among the variables.

Findings

Descriptive statistics

Communities on average underwent a decline in the number of establishments and paid employees while experiencing an increase in unemployment. Median household income rose by an average of $6264 for the sample communities (not controlling for inflation). Sampled communities had an average of 17% of employed residents employed in creative class occupations, but less than 1% of employed residents employed in bohemian occupations. On average, sampled communities were somewhat receptive to the idea of an employer locating to the community if the employer would attract a large number of African-Americans or Latinos to the community. In all, 78% of sampled communities were historically exclusive of African-Americans living within city limits. Because of the large number of historically exclusive communities in the sample, communities, on average, had only 1% of its residents identify as African-American. The range in community members aged 25 years or older with at least a bachelor's degree was quite large, ranging from 4 to 70%, with an average of 17%. On average, communities had just over 10% of their residents below poverty. In total 61% of communities had manufacturing as their major economic base, 24% were unspecialized, 8% were service-based, 5% had the government as the primary employer, 1% of communities had farming as their major economic base, and 1% were mining-oriented.

Predictors of economic development

Table 2 shows results from OLS regression models that predict the change in the number of establishments and paid employees. None of the independent variables were significantly related to change in businesses in the predicted direction. Surprisingly, communities with better quality infrastructural technologies were less likely to see business growth than communities with lower quality technology (β = −1.98, $p < .05$). Towns located in government and service counties were significantly less likely to experience growth in the number of establishments per 1000 residents (β = −7.84, $p < .05$; β = −9.46, $p < .01$ respectively).

Similarly, none of the independent variables were significantly related to change in paid employees. Towns located in farming, service, and unspecialized counties were

Table 2. Ordinary least squares regression of change in establishments per 1000 population and paid employees from 2000 to 2010 ($N = 217$).

Independent variables	Establishments per 1000 population	Paid employees
Creative class occupations	9.94	712.72
	−3(25.98)	(2646.70)
Bohemian occupations	422.23	34,789.50
	(377.59)	(38,609.61)
Current racial tolerance	1.16	175.29
	(1.24)	(127.39)
Historical racial tolerance	−2.96	339.31
	(4.48)	(455.97)
African-American (%)	−.02	−12.99
	(.25)	(25.23)
Human capital	.19	17.52
	(.12)	(12.11)
Technology	−1.98*	−39.80
	(.78)	(81.00)
Economic development strategies	1.22	−19.61
	(.87)	(88.81)
Bridging social capital (within)	1.03	88.35
	(.76)	(76.92)
Bridging social capital (outside)	−.46	−17.79
	(.80)	(82.31)
Poverty rate (%)	.16	12.38
	(.21)	(21.60)
Population	1.57	−13.94
	(1.32)	(134.92)
Farming	3.04	1296.82*
	(6.23)	(2.04)
Mining	−5.88	575.56
	(8.15)	(829.53)
Government	−7.84*	−141.78
	(3.78)	(385.75)
Service	−9.46**	725.67*
	(3.22)	(329.34)
Unspecialized	.58	640.98***
	(1.91)	(194.25)
R^2	.23	.18

Note: Robust standard errors are in parentheses.
*$p < .05$; **$p < .01$; ***$p < .001$.

significantly more likely to experience growth in paid employees than manufacturing counties (β = 1296.82, $p < .05$; β = 725.67, $p < .05$; β = 640.98, $p < .001$ respectively).

Table 3 shows results from OLS regression models that predict a change in the percentage of unemployed residents and a change in median household income. Human capital is positively related to employment; towns with a greater percentage of residents with a bachelor's degree or higher (β = −.10, $p < .01$) were less likely to have an increase in unemployed residents between the years 2000 and 2010. Economic development strategies are also positively related to employment; towns that employ more economic development strategies were less likely to have an increase in unemployed residents between the years 2000 and 2010 (β = −.51, $p < .10$). Counterintuitively, however, technology is positively related to unemployment; towns that have higher quality infrastructural technology were more likely to have an increase in unemployed residents

Table 3. Ordinary least squares regression of change in percent unemployed and median household income from 2000 to 2010 ($N = 217$).

Independent variables	Unemployment	Household income
Creative class occupations	10.66	−2262.51
	(8.42)	(11,596.72)
Bohemian occupations	−107.23	13,8093.66
	(122.34)	(16,8528.67)
Current racial tolerance	−.30	−23.25
	(.40)	(.97)
Historical racial tolerance	−.56	4026.58**
	(1.45)	(1999.58)
African-American (%)	.10	105.86
	(.08)	(110.66)
Human capital	−.10***	212.77***
	(.04)	(52.66)
Technology	.77***	−518.16
	(.25)	(349.90
Economic development strategies	−.51*	53.72
	(.28)	(389.44)
Bridging social capital (within)	−.22	200.83
	(.25)	(337.30)
Bridging social capital (outside)	.32	−111.78
	(.26)	(357.72)
Poverty rate (%)	.07	1.69
	(.07)	(94.71)
Population	−.09	−385.33
	(.43)	(590.18)
Farming	−1.08	2758.14
	(2.02)	(2778.78)
Mining	.19	4268.28
	(2.64)	(3637.79)
Government	−3.11**	2311.33
	(1.23)	(1688.28)
Service	−2.21	5205.83***
	1.04	(1435.03)
Unspecialized	−1.44**	1540.90
	(.62)	(850.39)
R^2	.25	.33

Note: Robust standard errors are in parentheses.
*$p < .10$; **$p < .05$; ***$p < .01$.

between the years 2000 and 2010 ($\beta = .77$, $p < .01$). Towns located in federal/state government-dependent and unspecialized counties were also less likely to have an increase in unemployed residents between those years ($\beta = -3.11$, $p < .05$; $\beta = -1.44$, $p < .05$ respectively).

Only one independent variable, human capital, was significantly related to the change in median household income in the expected direction ($\beta = 212.77$, $p < .01$). While historical racial tolerance is also positively related to a change in household income ($\beta = 4026.58$, $p < .05$), it is in the opposite direction than predicted. Communities that were historically exclusive of African-Americans saw a larger increase in median household income than towns that were historically inclusive (U.S. Census Bureau 1880, 1930, 2000). Towns located in service counties also experienced a larger increase in median household income between the years 2000 and 2010 ($\beta = 5205.83$, $p < .01$).

Discussion

We tested several community characteristics and economic development strategies to determine which were associated with greater economic well-being in rural communities, in part to see what actions would best benefit rural communities in an age of devolution. One method of economic development that has gained attention over the past few decades involves making a community desirable to attract the creative class of entrepreneurs. However, our study does not support the creative class theory: the near non-existence of bohemian occupations in rural areas shows how difficult it is for rural communities to attract this creative class subset.

Furthermore, measures of tolerance and technology did not have the predicted effect on economic development. Due to institutional discrimination, whites continue to have higher incomes than African-Americans. Furthermore, African-Americans are financially hit harder than whites during economic recessions, due to their lower levels of wealth (Soss et al., 2008). Therefore, historically tolerant communities may experience lower levels of certain measures of economic development (e.g. median income) compared with historically racially exclusive communities due to having larger numbers of African-Americans in their communities. As for technology not having the predicted effect on economic development, it may be that the types of technology available to rural communities do not have the same type of effect impact as technologies available to metropolitan areas, and further research is needed to tease out different technology's effects.

In fact, increasing formal education of residents was the only key variable significantly related to two of the measures of economic development in the predicted manner. Residents in towns with a higher percentage of residents with at least a bachelor-level degree experienced less unemployment and had higher median household incomes than residents in towns with less formal education, suggesting the continued importance of human capital in times of devolution.

Given that 78% of the sampled communities were historically exclusive of African-Americans, and on average communities in this sample had only 1% African-American residents, our sample captures a subset of rural America with a very specific racial history of exclusion and continued racial isolation. One of our goals was to test the effects of racial tolerance on economic development, which is why we chose our sample. Although our findings are not empirically generalizable to other communities, they are theoretically suggestive; by studying communities at far ends of a racial tolerance spectrum, we provide insight into what may be occurring in other rural communities across

America, depending upon their own histories of race relations. Because of government devolution, solutions to address various forms of institutional racism – many of which are economic – are increasingly found at the level of state, county, and municipal governments, as are efforts to facilitate economic development in general.

Despite this attempt, more research is needed to tease out the relationship between racial tolerance and human capital in rural communities. It may be the case that rural communities that are more tolerant attract more racial minorities that may need more training to fit the needs of employers. Institutional racism that exists at the macro level, which results in African-Americans having less education than whites on average, puts additional financial strain on tolerant communities and leaves less money for other economic development efforts.

Next, communities that implemented more economic development strategies had lower unemployment than communities with fewer economic development strategies. Given the numerous resources expended to entice employers to a community and to build local businesses, this is a positive outcome. However, the number of economic development strategies a community implemented was not related to the other measures of economic development. It could be the case that those communities facing broader political-economic challenges in the global economy are the ones most likely to pursue these endeavors based on need; however, these economic challenges (e.g. job loss due to industry going overseas, technological advances in resource extraction, new laws affecting resource extraction and production) might disadvantage some communities compared to communities that do not experience such challenges. Future research could use additional measures of economic development strategies, such as annual budgets allocated for such strategies and the number of employees whose tasks include increasing economic development, to assess each approach's relative impact.

Finally, our measures of bridging social capital were not significantly related to any of the four measures of economic development. Advocates of an asset-building approach to community development emphasize the need to build networks and enhance the voices of disadvantaged groups (Flora & Flora, 2008; Warner, 2003), but it may be harder for such efforts to translate into tangible measures of economic development in rural areas. Our results do not lend support to the idea that devolution succeeds by allowing local civic actors to flourish. Future research is needed to map power relations and network structures of a large sample of rural communities to better assess whether cross-network cooperation leads to economic development.

Policy implications

Beyond theoretical implications, these findings provide important insight for local officials and community volunteers. First, economic development in rural communities is a constant challenge that needs to be addressed at all levels. Between 2000 and 2010 (the last three years of this period affected by a recession), rural communities experienced a decrease in the number of establishments and paid employees and an increase in unemployment. Second, economic development strategies that succeed in urban areas may not necessarily benefit rural areas. By having low-density population, rural areas have a harder time creating the conditions needed to attract high-technology firms and people employed in bohemian occupations. Third, economic development is a complicated phenomenon with no magic formula to increase it. Given the financial strain placed on rural communities, increasing capacity in one area, such as infrastructural technology, may decrease capacity in other areas. As Warner (2003) notes, uneven capacity can become even more prominent under devolution.

Finally, our results suggest that devolution of economic responsibilities to towns and counties may not necessarily lead to stronger economic development. Given that many rural communities struggle with social divisions and a lack of local economic strengths, devolution may worsen, rather than strengthen, some local economies. Small communities often lack adequate resources to serve the social and economic needs of residents, and the additional responsibilities necessitated by devolution may simply exacerbate this financial strain. Accordingly, policymakers at the state and federal levels should consider greater economic assistance to rural communities. Grants and other forms of financial assistance may be beneficial, as might be consultation with skilled economic development strategists. Although devolution has the potential to benefit some local communities, the responsibilities devolved need to be carefully considered by both federal and state governments, and financial assistance should be made available to those communities that struggle with the demands of devolution.

Conclusion

This analysis provides insight into the roles that economic development strategies, the creative class, and bridging social capital play with respect to rural economic development. We focus on rural communities as our level of analysis because it is greatly under-researched, despite the need for data that will contribute to economic development efforts. In doing so, it is important to point out that these conclusions can only be generalized to communities with similar features to those in our study. Furthermore, much of the data were gathered during years impacted by a severe economic recession. Further examination using data from nonrecession years will be necessary to determine if similar analyses can be drawn. Additionally, we use quantitative analysis in this study, relying upon theory to provide an interpretation of the statistical findings, and thus future qualitative research would provide insight to communities within our study, and allow us to better understand nuances of economic development.

Disclosure statement

No potential conflict of interest was reported by the authors.

Notes

1. The term "nontraditional south" is used in this article to reference those states that bordered the Confederacy but still remained in the Union during the Civil War.
2. Towns needed to be incorporated and at least 1500 in population so that they could have the potential for meaningful economic development. To get a sample size large enough for statistical analyses with low sampling error, we included communities up to 17,000 residents. However, 75% of communities were between 1500 and 9300 residents.
3. Given the stratified sample, the sample was weighted by historical racial tolerance.
4. Most towns that were racially exclusive did so between 1890 and 1930 (Loewen, 2005). Therefore, we examine the 1880 census to see how racially tolerant a community was prior to the creation of sundown towns and again in 1930 to see if the racial make-up of a community changed.
5. Because there were so few small communities in the seven states that were racially inclusive, every community in these states is included in the sample. Since Kentucky had many more

communities that remained racially inclusive, a sample of such communities was taken for the study.

6. Because many sundown towns would allow for a few "special" African-Americans to live in the community (e.g. the town barber), a cut-off of five African-Americans is used for the years 1880 and 1930. By 2000, sundown laws were illegal; therefore, most prior sundown towns had more African-American residents than they did in 1880 or 1930. However, intolerance in most prior sundown towns carried on informally once sundown laws were made illegal, so most previous sundown towns still had very few African-Americans. Thus, we use the cut off of 1% African-American in 2000 as my third data point needed to label the town racially exclusive.
7. Refer to Crowe (2012) for an explanation of how nearly all of the all-white towns in the Midwest in the late twentieth century were racially exclusive in the early twentieth century.
8. In these six states, most towns were racially exclusive. Because of this large number of racially exclusive towns, a random sample is taken from these states. However, in Missouri and Kentucky, states in the nontraditional South, far fewer towns became racially exclusive. Therefore, in these two states, every racially exclusive town that fit the parameters is included in the study's sample.
9. We examine standard measures of job growth rather than growth in high-technology or highly skilled jobs. High-technology jobs cluster in urban areas, thus making it difficult for rural communities to entice them to their location. Furthermore, with jobs declining in manufacturing and natural resources, leaders often perceive job growth in any sector as positive for the community, as job growth in general will slow population decline.
10. There are several definitions of tolerance, but for this study, we use tolerance in a way similar to the acceptance of something harmful or unpleasant. Many white people in the late nineteenth and early twentieth centuries viewed African-Americans as harmful, unpleasant, or both. However, some communities allowed them to live, congregate, and work in the community while many communities banished African-Americans from the city limits. While some communities tolerated African-Americans enough to let them be part of the community, it was not the case that they fully accepted them as equal community members. In most towns, they were still segregated during this time period.
11. Ancestry.com provided historic census records through 1930, with the name, race, gender, and occupation of each resident broken up by household for each town.
12. Census records were acquired for the years 1880, 1930, and 2000. Towns that had African-American families living within city limits for all three decades were identified as towns with a consistent, significant African-American population.
13. For over a decade Loewen travelled to towns collecting evidence about their racial histories. This database documents reports by local residents who recall seeing signs that were posted to warn blacks/African-Americans to be out before sundown, remember being told that they were not welcome, or recall a general hostility toward African-Americans. All of the towns that, at one time, had African-American populations but had no African-American residents by 1930, were included in Dr. Loewen's database, in addition to many other towns that never had a significant African-American population.
14. Several towns in the sample had a significant African-American population in 1880 – over 50 residents, including several families – but did not have a single African-American resident in 1930. This indicates that the population was forced, either directly through physical means or indirectly through economic means, to move out of the town. Refer to Crowe (2012) for a mathematical explanation that indicates that African-American families were either indirectly or directly forced to move out of town.
15. Refer to Crowe (2012) for a list of economic development strategies.
16. Six dummy variables were used to code each community based on their dominant economic sector: farming, mining, manufacturing, services, federal/state government, or unspecialized (if they had no dominant industry).

References

Ancestry. (2015, July 26). Ancestry.com Home Page. Retrieved from http://www.ancestry.com/

Bartik, T. (1991). *Who benefits from state and local economic development policies?* Kalamazoo, MI: W.E. Upjohn Institute for Employment Research.

Bourdieu, P. (1979). Les trois etats du capital culturel [The three states of cultural capital]. *Actes de la recherche en sciences sociales [Social Science Research Acts], 30*, 3–6.

Coleman, J. (1988). Social capital in the creation of human capital. *American Journal of Sociology, 94*, S95–S120.

Conlan, T. (1998). *From new federalism to devolution: Twenty-five years of intergovernmental reform*. Washington, DC: Brookings Institution Press.

Crowe, J. (2008). Economic development in the nonmetropolitan west: The influence of built, natural, and social capital. *Community Development, 39*, 51–70.

Crowe, J. (2012). The influence of racial histories on economic development strategies. *Ethnic and Racial Studies, 35*, 1955–1973.

Crowe, J., & Ceresola, R. (2014). Racial history, legacy and economic development. *Patterns of Prejudice, 48*, 350–369.

Dillman, D., Smyth, J., & Christianson, L. (2008). *Internet, mail, and mixed-mode surveys: The tailor design method* (3rd ed.). New York, NY: Wiley.

Duncan, C. M. (2001). Social capital in America's poor rural communities. In S. Saegert, J. P. Thompson, & M. R. Warren (Eds.), *Social capital and poor communities* (pp. 60–86). New York, NY: Russell Sage Foundation.

Economic Research Service. (2004). *County typology codes*. Washington, DC: United States Department of Agriculture.

Emery, M., & Flora, C. (2006). Spiraling-up: Mapping community transformation with community capitals framework. *Community Development, 37*, 19–35.

Flora, C., & Flora, J. (2008). *Rural communities: Legacy and change* (3rd ed.). Boulder, CO: Westview Press.

Flora, J., Sharp, J., Flora, C., & Newlon, B. (1997). Entrepreneurial social infrastructure and locally initiated economic development in the nonmetropolitan United States. *The Sociological Quarterly, 38*, 623–645.

Florida, R. (2002). *The rise of the creative class: And how it's transforming work, leisure, community and everyday life*. New York, NY: Basic Books.

Florida, R. (2003). Cities and the creative class. *City and Community, 2*, 3–19.

Florida, R. (2005). *Cities and the creative class*. New York, NY: Routledge.

Gittell, R., & Thompson, J. P. (2002). Making social capital work: Social capital and community economic development. In S. Saegert, J. P. Thompson, & M. R. Warren (Eds.), *Social capital and poor communities* (pp. 115–135). New York, NY: Russell Sage Foundation.

Glaeser, E. (2000). The new economics of urban and regional growth. In C. Gordon, G. Meric, & M. Feldman (Eds.), *The Oxford handbook of economic geography* (pp. 83–98). Oxford: Oxford University Press.

Goetz, S., & Rupasingha, A. (2002). The new rural economy: High-tech firm clustering: Implications for rural areas. *American Journal of Agricultural Economics, 84*, 1229–1236.

Gordon, R. (2000). Does the "new economy" measure up to the great inventions of the past? *Journal of Economic Perspectives, 14*, 49–74.

Grisham, V., & Gurwitt, R. (1999). *Hand in hand: Community and economic development in Tupelo*. Washington, DC: The Aspen Institute.

Harrison, B. (1992). Industrial districts: Old wine in new bottles? *Regional Studies, 26*, 469–483.

Harvey, M. H. (2011). Welfare reform and household survival: The interaction of structure and network strength in the Rio Grande Valley, Texas. *Journal of Poverty, 15*, 43–64.

Herslund, L. (2012). The rural creative class: Counterurbanisation and entrepreneurship in the Danish Countryside. *Sociologia Ruralis, 52*, 235–255.

Hoyman, M., & Faricy, C. (2009). It takes a village: A test of the creative class, social capital, and human capital theories. *Urban Affairs Review, 44*, 311–333.

Letki, N. (2008). Does diversity erode social cohesion? Social capital and race in British neighbourhoods. *Political Studies, 56*, 99–126.

Loewen, J. (2005). *Sundown towns: A hidden dimension of American racism*. New York, NY: New Press.

Majee, W., & Hoyt, A. (2011). Cooperatives and community development: A perspective on the use of cooperatives in development. *Journal of Community Practice, 19*, 48–61.

McGranahan, D., & Wojan, T. (2007). The creative class: A key to rural growth. *Amber Waves, 5*, 16–21.

Moller, S. (2002). Supporting poor single mothers: Gender and race in the U.S. welfare state. *Gender & Society, 16*, 465–484.

Parisi, D., McLaughlin, D. K., Grice, S. M., Taquino, M., & Gill, D. A. (2003). TANF participation rates: Do community conditions matter? *Rural Sociology, 68*, 491–512.

Putnam, R. (1993). *Making democracy work: Civic traditions in modern Italy*. Princeton, NJ: Princeton University Press.

Putnam, R. (2007). E Pluribus Unum: Diversity and community in the twenty-first century: The 2006 Johan Skytte prize lecture. *Scandinavian Political Studies, 30*, 137–174.

Rainey, D. V., Robinson, K. L., Allen, I., & Christy, R. D. (2003). Essential forms of capital for sustainable community development. *American Journal of Agricultural Economics, 85*, 708–715.

Robichau, R. (2010). The effects of economic development strategies in local municipalities. *Perspectives in Public Affairs, 7*, 26–41.

Schultz, T. (1961). Investment in human capital. *American Economic Review, 51*, 1–17.

Sharp, E., & Joslyn, M. (2008). Culture, segregation, and tolerance in urban America. *Social Science Quarterly, 89*, 573–591.

Sharp, J., & Parisi, D. (2003). Devolution: Who is responsible for rural America? In D. Brown & L. Swanson (Eds.), *Challenges for rural America in the twenty-first century* (pp. 353–362). University Park, PA: Pennsylvania State University Press.

Soss, J., Fording, R., & Schram, S. (2008). The color of devolution: Race, federalism, and the politics of social control. *American Journal of Political Science, 52*, 536–553.

U.S. Census Bureau. (1880). Online database. Ancestry.com.

U.S. Census Bureau. (1930). Online database. Ancestry.com.

U.S. Census Bureau. (2000). *Summary file 1*. Washington, DC: Author.

U.S. Census Bureau. (2010). *American community survey: 2006–2010*. Washington, DC: Author.

U.S. Census Business Patterns. (2000). *2000 Zip Code Business Patterns*. Washington, DC: U.S. Census Bureau.

U.S. Census Business Patterns. (2010). *2010 Zip Code Business Patterns*. Washington, DC: U.S. Census Bureau.

Warner, M. (2003). Competition, cooperation, and local governance. In D. Brown & L. Swanson (Eds.), *Challenges for rural America in the twenty-first century* (pp. 252–261). University Park, PA: Pennsylvania State University Press.

Complex transactions: Community development financial institutions lending to ethnic entrepreneurs in Los Angeles

R. Varisa Patraporn

Despite federal and state efforts to ensure equal access to credit, ethnic disparities in financial capital remain. Community Development Financial Institutions (CDFIs) represent one type of institution working to address this inequality. Based on interviews with the staff of ten Los Angeles, CA (USA) area CDFIs, this article explores the unique way CDFIs lend to ethnic entrepreneurs. The findings highlight the role of CDFIs in providing extensive technical assistance, utilizing flexible lending criteria, and building co-ethnic weak ties. Furthermore, CDFI staff members' specialized knowledge about particular ethnic groups, shared cultural background, and/or language ability allow them to take on greater risk. As the demand for financial capital grows in a tight credit market, it will become increasingly important to understand these community institutions and their potential impact on community development more broadly.

Introduction

Despite the importance of small business in generating jobs in the overall economy and as a community economic development strategy, significant challenges exist in starting, growing, and sustaining small businesses (Fairlie & Robb, 2008). Among these challenges, access to financial capital is particularly difficult for ethnic entrepreneurs. They typically have little to no credit history, less experience, and/or face discrimination compared to their non-ethnic counterparts (Bates, Jackson, & Johnson, 2007; Blanchard, Zhao, & Yinger, 2008; Blanchflower, Levine, & Zimmerman, 2003; Cavalluzzo & Wolken, 2005). Even with federal and state efforts to ensure equal access to credit, ethnic disparities persist (Bates & Robb, 2013). Indeed, the California Reinvestment Coalition reports that from 2007 to 2012, while overall business loans approved dropped by 60% for all businesses, the percent of business loans approved to Latinos dropped by 73% and to African-Americans by 93% (Fisher, 2013).

Community Development Financial Institutions (CDFIs) represent one response to meet the credit needs of ethnic entrepreneurs. CDFIs first emerged as an alternative to banks providing over a billion dollars in loans and investments in economically distressed communities since 1992 (CDFI Coalition, 2014). Earlier forms of CDFIs began in the late 1960s and 1970s when community development corporations provided small business and affordable housing loans. With the establishment of United States Treasury

Department's CDFI Fund in 1994, the number of CDFIs has grown to over 1000 (CDFI Coalition, 2014; CDFI Fund, 2014). CDFIs provide an alternative to banks because they accept below market rate returns subsidized by acquiring lower cost capital from banks, foundations, and the government, all with the goal to further community economic development (Caskey & Hollister, 2001).

Prior research on CDFIs focuses on the industry as a whole and the impact on local economic development (Bates, 2000; Benjamin, Rubin, & Zielenbach, 2004). For instance, Benjamin et al.'s (2004) paper represents one of the first studies on the topic providing a thorough description of the range of institutions, including banks, credit unions, loan funds, and capital venture funds that are CDFIs. They also describe the range of products and services CDFIs have from deposits and checking accounts to consumer loans, individual development accounts, affordable housing, and entrepreneurial training.

Less is known about how such institutions work, especially the details of the lending process and how loan decisions get made (Frisch & Servon, 2006). Moreover, to the author's knowledge, Caskey and Hollister's (2001) is the only study to focus on small business lending CDFIs. They distinguish between two types of institutions. The first type provides loans to small businesses with typically three or more employees and needing more than $25,000. The second type provides what is known as microloans to primarily sole proprietorships in need of less than $25,000. Caskey and Hollister (2001) distinguished the former by calling them Business Development Financial Institutions and the latter as microcredit lenders.[1]

In comparison, a great deal of research examines lending in other institutions, including banks, ethnic banks, and among peer groups. A common theme found across these studies includes the importance of relationships and race/ethnicity in lending. For instance, the literature on banks and their lending process highlights the importance of length and quality of relationships for information exchange (Cole, Goldberg, & White, 2004; Ongena & Smith, 2001). The multiple and repeated interactions between loan officers and entrepreneurs creates a weak tie. Granovetter (1973) showed the relevance of weak ties in economic outcomes. Other sociologists also noted the relevance of co-ethnic strong ties in facilitating access to capital in peer lending groups, such as rotating credit and savings association (Light & Bonacich, 1988; Light, Kwuon, & Zhong, 1990). Similarly, the literature on bank mortgage lending finds that loan officers and borrowers being the same race/ethnicity results in more positive loan outcomes (Black, Collins, & Cyree, 1997; Hunter & Walker, 1996). Such positive loan outcomes occur within ethnic banks due to specialized knowledge and social capital that ensures loan repayment (Li, Dymski, Zhou, Chee, & Aldana, 2002). To what extent do similar relationships exist in CDFI loan processes? What is the role of race/ethnicity in the CDFI lending process, and does it influence loan outcomes? What does the CDFI loan process look like, and how does it compare to a bank?

This article expands our understanding of weak ties and co-ethnic ties by exploring the intersection of the two within CDFIs. The role of CDFIs in small business lending has increased in recent years due to bank tightening of the credit markets. Thus, it will become increasingly important to understand whether and to what degree they function similarly and differently from other institutions (Fisher, 2013; Quittner, 2014). In doing so, this study clarifies how the financial industry and policymakers can improve unequal access to credit (Blanchflower et al., 2003; Fairlie & Robb, 2008; Fisher, 2013). This is because CDFIs tend to operate at a local scale understanding community needs and culture in a way that larger commercial banks cannot, especially in the post-2007 regulatory environment. Moreover, while most studies have focused on CDFIs at the national level, this study explores CDFIs in Los Angeles, an economically and ethnically diverse area that is underrepresented in the academic literature (Caskey & Hollister, 2001).

The remainder of this paper proceeds in four parts. First is a discussion of prior research on various lending institutions, what we know about their loan processes, and the role of relationships and more specifically co-ethnic relationships in the lending process. The second part outlines the methods and provides a sample description. The methods section is followed by a discussion of key findings. The final part includes study limitations, future research recommendations, and policy implications.

Continuum of lending institutions

Entrepreneurs rely on a range of institutions and/or sources of capital, but mostly personal savings and/or family and friends and commercial banks (U.S. Bureau of the Census, 2007). Figure 1 presents a continuum of lending institutions from less-formal entities to more-formal entities based on the literature on various lending institutions. Less-formal entities include personal savings, money from family and friends, and rotating credit and saving associations (ROSCAs). At the far right end of the continuum are the most regulated entities, commercial banks. They are the most formal in their loan process and rely more on quantitative measures such as credit scores and financial modeling as compared to institutions toward the left of the figure (Altman, 1980; Chen, Guo, & Huang, 2009). Some CDFIs are not regulated, but apply similar practices as regulated entities.

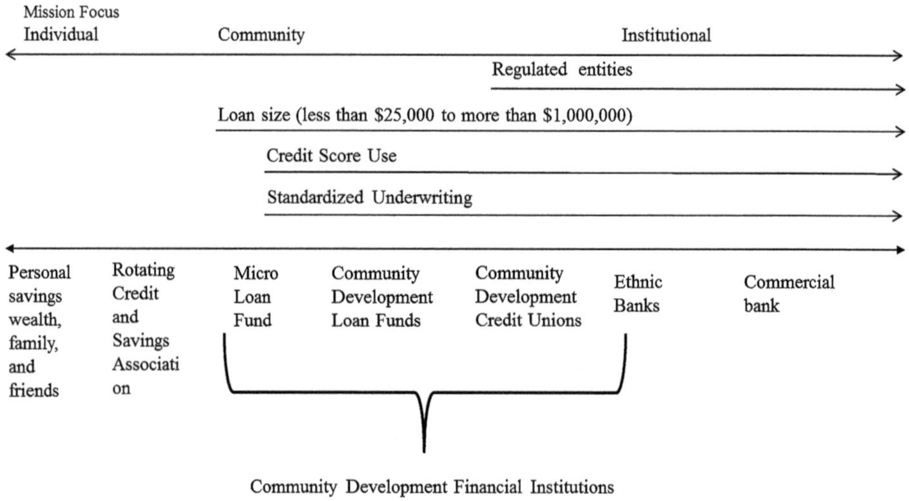

Figure 1. Continuum of lending institutions.

Institutions vary in their mission and corresponding loan amounts. Institutions on the left side of Figure 1 focus on individual economic success, while those at the far right emphasize profit for institutional success. CDFIs, located in the middle, have a mission to help individuals and/or communities (Benjamin et al., 2004). Documented loan amounts range from $500 among microcredit institutions to about $25,000 (Caskey & Hollister, 2001; Servon, 1997). On the other hand, while community development loan funds (CDLFs) and business loan funds vary, they range from $25,000 to greater than $1 million. In 2005, the median financing outstanding among business-focused CDLFs was close to $2.4 million (Rubin, 2008). With greater scale and assets, transnational ethnic banks and commercial banks can lend even greater amounts.

It should be noted that Figure 1 does not represent all the institutions. For instance, some ethnic banks are large transnational banks. These banks are distinctly different in terms of capital resources and function compared to smaller community-oriented ethnic banks. Instead, the figure should be understood as identifying general patterns seen in the existing literature.

Banks

Among the limited studies about the overall commercial bank lending process, the bank lending process is seen as relatively straightforward (Altman, 1980). Quantitative analysis drives the lending process, with financial forecasting beginning as early as the application stage (Frame, Srinivasan, & Woosley, 2001). While Altman (1980) acknowledges that banks use qualitative factors in decision-making, "The essence of good credit analysis is to determine repayment probabilities … to provide the basis for the lending decision and for the pricing and structuring of the loan agreement" (p. 814).

To conduct such financial forecasting, the bank collects firm and entrepreneur information, including profit, firm size, age, and industry (Cavalluzzo & Wolken, 2005). For entrepreneur characteristics, banks look at experience, education, and personal wealth (Cavalluzzo, Cavalluzzo, & Wolken, 2002; Frame et al., 2001). However, the most important factor is the credit score, a single quantitative measure that estimates the borrower's future loan performance. Banks often rely only on the credit score to initially screen for borrowers who do not meet the credit score minimum (Chen et al., 2009).

Banks also mitigate their risk by considering the 5 Cs of banking. Capacity is the entrepreneur's ability to pay back the loan based on business revenues. Collateral are assets such as real estate or equipment the bank can keep when there is no cash to pay back a loan. Capital is the amount of cash that is available and indicates how the entrepreneur is managing their finances. And while banks look at character, they often relate it to credit history (Chen et al., 2009).

Following credit analysis, a loan decision is typically made by a loan officer. After a positive loan decision, pricing and structuring of the loan occurs using data acquired from the credit evaluation stage. It is not clear from the literature whether there is any contact between the bank and entrepreneur following a loan denial. At least one study claims that banks are known to provide limited feedback post loan denial (Gray, Saunders, & Goregaokar, 2013).

Microcredit and rotating credit and savings associations

In comparison to banks, institutions on the less-formal end of the continuum are called microcredit institutions. Microcredit institutions typically provide smaller loans (under $25,000) to entrepreneurs (Servon, 1997, 1998, 1999; Wydick, 2001). Prior research discusses the potential to alleviate poverty and promote minority economic development (Bates, 1997, 2000; Servon, 1997, 1998). Some microcredit institutions use a peer group-lending model, providing very small amounts of capital (typically starting at $500) to new businesses considered high-risk investments (Ghatak, 1999; Hossain, 1988). Peer groups make lending decisions and assume responsibility for the collection of loans. Each group decides whether someone gets a loan and how to seek repayment and/or monitor loans (Anthony, 2005). As a result, no standard underwriting applies among such institutions as a whole.

Within peer group lending models, ROSCAs exist, consisting of individuals of the same racial/ethnic group lending money to each other by taking turns. This form of lending institution is perhaps the least regulated. Most of this research identifies immigrants from Asia as practicing this strategy as a way to secure capital for small business (Light & Bonacich, 1988; Light et al., 1990; Min, 2008).

CDFIs

CDFIs represent a range of institutions, including banks, credit unions, loan funds, and capital venture funds (Benjamin et al., 2004). They provide a range of products and services from checking accounts to consumer loans, individual development accounts, affordable housing development loans, and entrepreneurial training (Benjamin et al., 2004; Rubin, 2008).

Frisch and Servon's (2006) survey of prior research on community development system components found only two studies about CDFIs and eight on microenterprise and entrepreneurship programs. Since then more research has been produced furthering our understanding of such institutions and their impacts more broadly. For instance, some scholars have focused on CDLFs as one type of CDFI (Rubin, 2008; Rubin, Caskey, Dickstein, & Zielenbach, 2008). And while such studies expand our understanding of the broad impact of such institutions, they do not provide an in-depth understanding of how such institutions function and make lending decisions.

Even less is known about CDFIs that work with entrepreneurs. To date, the author is aware of one study that focuses solely on CDFIs lending to entrepreneurs (Caskey & Hollister, 2001). Caskey and Hollister (2001) provide a description about how business-focused loan funds work, including funding sources and the potential social impact of such institutions.

Race/ethnicity, relationships, and lending

Social networks are individual connections that form a web of relationships. These relationships are important because they are critical to knowledge creation and transfer, and sharing and exchanging information (Coleman, 1988; Levin & Cross, 2004; Portes, 1998). This knowledge and information can be utilized to identify and secure economic opportunities.

Having a larger social network would presumably mean greater opportunity for an individual to become economically mobile. However, one's social network is based not only on how many relationships one has, but also the diversity of that network (Granovetter, 1973; Lin, 1999). Individuals with not just strong, but also weak ties presumably have access to higher quality information (Granovetter, 1995; Montgomery, 1992).

Weak ties are relationships outside one's regular day-to-day community and/or ethnic group. Thus, for ethnic entrepreneurs, having weak ties would mean more relationships with Whites because as Flores-Yeffal and Zhang (2012) explain "as the majority US population, Whites [have] formed their own exclusive networks due to their privileged social and economic position and power" (p. 237). Thus, compared to other racial groups, ties with Whites should result in better quality information and resources. Weak ties also provide a bridge and link to individuals in other social circles beyond family or close friends that can result in positive economic outcomes (Granovetter, 1973).

In the banking literature, the repeated interaction between the two prior to a loan application submission creates a weak tie. This research identifies the importance of such ties in entrepreneurs applying for, receiving, and paying back loans (Cole, 1998; Frame et al., 2001; Ongena & Smith, 2001). Relationships also provide banks with additional "soft" information acquired through multiple interactions beyond the quantitative information that can then be used in the application evaluation.

Other scholars argue the importance and usefulness of "strong ties" within an ethnic group for entrepreneurship (Light, 1972; Portes & Bach, 1985; Portes & Sensenbrenner, 1993). For instance, Light and Bonacich's (1988) study of Koreans found that strong ties within an ethnic group can act as a resource for information about how to run businesses and provide capital for business.

The literature on ethnic banks also discusses the benefits of such co-ethnic relationships. Such studies examine how ethnic banks identify additional "soft information" about borrowers of the same ethnicity (Dymski & Mohanty, 1999; Hum, 2010; Li et al., 2002; Zonta, 2004). They conclude that the source of "soft information" comes from the ethnic bank's ability to capitalize on its specialized knowledge of its customer base. Co-ethnic relationships are inherent in this business, and ethnic banks use informal information based on locational proximity and reputation in the community as identified by business networks (Dymski & Mohanty, 1999). Thus, social capital within a community allows ethnic banks unique access to certain resources.

Research on banks and ethnic banks also shows the positive impacts of social capital, specialized knowledge, and co-ethnic relationships in loan outcomes. While mostly focused on mortgage lending, the research testing the cultural affinity hypothesis demonstrates that co-ethnic relationships positively impact loan outcomes. This happens because the lender prefers to lend to individuals of the same ethnicity or they have better access to information about the borrower (Black et al., 1997; Hunter & Walker, 1996; Zonta, 2004).

This study builds on research concerning small business lending by exploring the lending process within an understudied institution, CDFIs. It also expands on the literature on strong and weak ties by testing the existence of either and/or both within the CDFI lending process. Essentially, is there a relationship between the CDFI staff and the entrepreneur? If so, are these strong or weak ties? What is the ethnic nature of these ties? How do such ties contribute to the loan decision process?

Methods

To better understand the CDFI loan processes and how they connect to co-ethnic and weak ties, 12 in-depth semi-structured interviews with key staff of 10 Los Angeles, CA area CDFIs were conducted. While interviews were with individual staff members, the study unit of analysis is the CDFI because interviewees were asked about the CDFI and its lending practices.

There are several reasons the Los Angeles area was chosen. First, Los Angeles is a region where the number of ethnic entrepreneurs is growing and has persisted. Despite moderate growth of entrepreneurs, Los Angeles County continues to have the most minority-owned firms of all United States counties (U.S. Bureau of the Census, 2011). From 2002 to 2007, the number of African-American firms increased from 52,699 to 59,677 while Hispanic or Latino firms grew from 188,422 to 225,791; a 13 and 20% change for African-Americans and Latinos, respectively. Asian American entrepreneurs experienced the largest growth (30%) representing an increase from 140,461 to 183,090 entrepreneurs (U.S. Bureau of the Census, 2002, 2007). Thus, Los Angeles area CDFIs are more likely to serve racial and ethnic minorities. Second, while the overall CDFI industry has a larger historical presence in the Northeast, the industry growth in the West and the South are commensurate with population growth among immigrants and racial minorities in these regions.[2] Finally, focusing on the Los Angeles area allowed for all of the interviews to occur face-to-face with limited resources.

The Department of Treasury CDFI Fund, Association for Enterprise Opportunity, and CDFI Coalition websites provided a source to identify CDFIs in the Los Angeles area. From there, the list focused on CDFIs serving ethnic entrepreneurs.[3] Of 15 potential organizations, seven responded with interest by email and/or phone. The use of snowball sampling identified three more organizations. Despite the small sample size and potential bias due to snowball sampling, this study captured nearly 50% of the universe of Los Angeles area CDFIs providing small business loans at the time. A liberal estimate of CDFIs operating loan funds puts the count at 23 in 2006 (Abramowitz, Edwards, & Melford, 2006).[4]

To determine eligibility of the CDFI for the study, there were three criteria. First, they needed to serve the Los Angeles area. Second, CDFIs had to provide some level of financial capital to entrepreneurs and not just provide development services. Third, they should have been in operation for at least one year at the time of the interview.

Once a CDFI was eligible, the author identified the appropriate person to interview. The author asked to speak with the staff person who has the most direct contact with entrepreneurs, which was often a loan officer. Due to the organizational structure and size of CDFIs, some individuals interviewed did not have the title of loan officer, but performed the same function. These individuals include executive directors and program directors.

By relying on in-depth interviews, this study provides an understanding of the complex and personal nature of social processes that are part of lending. As a result, findings provide a more refined analysis of CDFI lender–entrepreneur relationships than possible with quantitative tools, despite the small sample size limiting generalizability (Miles & Huberman, 1984). This method also identifies relevant actors, resources, and relationships that might not otherwise be expected in an area of research that has produced very little on the subject (Frisch & Servon, 2006).

The semi-structured interview guide had three sets of questions. The first set of questions focused on a broad understanding of the overall loan process. Respondents provided an account of the overall loan process from when someone "enters their door" to when they close a loan. They were also asked directly about whether they saw the process as different from a bank's and if so, in what ways. Probes utilized allowed for greater detail about how long they spent on technical assistance and the kinds of technical assistance they provided.

The second set of questions focused on understanding the role of race as it relates to relationship building and information gathering. Respondents were asked about the racial/ethnic background of clients and staff as well as staff's knowledge regarding the individuals they serve. The author had them consider whether or not their own race, similar or different from the entrepreneurs, mattered in how they provided services and if so, in what ways.

The last set of questions discussed characteristics of the organization itself, including average loan size, staff size, sources of capital, and default rates. The author collected contextual information at the beginning of the interview, including an overview of the organization, its mission, and the participant's role in the organization. Staff were also asked to share a bit about their background with entrepreneurship and small business lending.

All interviews took place face-to-face and on-site at the CDFI office location within a private office and/or conference room between March 2006 and December 2007. All interviews were recorded and notes were taken on a notepad. Interview time ranged from one hour to three hours. To analyze transcriptions from interviews, the author used open coding. From open coding, the author drew out themes that were consistent across organizations.

Since there are a small number of community lenders that provide business loans to ethnic entrepreneurs in the Los Angeles area, descriptive information about individuals and organizations provided is limited. This approach protects the internal confidentiality of both individual staff members and organizations (Tolich, 2004).

Sample description

Almost all of the CDFIs included in this study operate business loan funds, opposed to microcredit institutions. Only two of the CDFIs interviewed could be defined as micro loan funds, making loans under $25,000 (Benjamin et al., 2004; Caskey & Hollister, 2001). The number of business loans made to entrepreneurs in one calendar year averaged from 6 to 241, for a total of up to $13 million. The CDFI asset size in this sample ranged from about $200,000 to $15 million. Eight out of ten CDFIs receive funding from multiple sources, including banks, federal, state, and local government, and philanthropy. The remaining two CDFIs are self-sufficient and rely solely on the profits made from lending.

CDFIs in this study seek to help those who are disadvantaged in access to credit and/or to facilitate community development for low-to-moderate income communities. Some CDFIs are explicit in their mission about helping those businesses "which do not easily meet the lending criteria of commercial banks" or "borrowers that could not secure financing through traditional main stream banks." Only one CDFI focused on community development broadly, stating that they "provide capital and advisory services to foster positive community development impacts in distressed neighborhoods."

All CDFIs in the sample serve ethnic entrepreneurs, with most groups serving primarily one group and/or a specific geographic area, which has a concentration of a particular racial/ethnic group. Similarly, all CDFIs in the sample provide technical assistance at varying levels, with some providing more one-on-one assistance than others (Table 1).

Table 1. Description of CDFIs in sample ($N = 10$).

Average loan size is less than $30,000	2
Average loan size is $1,000,000	2
Provides microloans and business loans greater than $30,000	8
Provide workshops, classes and/or training for entrepreneurs	5
Provides one on one technical assistance beyond completing application	8
Average time it takes to provide a loan more than two months	5
Loan committee makes final loan decision	10
Serve mostly ethnic entrepreneurs (75% or more)	8
Staff race/ethnicity is the same as the majority of entrepreneurs	8

On average, the CDFIs in the sample have very few staff. Staff size ranged from one to a maximum of twenty staff in the sample. Due to the often small staff size, most CDFIs also employ consultants. The number of consultants ranged from one to five working for a CDFI at any given point in time. The length of time each staff person had worked for the CDFI ranged from one year to 12 years. In addition to their current position, most staff also had prior experience lending to entrepreneurs. The staff members that were interviewed represent a diverse group of African-American, Latino, and Asian American loan officers, program directors, and executive directors. Ten of the twelve CDFI staff interviewed share the same ethnicity as those entrepreneurs they predominantly serve.

Findings

CDFI loan process

According to CDFI staff, the CDFI loan process for entrepreneurs contains elements similar to that of a bank loan process. This would include a typical initial intake process, gathering of information for the application, and loan decision (Cavalluzzo & Wolken, 2005; Cole et al., 2004; Frame et al., 2001). Figure 2 below shows the CDFI loan process as described by staff from the time an entrepreneur seeks a loan to after a loan is disbursed. In comparison, Figure 3 shows the four major steps within a commercial bank.

The first stage in the CDFI loan process is the initial inquiry and screening stage. During this stage, CDFI loan officers begin to collect information about the entrepreneur and business. Even at this early stage, CDFI loan officers begin assessing whether the loan is "doable" and/or a good match for the CDFI. A loan is "doable" based on the

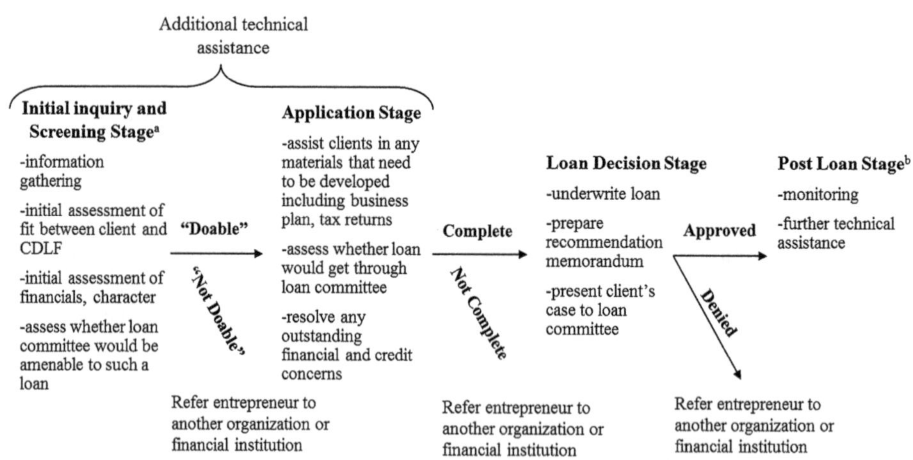

Notes: a Information and assessment is made by various methods of communication including phone, email, in writing, and in person. Most occur over the phone or in person. b Monitoring and technical assistance is also provided through various means including over the phone and in person. In some cases staff may refer individuals to appropriate further assistance that they might need including certified public accountants and attorneys.

Figure 2. Stages of CDFI lending process (from perspective of lender).

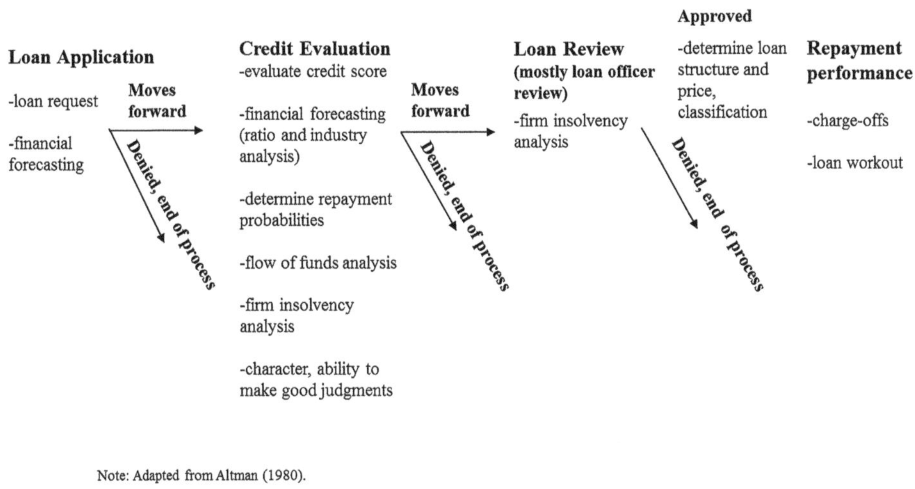

Figure 3. Stages of bank lending process.

loan request (amount, terms, purpose), but also based on the financial background and characteristics of the business and entrepreneur. CDFI staff describes doable as the degree to which the entrepreneur and the "deal" are a good fit with the CDFI's area of expertise in terms of loan, business, and/or existing borrower types. Once the CDFI loan officer decides the loan is "doable" and a good fit, he or she proceeds to gather more information and asks the entrepreneur to complete an application. Staff determination of what is "doable" is also influenced by their assessment of potential loan committee approval. An African-American Vice President of a CDFI serving mostly African-Americans described this sentiment: "It shakes out to where anything that goes to loan committee for the most part we strongly feel it's going to get passed. Um, that they're willing and able to pay us back. We do a lot of pre-screening."

The majority of CDFI staff interviewed said they paid close attention to loan committee concerns and adjust recommendations accordingly. A Latina loan officer of a Latino and African-American serving CDFI expressed the influence of the loan committee on her decision-making:

> Um not too often because like I said, because I've been there for eight years, I know most of them are, we have about three of them that have been there for the amount of time I've been there. So I know what they're looking for and all we need is the majority. So the majority at least, right now, are three. So when I present, I try to present something that I think they are going to do.

Relationships formed between staff and entrepreneurs result in a weak tie. Relationships begin to form between staff and the entrepreneur during the second stage of the loan process when applications get completed. In comparison, banking relationships typically exist prior to a loan application being complete (Ongena & Smith, 2001). CDFI staff collect information through email, phone, and in-person interviews and inquiries, on site visits at the business, and from financial and personal documents. The application stage is especially important because of the amount of information gathered. All staff interviewed expressed the significant time this stage takes from an average of 2–6 months, with one case mentioned taking as long as 18 months. The back and forth information sharing, discussion, and technical assistance forms a weak tie between staff and entrepreneur. An African-American program manager at a CDFI serving mostly African-Americans and Latinos describes the process:

> It can take forever for them [entrepreneurs] to produce that type of stuff [financial statements] … you know, its gonna take at least two months for us to get from start to finish, even if you're the best borrower ever and give me everything I need right away … you get to know them really well, have a very good understanding of the borrower and the business to overcome the objections that might come up, because they're all bankers on my loan committee.

Technical assistance at this stage includes cleaning up financial statements and resolving existing credit issues. Staff mentioned the use of credit scores and noted credit score as an issue for most entrepreneurs. As a result, they de-emphasize the credit score, whereas in banks, the credit score drives a decision even at the application stage (Altman, 1980; Chen et al., 2009).

Sometimes a loan officer concludes that financial issues/concerns cannot be resolved and/or that the loan committee would not approve such a loan. CDFI staff may decide at any point to not proceed with the application. Following this decision, CDFI staff typically refer entrepreneurs to other financial and/or community institutions. In contrast, there appears to be no technical assistance provision in banks and no referrals provided (see Figure 3) (Altman, 1980; Chen et al., 2009; Gray et al., 2013).

The last major stage of the loan process is the loan decision. An entrepreneur reaches the loan decision stage once all information is collected and any remaining concerns have been resolved or overcome. One of the major distinctions between CDFIs and banks is who makes the loan decision. Figure 3 shows that loan officers often make the final loan decision. In comparison, loan committees make loan decisions in all the CDFIs in the study. Having such committees allows CDFIs the ability to minimize risk and fulfill their mission by having individuals with a variety of experiences, including prior lending and/or entrepreneurship.

Typically, a CDFI staff member prepares a recommendation memorandum and provides an oral presentation to the loan committee. Once a loan is presented to the loan committee, the loan committee may approve, deny, or provide a conditional loan. Most cases presented to the loan committee have positive recommendations from staff. Negative recommendations are rare and typically filtered out by CDFI staff prior to reaching this stage.

Comprehensive, extensive technical assistance and flexible lending

While similar elements exist in the CDFI and the bank loaning process, there are some distinctions in process implementation. These distinctions include extensive technical assistance provision and flexible underwriting. While prior research described the kind of technical assistance provided by CDFIs, the findings here extrapolate in more detail how technical assistance is provided and in what cases (Benjamin et al., 2004; Caskey & Hollister, 2001; Rubin, 2008) (Figure 4).

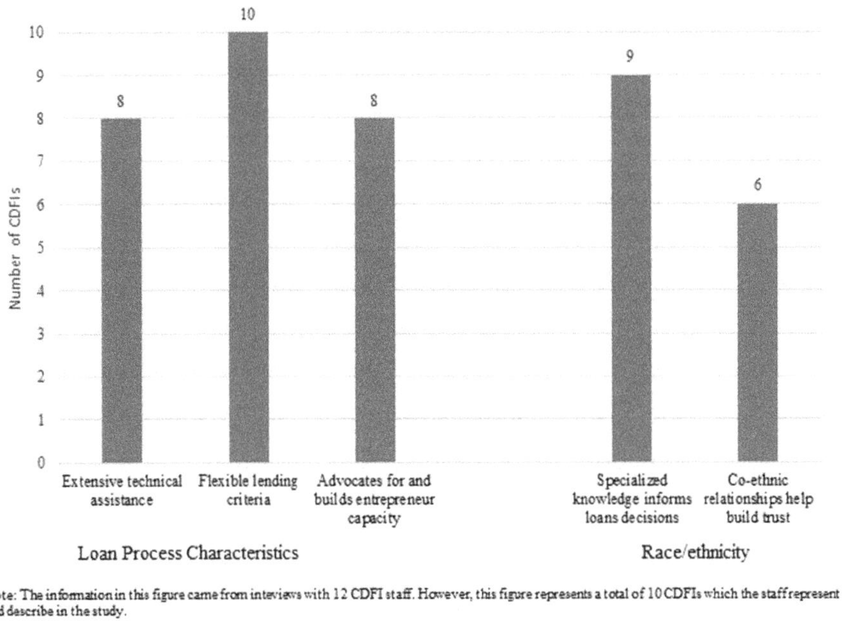

Figure 4. CDFI staff reflections on loan process ($N = 10$).

Technical assistance is extensive both due to the range of topics CDFIs assist entrepreneurs with, as well as the amount of staff time spent providing such assistance. The broad range of financial issues and concerns addressed include problems with liens, debt, poor or no credit, lack of audited financial statements, and/or not paying taxes. One-on-one assistance takes place on the phone, in person, and/or through email. An African-American loan officer with a mostly Latino and African-American serving CDFI conveyed the kind of assistance they provide:

> They come to us, and not only do we do the technical assistance … we're going to point you in the right direction. And we try to give them a loan, take a risk on them with a loan. And you know keep on top of the collections, making sure that they're okay getting their financials at the end of the year … and they're following what we initially said they should. And that's the difference. The handholding, we do a lot of it – A lot of it.

In total, CDFI staff estimate that entrepreneurs receive on average anywhere from 10 to 60 hours of technical assistance prior to and during the loan process. Beyond one-on-one assistance, CDFI staff also provide workshops and seminars. Workshops and seminars offer broad training such as financial management or more specific training such as marketing strategies. For instance, one CDFI explained that entrepreneurs go through a two-day workshop training to learn about American labor laws, the importance of insurance, paying taxes, and how to write a business plan.

Overall, the extensive technical assistance provided by CDFIs does more than just make entrepreneurs ready for a loan. The assistance also results in borrowers with improved financial and business skills. CDFI staff view technical assistance provision as a way to ensure greater success down the line, whether it is with them or another lending institution. This view is consistent with the mission of many CDFIs to serve those who did not meet traditional lending institution standards or to improve individual access to "mainstream" lending institutions.

Due to the extensive technical assistance provided, staff members develop strong relationships with entrepreneurs. Many see their role as an advocate for the entrepreneurs, particularly when loan applications are presented to the loan committee. A Latina President of CDFI serving mostly Asian American and Latinos exemplified this feeling that many CDFI staff mentioned:

> I consider my role to be the advocate for the borrower, and for my shareholders … So you know I'm cautious in that sense and don't take on anybody, but I view my role as the advocate to the borrower for loan committee. Yeah, they have this credit issue, but here's what happened, this is why I believe them, and you know, here's the argument of the current trend, you know, to offset their previously you know bad history kind of thing, you know, taking the time to argue for the borrower.

It is through technical assistance that a weak tie is formed between entrepreneurs and CDFI staff.

Another way CDFIs appear to distinguish themselves from banks is by using flexible underwriting. CDFIs accomplish this by how they examine, evaluate, and weight information. First, CDFI staff believe they take more time to inquire more deeply about the borrower's capital need, business, financial, and personal situations. While banks may deny a loan based on bad credit, insufficient cash, or lack of collateral, CDFI staff explained that they will question such "red flags." They provide entrepreneurs an opportunity to explain their situation. A Latino Vice President at a CDFI serving Asian Americans and Latinos explained:

> The typical person … They don't qualify for traditional loans, okay so a lot of people that we do loans for, their credit is probably horrible, but what was different between us and other lenders is that I'll listen to the reason, give me a reason, there are several reasons that are valid, divorce for one … you got hurt and couldn't work anymore … there's reasons for bad credit, as long as we can understand it, and we don't see a pattern. But we are more flexible in certain areas than the banks would be. And so, if you have a good explanation, we'll do the loan. If you're just getting started obviously, if you have a good plan also, we may do it where a bank wouldn't do it.

An African-American President of a CDFI provides an example of flexible lending criteria utilized:

> When you look at credit score, it's looking at all of their credit, now some people will make their house payment before they make their visa payment. You want to give those people a loan on their house. Why? Because they are going to make payments on their house before their Visa. But credit scoring is for all creditors so a mainstream bank will look at a 568 score based on missed Visa payments. This guy missed three Visa payments, but his house payment has never been late, so they are going to turn him down because his credit score is not high enough … I'm not gonna look at your credit score, I'm gonna look at what you paid for.

In addition to the amount, depth of inquiry, and information acquired, CDFI staff report flexibility in considering not only past but future potential as well. For instance, if an entrepreneur had a prior business fail, but the new current business shows profits, the staff would consider the newer pattern of profits. Another example could be a business that has minimal profits over the last ten years, but perhaps shows increasing gains in profit in the last four or five years.

The third major way that CDFI staff exercise flexibility is in the weight they give to an entrepreneur's character. CDFI staff express that while they consider credit score, cash flow, credit, collateral, and character, they put more weight on character. Character, according to CDFI staff in this study, is one of the main factors that helps an entrepreneur overcome other weak financial or firm factors. A Latino director of a CDFI serving mostly Latinos shared how he sees their process compared to a bank's process:

> And so, the process of analyzing the loan is the same. We don't cut corners there at all. Except for we're way more flexible when it comes to if they're weak in one area but maybe stronger in another area. We touch every deal. Touch and feel it. We get to know the borrower, look at the character as a very big indicator as where the loan is going to go.

Assessing character is a qualitative process that is more difficult to quantify as part of a loan application evaluation. CDFIs have come up with their own criteria and set of questions for assessing character and business success. For instance, staff identify and determine entrepreneur motivation to start and sustain business, the degree to which they understand and/or are knowledgeable about their business, and the level of commitment and confidence an entrepreneur has in their business. In Figure 3, character falls into qualitative factors considered by banks in the credit evaluation stage. Figure 3 also highlights the prevalence of quantitative factors considered relative to qualitative factors.

Race/ethnicity in CDFI lending: Looking like, speaking like, and knowing the entrepreneur

Race/ethnicity impacts the loan process in several ways. First, there is an initial comfort and trust entrepreneurs feel when working with someone of the same race/ethnicity. The trust and comfort between the entrepreneur and the lender is key to even starting the conversation about a loan. A Latino Vice President at CDFI serving racial minorities clarifies, "we have to go back to the trust issue. So it has to be people that speak the language, look like them and people that are very personable. So that's one of the things with the Hispanic community." Similarly, an Asian American Executive Director of an Asian American serving CDFI shared a similar assessment of the Asian entrepreneurs, stating,

> You stand a Caucasian guy and an Asian guy with the same deal, the Asian guys gonna get the deal most likely. I mean [Asians] they feel a lot more comfortable dealing with a person who either speaks the language or looks the same.

This desire to work with co-ethnics may have to do with entrepreneurs' experiences with banks. All of the CDFIs shared that the majority of their clients have already gone to and been rejected by a bank prior to coming to them. Some CDFIs have a requirement or it is part of their mission to serve those without access to traditional institutions or that banks have rejected.

Second, speaking the same language is important due to the highly immigrant nature of ethnic entrepreneurs in Los Angeles. Eight of the ten CDFIs have staff that can communicate in the same language as the majority of their ethnic entrepreneurs (Table 1). Language barriers identified by CDFIs include not speaking English, speaking

English with an accent, and/or limited comprehension. As a Latina loan officer of a CDFI serving African-Americans and Latinos explains:

> Latino clients come in and have more challenges sometimes because of the language barrier. So everywhere they go, they have an interpreter. For them, their interpreter is like their nine-ten year old son or daughter that probably won't interpret everything exactly like its being said. So they make a decision based on the interpretation and it's not what they should be making decisions on.

Language becomes an important part of the loan process in acquiring the correct information and in understanding agreements being made by the entrepreneur and the staff member.

The other way ethnicity plays a role in the loan process is based on how well CDFI staff know the culture, attitudes, and experiences in the home country of a particular ethnic entrepreneur. The use of specialized knowledge in CDFIs appears similar to that identified by Li et al. (2002) in ethnic banks and by Hunter and Walker (1996) in mortgage lending by banks. For instance, for CDFIs serving Latinos, staff has an understanding of business in the home country and how that may or may not apply in the United States. A Latina loan officer at another African-American and Latino serving organization explains how this information is utilized to assess the potential of the business in the United States:

> You know, for example, some of the borrowers out here … maybe immigrants from Mexico. So they may have language barriers, but would be very good business people and had been business people in Mexico. And so we're able to make a deal happen. We're able to ask them, "What is your history? What have you done in Mexico?" … Whereas they may not be as comfortable saying that to the bank or another financial institution because they are not of the same culture.

In another example, a Latino program director of a Latino serving CDFI recalls a conversation he had with an entrepreneur of the same ethnicity. He states that

> I come from the same area, same process. So when he says, "Look I had a business in Guadalajara for ten years. I know how to run it. This is my background. I have a business degree from the university" … we can make the case for them, where it wouldn't necessarily be made.

Because of the program director's specialized knowledge, he considered this information in a positive way.

Another way specialized knowledge may result in more positive loan outcomes is due to perceived values and attitudes about borrowing. CDFI staff characterized both Asian American and Latino entrepreneurs as being debt adverse. A Latino program director of an Asian American and Latino serving CDFI provided the following description about Asian Americans: "Well a lot of Asians I've talked to before, they said, 'I don't want to borrow money. I don't want to owe people money. The sooner I can pay you back the better.' which is perfect for us." The Vice President sees this attitude among Asian Americans as positive, and as a result was more likely to lend to Asian American entrepreneurs. In another example, a Latina loan officer in a Latino serving CDFI described Latinos,

> They don't like to owe people money. They like to pay when they're supposed to pay. And so when they see you, it's more like as if they were lending to or borrowing from their, what they call their compadre ... there's a sense of shame if they don't pay their share.

This loan officer sees this attitude as a cultural strength that would result in a more favorable loan outcome.

Discussion and conclusion

Overall, this study finds that CDFIs share some processes and policies found in regulated commercial banks. The distinction is in how CDFIs implement such processes and policies. CDFIs use more flexible underwriting and provide extensive technical assistance. They also consistently refer entrepreneurs to other sources of assistance or capital throughout the lending process.

The extensive technical assistance found confirms prior research and extends it by showing how staff tailor technical assistance provision by utilizing specialized knowledge gained through co-ethnic weak ties (Benjamin et al., 2004; Caskey & Hollister, 2001; Rubin, 2008). Specialized knowledge based on the co-ethnic nature of relationships improves the ability to exercise flexible lending criteria, allowing CDFIs to take on greater risk that more regulated entities are unlikely to take on. The use of specialized knowledge is similar to that found among ethnic banks.[5] However, the co-ethnic ties within an ethnic community, called social capital by Li et al. (2002), was not found among CDFIs in this study.

CDFI staff instead rely on a weak tie to offer capital and ensure repayment. This makes the role of social ties in CDFI lending practices different from microcredit and rotating credit and savings associations that rely on strong ties among co-ethnics for repayment (Light et al., 1990). Another distinction is how CDFI lending results in the formation of weak ties, opposed to banks, where the weak tie often exists prior to lending (Cole, 1998; Ongena & Smith, 2001).

Being of the same ethnicity and speaking the same language is important at the start of the CDFI loan process. However, feelings of reciprocity that result from the weak tie formed as a result of technical assistance provision become equally important toward the end of the loan process. Feelings of ethnic solidarity and pride (i.e. not letting the other person down) become intertwined with feelings of reciprocity. Together, they become equally important in influencing entrepreneur behaviors including repayment.

The CDFI lending process also identifies the importance of the intersection between weak ties and co-ethnic relationships. This study shows that weak ties with Whites, as the most privileged in society, may not be the most beneficial in the short term for ethnic entrepreneurs. In fact, weak ties with co-ethnics are equally if not more important in order to bridge the financing gap and access to mainstream institutions.

The combination of extensive technical assistance, flexible lending criteria, and specialized knowledge about cultural attitudes and behaviors, home country experiences, and language engender more and higher quality information that can be utilized to lend towards success. CDFIs in the study are successful with default rates below 3%. In comparison, the U.S. Small Business Administration (SBA) reported default rates as high as 11.9% in 2009 (Maltby, 2009). And while the overall CDFI default rate in 2010 was 1.9%, this rate does not distinguish loan fund type including some with less risk such as housing loan funds (Swack, Northrup, & Hangen, 2012). Thus, any conclusions about success and positive outcomes must be considered with caution.

The findings from this study should be considered in the context of its methodological limitations. The small sample size limits its generalizability. Thus, future research would greatly benefit from additional data beyond Los Angeles CDFIs. Second, findings should also be considered in light of the highly ethnic serving nature of the sample. Ideally, there would be data on CDFIs that do not serve ethnic entrepreneurs in high proportions as a source of comparison.

Third, due to the sensitivity around discussing interactions with clients, including the role of race/ethnicity, some staff members may have refrained from speaking as directly or as freely about their experiences. Future research should consider using additional methods such as observations and experimental designs that have been utilized in mortgage lending studies to improve internal validity.

Finally, this study would benefit from different perspectives, particularly those of ethnic entrepreneurs themselves and loan officers in banking institutions. For instance, it would be helpful to know from the perspective of the entrepreneur whether the observations of the staff resonate with their own experience. Do they trust someone more because they are the same ethnicity? Or is it based on something else? Gaining the answers to such questions would allow a more comprehensive picture of the loan process.

Despite these limitations, this research expands our understanding of a growing industry, demonstrates the complexity of the financial world, and highlights the social nature of the lending process. CDFIs mitigate risk through extensive technical assistance and specialized knowledge, but this comes at a cost. Most CDFIs find ways to subsidize technical assistance provision through profits, foundations, government funding, and/or bank partnerships (Rubin, 2008). However, CDFIs and policymakers should continue to look at and grow partnerships with banks (Smith & Zielenbach, 2010).

Exercising flexible lending criteria is also costly due to the time spent collecting additional information from entrepreneurs. However, there are less costly parts of exercising flexible criteria that other institutions could adopt, such as inquiring further about credit history and allowing entrepreneurs to offer explanations. Perhaps there is a list of possible reasons an entrepreneur could give that would be deemed acceptable. Additional research on CDFI and similar institutional practices around flexible lending criteria should create more confidence about broader adoption of such policies.

Finally, banks and other institutions have already begun to hire more bilingual staff to serve clients, and from this study, it is clear that employing bicultural staff with specialized knowledge about clients is equally, if not more, important. Specialized knowledge comes from significant experience in lending to and serving a particular ethnic community not just from being of the same ethnicity and speaking the same language. This experience is how staff members develop a true and deep sense of what to look for and consider in ethnic entrepreneurs. Hiring individuals who understand entrepreneurs' cultural norms and attitudes would be encouraging to the entrepreneurs and advantageous for the banks in mitigating risk.

Until banks and more mainstream financial institutions change their policies and practices, alternative institutions will need to continue to meet the demand for business capital. As such, policymakers and the federal government should continue to support CDFIs as they are providing much-needed services and products. The strength of the CDFI industry and its ability to meet credit needs will be especially important to ethnic entrepreneurs. Policymakers and leaders certainly have a challenge ahead of them as the demand for capital grows in an ever increasingly diverse and unequal society.

Disclosure statement

No potential conflict of interest was reported by the author.

Notes

1. A similar distinction was made by Benjamin et al. (2004) in discussing various CDFIs.
2. As of 2013, New York has the largest number of certified CDFIs, 65. California is next with 37 certified CDFIs. Pennsylvania and Texas follow New York and California with 30 and 25, respectively. Certified CDFIs have to be approved by the Treasury Department's CDFIs Fund.
3. Based on professional expertise regarding CDFIs, I identified CDFIs on the list serving a high proportion (more than 50%) of ethnic entrepreneurs. I also sent this list to a CDFI Fund program manager to review. Finally, I confirmed my list based by asking interviewees the names of other CDFIs serving ethnic entrepreneurs.
4. This report included CDFIs in Southern California beyond Los Angeles. In addition, the inclusion of loan funds beyond those providing business loans such as affordable housing also makes this estimate more liberal.
5. See Li et al. (2002), Dymski and Mohanty (1999), and Hum (2010).

References

Abramowitz, A., Edwards, B., & Melford, G. (2006). Community development finance in Los Angeles: Challenges and responses. *Opportunity Finance Network*. Retrieved from http://community-wealth.org/sites/clone.community-wealth.org/files/downloads/paper-abramowitz-et-al.pdf

Altman, E. (1980). Commercial bank lending: Process, credit scoring, and costs of errors in lending. *The Journal of Financial and Quantitative Analysis, 15*, 813–833.

Anthony, D. (2005). Cooperation in microcredit borrowing groups: Identity, sanctions, and reciprocity in the production of collective goods. *American Sociological Review, 70*, 496–515.

Bates, T. (1997). *Race, self-employment, and upward mobility*. Baltimore, MD: John Hopkins University Press.

Bates, T. (2000). Financing the development of urban minority communities: Lessons of history. *Economic Development Quarterly, 14*, 227–242.

Bates, T., Jackson, W. E., & Johnson, J. H. (2007). Advancing research on minority entrepreneurship. *The Annals of the American Academy of Political and Social Science, 613*, 10–17.

Bates, T., & Robb, A. (2013). Greater access to capital is needed to unleash the local economic development potential of minority-owned businesses. *Economic Development Quarterly, 27*, 250–259. doi:10.11770891242413477188

Benjamin, L., Rubin, J. S., & Zielenbach, S. (2004). Community development financial institutions: Current issues and future prospects. *Journal of Urban Affairs, 26*, 177–195.

Black, H. A., Collins, M. C., & Cyree, K. B. (1997). Do black-owned banks discriminate against black borrowers? *Journal of Financial Services Research, 11*, 189–204.

Blanchard, L., Zhao, B., & Yinger, J. (2008). Do lenders discriminate against minority and woman entrepreneurs? *Journal of Urban Economics, 63*, 467–497.

Blanchflower, D. G., Levine, P. B., & Zimmerman, D. J. (2003). Discrimination in the small-business credit market. *Review of Economics and Statistics, 85*, 930–943.

Caskey, J. P., & Hollister, R. G. (2001). *Business development financial institutions: Theory, practice and impact*. Madison, WI: University of Wisconsin-Madison, Institute for Research on Poverty.

Cavalluzzo, K. S., Cavalluzzo, L. C., & Wolken, J. D. (2002). Competition, small business financing, and discrimination: Evidence from a new survey. *The Journal of Business, 75*, 641–679.

Cavalluzzo, K., & Wolken, J. (2005). Small business loan turndowns, personal wealth, and discrimination. *The Journal of Business, 78*, 2153–2178. Retrieved from http://www.jstor.org/stable/10.1086/497045

CDFI Coalition. (2014). About CDFI coalition. *CDFI Coalition of Community Development Financial Institutions*. Retrieved from http://www.cdfi.org/about-cdfi-coalition/history/

CDFI Fund. (2014). *Certified CDFIs as of November 2014*. Retrieved from http://www.cdfifund.gov/docs/2014/Cert/CDFI%20List%2011-30-14.xls

Chen, Y., Guo, R. J., & Huang, R. L. (2009). Two stages credit evaluation in bank loan appraisal. *Economic Modelling, 26*, 63–70.

Cole, R. A. (1998). The importance of relationships to the availability of credit. *Journal of Banking & Finance, 22*, 959–977.

Cole, R. A., Goldberg, L. G., & White, L. J. (2004). Cookie cutter vs. character: The micro structure of small business lending by large and small banks. *Journal of Financial and Quantitative Analysis, 39*, 227–251.

Coleman, J. (1988). Social capital in the creation of human capital. *American Journal of Sociology, 94*, S95–S120.

Dymski, G., & Mohanty, L. (1999). Credit and banking structure: Asian and African-American experience in Los Angeles. *American Economic Review, 89*, 362–366.

Fairlie, R., & Robb, A. (2008). *Race and entrepreneurial success: Black-, Asian-, and white-owned businesses in the United States*. Cambridge: Massachusetts Institute of Technology Press Books.

Fisher, A. (2013, December 23). *Small business access to credit: The little engine that could: If banks helped* (Report). San Francisco, CA: Community Reinvestment Coalition. Retrieved from http://calreinvest.org/publications/california-reinvestment-coalition-research

Flores-Yeffal, N. Y., & Zhang, L. (2012). The role of social networks in determining earnings: A comparison analysis of four racial and ethnic groups. *Sociology Mind, 2*, 235–246.

Frame, W. S., Srinivasan, A., & Woosley, L. (2001). The effect of credit scoring on small-business lending. *Journal of Money, Credit and Banking, 33*, 813–825.

Frisch, M., & Servon, L. J. (2006). CDCs and the changing context for urban community development: A review of the field and the environment. *Community Development, 37*, 88–108.

Ghatak, M. (1999). Group lending, local information and peer selection. *Journal of Development Economics, 60*, 27–50.

Granovetter, M. (1973). The strength of weak ties. *American Journal of Sociology, 78*, 1360–1380.

Granovetter, M. (1995). The economic sociology of firms and entrepreneurs. In A. Portes (Ed.), *The economic sociology of immigration: Essays in networks, ethnicity and entrepreneurship* (pp. 128–165). New York, NY: Russell Sage Foundation.

Gray, D., Saunders, M., & Goregaokar, H. (2013). *Small and medium sized enterprises success in challenging times: Bank finance – Lost in translation* (Project report). Retrieved from http://epubs.surrey.ac.uk/804540/

Hossain, M. (1988, February). *Credit for alleviation of rural poverty: The Grameen Bank in Bangladesh* (Research report). Retrieved from http://www.ifpri.org/publication/

Hum, T. (2010). Minority banks in New York City: Is the community reinvestment act relevant. *Journal of Civil Rights & Economic Development, 25*, 501–524.

Hunter, W. C., & Walker, M. B. (1996). The cultural affinity hypothesis and mortgage lending decisions. *The Journal of Real Estate Finance and Economics, 13*, 57–70.

Levin, D., & Cross, R. (2004). The strength of weak ties you can trust: The mediating role of trust in effective knowledge transfer. *Management Science, 50*, 1477–1490.

Li, W., Dymski, G., Zhou, Y., Chee, M., & Aldana, C. (2002). Chinese-American banking and community development in Los Angeles County. *Annals of the Association of American Geographers, 92*, 777–796.

Light, L. (1972). *Ethnic enterprise in America: Business and welfare among Chinese, Japanese, and Blacks*. Berkeley: University of California Press.

Light, I. H., & Bonacich, E. (1988). *Immigrant entrepreneurs: Koreans in Los Angeles, 1965–1982*. Berkeley: University of California Press.

Light, I., Kwuon, I. J., & Zhong, D. (1990). Korean rotating credit associations in Los Angeles. *Amerasia Journal, 16*, 35–54.

Lin, N. (1999). Social networks and status attainment. *Annual Review of Sociology, 25*, 467–487.

Maltby, E. (2009, February 25). Small biz loan failure rate hits 12%. *CNNMoney.com*. Retrieved from http://money.cnn.com/2009/02/25/smallbusiness/smallbiz_loan_defaults_soar.smb/

Miles, M. B., & Huberman, A. M. (1984). *Qualitative data analysis: A sourcebook of new methods*. Thousand Oaks, CA: Sage.

Min, P. G. (2008). *Ethnic solidarity for economic survival: Korean greengrocers in New York City*. New York, NY: Russell Sage Foundation.

Montgomery, J. (1992). Job search and network composition: Implications of the strength-of-weak-ties hypothesis. *American Sociological Review, 57*, 586–596.

Ongena, S., & Smith, D. C. (2001). The duration of bank relationships. *Journal of Financial Economics, 61*, 449–475.

Portes, A. (1998). Social capital: Its origins and applications in modern sociology. *Annual Review of Sociology, 24*, 1–24.

Portes, A., & Bach, R. (1985). *Latin journey: Cuban and Mexican immigrants in the United States*. Berkeley: University of California Press.

Portes, A., & Sensenbrenner, J. (1993). Embeddedness and immigration: Notes on the social determinants of economic action. *American Journal of Sociology, 98*, 1320–1350.

Quittner, J. (2014, July 22). Former SBA chief raises alarm over still tight credit market for small businesses. *Inc.com*. Retrieved from http://www.inc.com/jeremy-quittner/karen-mills-harvard-business-school-small-business-lending.html

Rubin, J. S. (2008). Adaptation or extinction? Community development loan funds at a crossroads. *Journal of Urban Affairs, 30*, 191–220.

Rubin, J. S., Caskey, J. P., Dickstein, C., & Zielenbach, S. (2008). *Assessing the systemic impacts of community development loan funds*. Washington, DC: Department of Treasury Community Development Financial Institutions Fund Research Initiative. Retrieved from http://community-wealth.org/content/assessing-systematic-impact-community-development-loan-funds

Servon, L. J. (1997). Microenterprise programs in U.S. inner cities: Economic development or social welfare? *Economic Development Quarterly, 11*, 166–180.

Servon, L. J. (1998). Credit and social capital: The community development potential of U.S. microenterprise programs. *Housing Policy Debate, 9*, 115–149.

Servon, L. J. (1999). *Bootstrap capital: Microenterprises and the American poor*. Washington, DC: Brookings Institution Press.

Smith, G., & Zielenbach, S. (2010, Winter). Lending to small business: The evolving bank-non-profit lender relationship. In *Communities & banking* (pp. 29–31). Boston, MA: Federal Reserve Bank of Boston. Retrieved from http://www.bostonfed.org/commdev/c&b/2010/winter/Geoff_Smith_Sean_Zielenbach_CDFI.pdf

Swack, M., Northrup, J., & Hangen, E. (2012, Spring). *CDFI Industry Analysis Summary Report*. CDFI Fund and Carsey Institute. Retrieved from https://carsey.unh.edu/sites/carsey.unh.edu/files/media/pdf/report-swack-cdfi-industry-analysis-final.pdf

Tolich, M. (2004). Internal confidentiality: When confidentiality assurances fail relational informants. *Qualitative Sociology, 27*, 101–106.

U.S. Bureau of the Census. (2002). *Survey of business owners: Geographic area series: Economy-wide estimates of business ownership by gender, Hispanic or Latino Origin, and race: 2001*. Table SB0200A1. Retrieved from http://factfinder.census.gov

U.S. Bureau of the Census. (2007). *Survey of business owners: Statistics for all U.S. firms by industry, gender, ethnicity, and race for the U.S., states, metro areas, counties, and places: 2007*. Table SBO700CSA01. Retrieved from http://factfinder.census.gov

U.S. Bureau of the Census. (2011, June). *Census Bureau Reports Number of Minority-Owned Firms Increased at More than Double the Rate of All U.S. Businesses From 2002–2007*. U.S. Bureau of the Census CB11-103. Retrieved from https://www.census.gov/newsroom/releases/archives/business_ownership/cb11-103.html

Wydick, B. (2001). Group lending under dynamic incentives as a borrower discipline device. *Review of Development Economics, 5*, 406–420.

Zonta, M. (2004). *The role of ethnic banks in the residential patterns of Asian Americans: The case of Los Angeles* (Unpublished doctoral dissertation). Department of Urban Planning, University of California, Los Angeles.

Invisible struggles: the representation of ethnic entrepreneurship in US newspapers

Leona Achtenhagen and Cindy J. Price Schultz

How entrepreneurship is portrayed in media can play an important role for how attractive it is perceived as a career and/or investment option. Communities need people of all ethnicities to be interested in starting businesses because economic development is tied so closely to community development. To date, little to no community development literature has been published about how newspapers frame ethnic minority entrepreneurs and how that might affect the community. This article examined such framing and its implications. This article presents a textual analysis of how ethnic minority entrepreneurship is represented in US newspapers included in the LexisNexis Academic Database from 2003 to 2008. Overall, ethnic minority entrepreneurship, including the struggles the entrepreneurs face, is almost invisible in the newspapers, despite its importance for the economy. From the articles that were published in this field, important patterns were identified. The article concludes with suggestions about how community development officials can assist ethnic minority entrepreneurs.

The decline of some urban centers in the USA is of great concern to community development officials (cf. Rosenthal, 2008). Evidence suggests that by encouraging the people who live in the inner city, often ethnic minority groups, to get involved in entrepreneurship, this decline can be slowed down or even reversed (cf. Sriram, Mersha, & Herron, 2007). Community development and economic development go hand in hand (Wallace, 1999), because "locally groomed entrepreneurs have commitment to their communities, and if they are successful, the returns to the community on investment are substantial" (Korsching, Allen, Vogt, & Sapp, 2007, p. 40). In the USA alone, minority-owned businesses contribute more than $1 trillion in annual economic output and account for more than 6 million jobs (MBDA Annual Performance Report, 2012).

Yet, the decision to become self-employed depends on several different factors. One factor that is sometimes overlooked is the existing image of entrepreneurs in a community – and this holds true also for ethnic minority entrepreneurs. Newspapers reflect public perceptions of what is desirable in a society, as well as impact these perceptions (Habermas, 1991), and "most of what the public learns is still overwhelmingly driven by traditional media – particularly newspapers" (Rogers, 2010, p. 1). Media thus contribute to the social construction of entrepreneurial activities by ethnic minority groups (e.g. Achtenhagen & Welter, 2011; Radu & Redien-Collot, 2008). People interpret events through the way they picture or frame them (Goffman, 1986). Community developers should care about the frames a community has created because shared rules establish a social reality (Hustedde & Ganowicz, 2002).

Limited research has been done to determine how newspaper discourses affect a community's social reality. Therefore, the purpose of this study is to examine how ethnic minority entrepreneurs are represented through newspapers and how those representations may influence community development. We assess whether the resulting social construction of the phenomenon bears potential to attract novice entrepreneurs from ethnic minority groups. As communication is vital to the understanding of what community is (Procter, 2004), and because a supportive local environment is "a critical factor in the founding of new businesses" (Korsching et al., 2007, p. 28), it is important to see what is being communicated about ethnic minority entrepreneurs through newspapers to determine if this mediated communication is providing a supportive environment.

The remainder of this article is structured as follows. We begin by presenting the relevance of ethnic minority entrepreneurship in the USA, while examining a gap in understanding how the phenomenon is covered in media. Then we present previous research investigating media portraits of entrepreneurship before explaining our methods, empirical study, and its results. While there is an emerging consensus among social scientists that ethnic minority entrepreneurship is playing a crucial role in the restructuring of Western industrial economies (see discussion in Fregetto, 2004), we find that the phenomenon of ethnic minority entrepreneurship and its struggles is not very extensively covered in media discourse. Yet, the existing reporting draws a largely positive image of the contribution of ethnic minority entrepreneurs to community development. We end with suggestions for development officials to enhance the perception of entrepreneurship for their communities.

Ethnic minority entrepreneurship in the USA

Whether or not to become an entrepreneur is an important career decision. Governments create policies to encourage people to become entrepreneurially active. According to the Global Entrepreneurship Monitor (GEM), opportunity-based entrepreneurship exploits business opportunities and plays a leading role in job creation and economic development (Acs, 2006). What the GEM has framed as necessity-based entrepreneurship (i.e. when no other options for work are available or satisfactory; see Bosma & Harding, 2006) is considered to be less important for economic development (Acs & Varga, 2005). This polar dichotomy between opportunity- and necessity-based entrepreneurship is increasingly questioned (Smallbone & Welter, 2006), even though it has been the basis of policy decisions that have affected minority entrepreneurs. For example, the US Minority Business Development Agency said minority businesses could have a stronger contribution to the economy without all of the hindrances that these entrepreneurs have to face. "[I]t is critical that the public and private sector work more closely together to ensure the value these companies bring to the US economy is not constrained" (MBDA Annual Performance Report, 2012, p. 3).

Academic research has shown the positive impact of ethnic minority entrepreneurship, defined as any "business ownership among immigrants, ethnic-group members, or both" (Valdez, 2008, p. 956), to economic growth (e.g. Sriram et al., 2007). Ethnic minority groups are more likely to become entrepreneurs and, therefore, can be a community resource (US International Trade Commission, 2010; Waldinger, 2001). In the USA, non-native-born people were 16.7% of all self-employed in 2008, an increase from 12.7% in 2000. Of the 15.5 million self-employed, 10% were Hispanic, and 5% each were black and Asian. While minority-owned businesses were more likely to close than their nonminority counterparts, they had consistently higher rates of job creation due to the expansion of their businesses (Small Business Association Office of Advocacy, 2010). Businesses of 10 employees or less, the size of many ethnic minority startups, are a significant contributor to economic development and they often need more help to get started (MBDA Annual Performance Report, 2012; Muske & Woods, 2004).

Public policies to support ethnic minority entrepreneurs were initiated by President Richard Nixon in 1969, when he signed an executive order to create an Office of Minority Business Enterprise (later renamed to Minority Business Development Agency, MBDA) in the US Department of Commerce (Waldinger et al., 1990). The MBDA coordinates activities related to investments and loans, assistance in providing market access (including export opportunities), and providing support to improve access to state and local government contracts (www.mbda.gov). Comparable programs also exist at state and municipality levels; for example, already by the early 1980s, 30 out of the 33 biggest cities operated major programs to support ethnic minority business (Waldinger et al., 1990). Despite the documented impact of ethnic minority businesses, some critics provokingly argue that such programs are bad public policy, because they would attract the least-skilled entrepreneurs who contribute little to generating innovation; and propose that instead only high-growth firms should be supported (Shane, 2009). However, Muske and Woods (2004) confirm for microbusinesses to develop that "beneficial regulations and laws are important as well as the creation of networking opportunities" (p. 99). They found the most requested assistance to be for help to understand government regulations as well as programs to build the person's business skill sets. Lichtenstein, Lyons, and Kutzhanova (2004) proposed that entrepreneurship should be encouraged at the community level instead of waiting for people to start businesses, then having them come for help. They also argued that each community must customize its entrepreneurial development to meet its own needs.

Media portraits of entrepreneurship

Recent research posits that entrepreneurship needs to be analyzed in its societal context to capture its diverse facets (Welter, 2011). Communities can legitimize or restrict entrepreneurship because culturally accepted role models influence the recognition of entrepreneurship as a viable career option, as well as the types that might be considered as interesting to pursue (Achtenhagen & Welter, 2011). Public discourses as sent by media, and especially newspapers, play an important role. Newspapers are authoritative producers and circulators of public discourse on entrepreneurship in that they impact our ways of talking about reality and have a powerful role in creating public discourses (e.g. Rindova, Pollock, & Hayward, 2006). Bruni, Gherardi, and Poggio (2004) suggest that the role of media is important for the social construction of the image of entrepreneurship because they popularize themes in their communities.

Newspapers attempt to provoke personal identification with their stories (Lippmann, 1922) by finding a point of reference that can be transferred through the use of metaphors. Finding such reference points alone may not lead people to change their opinion towards wanting to become entrepreneurially active. However, the more interested the audience becomes in what they have read, the more likely they are to discuss this with others. Such discussions can expand from the original newspaper article to surrounding issues, and through discussing clashing opinions, a collective opinion can eventually be reached (Park, 1940). By publishing articles fueling this discussion, newspapers can play an important role in this process of framing the public opinion of a community – impacting the image of ethnic minority entrepreneurship in that community and an individual's propensity to engage in it. This is especially true when media coverage of minority groups in general has been shown to sometimes be racist or depict these groups as being at fault for their poor economic conditions (Ojo, 2006).

For the last 100 years, journalism has been considered to be a Fourth Estate, monitoring what the government and community are doing and reporting about it in an objective manner (Baran & Davis, 2012). In fact, objectivity is often considered to be the most important professional norm for journalists (Soloski, 1989). And although many millennials use digital media, a 2014 study showed that that group of 18–34-year olds rely on newspaper media to be informed about their communities (Little, 2014). However, the idea of community journalism, sometimes called public or civic journalism, began in the mid-1990s when newspapers decided to create projects to help their communities and reconnect with their audiences (Fouhy, 1994). The notion of hosting projects for communities has faded, but the ideas behind this type of journalism are still alive. Nip (2006) said the newest way of thinking about community journalism includes examining different ways to frame stories about community issues, choosing frames that help citizens discuss and understand issues, and helping the community deliberate and search for solutions. Another aspect is citizen journalism, where unpaid members of a community can write articles for the newspaper's print or online editions. Therefore, with this new thinking about journalism, newspapers and community participants can work together to develop their communities. The main research question addressed in this article thus asks how newspapers communicate about ethnic minority entrepreneurs to analyze whether and how this mediated communication is providing a supportive environment.

Methods and data

The research we present here consisted of a systematic analysis of US newspaper articles chosen using ethnic minority entrepreneurship terms. The LexisNexis Academic Database was used to select full-text articles by using the terms "ethnic entrepreneur*" or "minority entrepreneur*" – terms commonly used since Light (1972) began the academic research agenda on this topic.[1]

This database is composed of 340 of the approximately 1400 daily newspapers, including all major newspapers in cities with a higher percentage of ethnic minority individuals. Because most businesses in the USA had hardships after the economic downturn of 2008, we studied the period *before* that time to get a clearer picture of more typical frames of minority entrepreneurs. We examined the five-year period between October 2003 and October 2008, focusing the analysis on general *patterns* of representation in the newspapers as well as on the *content* of the discussion of ethnic minority entrepreneurship (see Achtenhagen & Welter, 2007, 2011). Focusing on the 2003–2008 period provided information about portrayals of entrepreneurship prior to the recession, and it is likely that these perceptions influenced and continue to influence cultural understandings of business, even after the advent of social media. Five years of articles were pooled to have a substantial sample for analysis. Like Langowitz and Morgan (2003) suggested, the current study only used articles that had 450 words or more to ensure the news accounts were not just briefs. Altogether, 110 articles were downloaded from 23 newspapers in 20 cities. As noted in Table 1, only a few of the 340 daily newspapers found on the LexisNexis database published articles about ethnic minority entrepreneurship during the five years of our study.[2]

We examined the newspaper articles using textual analysis, which allowed us to describe their content in a systematic fashion. Like established methods of content analysis, we developed categories for classifying the information in the newspaper articles based on topics identified as relevant to ethnic minority entrepreneurship or general entrepreneurship (see Achtenhagen & Welter, 2007; Langowitz & Morgan, 2003), such as background information about the entrepreneur, including relevant prior experience, gender, the country of origin, race, or ethnic minority group, religion, motive for starting the venture, type of financing, plans for the future of the business, and profitability of the business. Also, drawing on the work of Achtenhagen and Welter (2011), we coded whether reporting was positive, neutral, or negative. For this study, we defined positive articles as portraying entrepreneurship as generally good for the entrepreneur(s), the economy, and/or overall society. Similarly, we defined negative articles as portraying entrepreneurship as generally bad for the entrepreneur(s), the economy, and/or overall society. Neutral articles were defined as using neither an extraordinary amount of positive or negative words or as containing a balance of both positive and negative comments.

Table 1. Newspapers and the number of articles published about ethnic minority entrepreneurs.

State	Newspaper	City	Number of articles	Number of minority businesses*
AL	Birmingham News	Birmingham	5	70,538
DC	Washington Post/Washington Times	Washington	4	22,505
MD	The Capital	Annapolis	2	164,130
	Baltimore Daily Record	Baltimore	3	
MA	Boston Globe	Boston	5	64,998
MN	St. Paul Pioneer Press/ Minneapolis Star Tribune	St. Paul & Minneapolis	11	31,074
MO	St. Louis Post Dispatch	St. Louis	2	42,744
NJ	The Record	Bergen County	3	182,489
NM	Albuquerque Journal	Albuquerque	2	48,976
NY	Buffalo Daily News	Buffalo	4	537,544
	New York Post/New York Times	New York City	5	
OR	Portland Oregonian/ Portland Daily Journal of Commerce	Portland	17	31,313
PA	Philadelphia Inquirer	Philadelphia	3	96,208
SC	Charleston Post and Courier	Charleston	2	57,557
TX	Houston Chronicle	Houston	3	723,057
VA	Richmond Times Dispatch	Richmond	4	138,256
WI	Madison Capital Times	Madison	2	26,030
	Milwaukee Journal Sentinel	Milwaukee	28	
National	USA Today	Largest national newspaper; published in Virginia	5	

*2007 data on number of minority-owned businesses by state and group, www.mbda.gov.

An important aspect in the discussion of ethnic minority entrepreneurship is the reason for becoming entrepreneurially active, especially whether this is done out of necessity or because an opportunity is recognized. We coded necessity-based entrepreneurship on descriptions such as no other job found, discriminated in previous job, did not fit in with organizational/work culture, jobs never work out, and entrepreneurship was the last resort. Opportunity-based entrepreneurship was coded on descriptions such as recognized business opportunity, realized market potential, and value creating. Both could be mentioned in the same article. As many policy measures have been initiated to support entrepreneurship in general and ethnic minority entrepreneurship in particular, we also analyzed how such measures were discussed, including government and non-government assistance programs for ethnic minority entrepreneurs. In addition, we studied challenges faced by this group of entrepreneurs, as well as their impact on society and the economy.

All articles were coded by one of the authors, while 21% were also coded by the other author to determine inter-coder reliability. Positive, neutral, or negative framing of the articles had 94% agreement. Necessity vs. opportunity in starting businesses had 90% agreement. The other inter-coder reliability agreements were 88% regarding challenges, 82% regarding the impact on the society and economy, 100% regarding policy support measures, and 86% regarding other government policies. Because of the low level of variance in interpretation, codings related to the topics background of the entrepreneur, gender, race, and financing had 100% agreement.[3]

Findings

General analysis of the dataset

Drawing attention to the relevance of ethnic minority entrepreneurs for community development, this article focused on the reporting on ethnic minority entrepreneurs in their own right, i.e. not in comparison to entrepreneurship more generally, which is beyond the scope of this article. However, to assess how our findings would have compared to the reporting on entrepreneurship in general, we checked in the same database and timeframe how many articles were published on entrepreneurship as such (using "entrepreneur*" as search term). We found 140 more articles on that topic, compared to 110 articles on ethnic minority entrepreneurship, rather surprising and signaling a relatively small representation of ethnic minority entrepreneurship in the public discourse (considering that there are 5.8 million minority-owned business activities compared to 20.1 million non-minority firms,[4] a relatively equal representation of ethnic entrepreneurs and entrepreneurs as such would require 381 articles to be published on entrepreneurs). This finding is even more interesting as only 23 newspapers out of the 340 included in the database published articles on the phenomenon of ethnic minority entrepreneurship.

Of the 110 articles, 47 discussed individual ethnic minority entrepreneurs, often by portraying their venture activities and providing examples of what they do. Forty-nine articles described policy programs to support ethnic minority entrepreneurship, but did not discuss entrepreneurs specifically. Articles varied between 450 and 3153 words in length, but only 7 had 1500 words or more, with an average of 959 words. As shown in Table 2, 74 articles were positive about ethnic minority entrepreneurs, 23 were neutral, and 13 pointed out mainly negative aspects of entrepreneurship.

Table 2. Framing of newspaper articles as positive, neutral, or negative per year.

Framing	From 10/2003	2004	2005	2006	2007	Until 10/2008	Total
Positive	5	10	14	15	18	12	74
Neutral	0	3	9	6	2	3	23
Negative	0	5	1	3	3	1	13
Total	5	18	24	24	23	16	110

Background of the entrepreneur

Entrepreneurs in 20 articles had relevant prior industry experience, and two articles described previous entrepreneurial experience. All but three articles (which were neutral) were framed positively. Twenty-one articles discussed black entrepreneurs, nine entrepreneurs of Hispanic origin, four entrepreneurs of Asian origin, and one each of Eastern European, Middle Eastern, and mixed race/ethnic origins, respectively. The remaining articles do not specify any racial/ethnic background. Regarding the entrepreneurs' religion, two articles pointed out their evangelical belief, and one article each referred to Jewish, Muslim, and Protestant entrepreneurs.

Gender and family issues

Male entrepreneurs were mentioned in 42 articles, while 16 female entrepreneurs were featured. This roughly corresponds to the share of women among total entrepreneurial activity (which in the USA is 35.3%; see Mitchell, 2011), implying that ethnic minority women entrepreneurs are not more underrepresented in the public discourse than their male counterparts – juxtaposing a pattern observed in other countries (see e.g. Achtenhagen & Welter, 2011, for the situation in Germany). Generally, the portraits of female entrepreneurs were positive in tone. Several articles depicted women as smart business people in industries (even male-dominated ones) and avoided overly stereotypical images. Another positively framed a businesswoman as actively trying to break common stereotypes about minorities and women. One article presented a woman in her struggles against the prejudice that Asian women would not be successful entrepreneurs, and other texts pointed out challenges posed by the specific life situation of the entrepreneurs, such as being a single mom.

In portraits of male entrepreneurs, six articles mentioned the wife's involvement in the business, which often included co-ownership, but she did not participate in the interview. In two cases, the husband was mentioned as co-owner without being part of the interview. In seven articles, the wife is mentioned, but with no involvement in the business. In a broader perspective, other family members are mentioned to be co-owners or employees of the company and as working alongside their entrepreneurial family members, sometimes even being interviewed for the portrayals. Being a family business is mentioned in few articles, which is surprising considering that about 90% of all US businesses feature family involvement (Dascher & Jens, 1999) and the importance of family networks for the development of ethnic minority businesses has been pointed out in several studies (e.g. Bagwell, 2008). For example, one article described a fourth-generation ethnic minority business. Eight entrepreneurs explained their plans to maintain the business within the family, but only one already had a clear succession plan.

Access to financing

Academic literature has pointed out the difficulty of ethnic minority entrepreneurs to receive financing (e.g. Deakins, Ishaq, Smallbone, Whittam, & Wyper, 2007), even for highly successful firms (Ram, Smallbone, Deakins, & Jones, 2003). In comparison, only very few small non-ethnic businesses in the USA said that they did not receive the financing they wanted (Levenson & Willard, 2000). Of the articles mentioning financing, 14 stated that ethnic minority entrepreneurs relied on personal savings, four received funding from family and friends, nine received funding by corporate or private investors, six got business bank loans, two used personal bank loans, and one used personal credit. In eight articles, the entrepreneurs received government-supported financing, while no article discussed funding provided by the ethnic community, though academic research suggests that ethnic resources are critical, especially in early phases of developing immigrant businesses (e.g. Zonta, 2012). Entrepreneurs portrayed in 11 articles received specific funding for ethnic minority entrepreneurs, as provided through the MBDA or other sources (see www.mbda.gov for more information on the different finance schemes available for ethnic minority entrepreneurs).

The motive for becoming entrepreneurially active

As stated in the literature review, the motives for becoming entrepreneurially active are often divided into opportunity- or necessity-based. In 28 articles, ethnic minority entrepreneurs were portrayed as running opportunity-based ventures and 52 articles referred to a combination of opportunity and necessity. Seven articles described how the entrepreneurs identified their business opportunity and eight articles described that opportunity as unique.

Portraits of opportunity-based entrepreneurship typically show that entrepreneurs want to run their own business instead of being employed (Hisrich, 1985). The articles included a female entrepreneur who worked for different real estate agencies until she realized she wanted to run her own company. Another entrepreneur saved money during his previous career in order to buy a restaurant when coming to the USA, thereby portraying how an entrepreneurial career was already planned before emigrating from an origin country. Other articles described how gaps in the market were identified, such as vegan food, low-fat dairy products, or small grocery stores. Some articles discussed the yearning for home as a driver for opening ethnic restaurants, where entrepreneurs can offer the feeling of home and have their own business. Showing the world that ethnic minority-owned businesses could also "do the job" appeared as a strong force for opening a business in several articles. An interesting aspect focused on how entrepreneurs start small by experimenting with an idea, and then expand. For example, one entrepreneur started a business cooking in a church kitchen, and then expanded to catering for schools.

The majority of the articles portrayed low-threshold businesses, such as the restaurant or small-shop sectors, which have also been the focus of research due to their disproportionate concentration of ethnic minority entrepreneurs (e.g. Ram, Sanghera, Abbas, Barlow, & Jones, 2000). However, many articles described how the entrepreneurs desired to be self-employed and therefore actively searched for business opportunities. Reasons for founding ventures were diverse, including altruistic motives of helping the community by providing certain services. But forms of racial discrimination were mentioned as pushing people into entrepreneurship, supporting academic findings (e.g. Ram, 1994). In addition, different forms of franchising were described as business opportunities, especially because this eliminated the need of developing an individual brand. Some portraits of necessity-based entrepreneurship described how entrepreneurs started their ventures, because they had low-paying jobs, but could not find better-paying jobs. The necessity of having a job that allowed for adjusting the work to physical impairments was another reason for starting a business.

In entrepreneurship literature, the dichotomy between necessity- and opportunity-based entrepreneurship is commonly seen as static (e.g. Reynolds et al., 2005), but in the newspaper articles, a different picture emerged. Twenty-nine articles described how entrepreneurial ventures that were founded out of necessity became more opportunity-driven over time. For example, the ethnic minority entrepreneurs developed and expanded their businesses, and acted on emerging business opportunities to diversify themselves. Six articles described how ethnic minority entrepreneurs were poverty-stricken when they founded the venture, clearly out of necessity, which they then turned into profitable businesses by acting on opportunities.

Support for ethnic minority entrepreneurs

Getting more ethnic minority people involved in entrepreneurial activities was a recurrent theme, both in articles portraying entrepreneurs and those discussing policy support measures. Articles about programs supporting ethnic minority entrepreneurship typically focused on necessity-based entrepreneurship, such as when they described how the programs should help to create jobs in crime-ridden neighborhoods in impoverished city centers. Another program described matching minority entrepreneurs with community government officials to help them establish relevant contacts. Descriptions of support measures for ethnic minority entrepreneurs typically had a very positive tone and gave the impression of tax money well invested. For example, one article described an organization created to help certify ethnic minority entrepreneurs so that they could get business contracts. Another discussed an expo for ethnic minority entrepreneurs, referring to both opportunity- and necessity-based entrepreneurship, while another presented a program that was created to help minority entrepreneurs attract financing and keep businesses going. A university program targeting ethnic minority entrepreneurs was also described.

One recurrent theme in the articles was that ethnic minority ventures needed help or else they would fail, thus implicitly drawing on the underperformance hypothesis common to the discussion of ethnic minority entrepreneurship (cf. Ndofor & Priem, 2011). Often, programs addressed in the newspaper articles aimed at assisting women and minority entrepreneurs in developing the skills necessary to create and run businesses, such as helping them identify a business opportunity and getting financing. Forty-three articles referred to local or regional governmental support programs for ethnic minority entrepreneurs, 11 referred to national governmental support programs, and eight to both local and national programs (for an overview of different existing programs, please see www.mbda.gov). Some policy initiatives were aimed at facilitating activities of ethnic minority entrepreneurs who already are active by matching small and big businesses. In comparison, 47 articles did not make reference to support programs.

More informal initiatives were described that help either ethnic minority people or other disadvantaged groups, such as one woman running workshops to help minority entrepreneurs develop skills to succeed in business. Another initiative was a fair where entrepreneurs could display their wares to help them get more well-known and sell more, while another business conference for minorities helped them both with financing and with finding opportunities to get contracts and customers. One article told the story of a program created to help minority entrepreneurs that turned into a program to educate entrepreneurs about consumer debts so that they can keep or start businesses. In 11 of the articles, entrepreneurs talked about their mentor as an important person for their business development. Mentoring is used as a common means of entrepreneurial support (Bisk, 2002).

The value of ethnic minority entrepreneurship

The positive impact made by ethnic minority entrepreneurs was stressed in several articles. One described how an entrepreneur revitalized parts of Washington, DC, by paying for the renovation of the professional basketball arena. Another stressed the positive contribution of ethnic minority entrepreneurs in reaction to a report released by the Minnesota's governor's office that focused on the drain that illegal immigrants had on the economy. Another article had a more pronounced political dimension, such as when candidates running for a county position both stated that they would be committed to have the county support women and minority entrepreneurs. Regarding future plans with the venture, no articles stated that the entrepreneur feared having to close down the business, while 36 articles reported on plans to expand the business. This is an interesting and encouraging contrast to research on black entrepreneurs from the US finding that while they are 50% more likely to engage in entrepreneurship than white entrepreneurs, their businesses would grow less and be less profitable (Edelman, Brush, Manolova, & Greene, 2010).

However, a number of articles focused on some negative aspects of ethnic minority entrepreneurship. Some pointed out that as ethnic minority entrepreneurs do not have as much access to funding, they sometimes refrained from starting businesses. A national report was described that showed how ethnic minority entrepreneurs need more information to have a better opportunity to grow beyond the sole proprietorship model. Several articles discussed the problems encountered by minority entrepreneurs in sustaining their businesses, claiming that they grew less, made less use of growth strategies than "other" businesses, and failed more often because they would take higher risks due to lacking opportunities, sometimes pointing out the need to learn management skills. These articles appeared to confirm critics of existing entrepreneurship support policies, claiming that these programs do not create enough impact (Waldinger et al., 1990).

Challenges faced by ethnic minority entrepreneurs

A number of challenges that ethnic minority entrepreneurs face were presented in the articles. One overarching challenge was the monetary concerns of these entrepreneurs, and how more businesses run by ethnic minority entrepreneurs go under because of lacking availability to get financing. Financing programs, such as micro-loans, were described in a few of the articles. One article discussed an entrepreneur who told how difficult it is to get started in the food industry, as the profit margins are very small and access to financing difficult, so the help of support programs was necessary. One entrepreneur wanted to buy the building he was leasing, but had trouble getting financing for it. Another challenge was finding business partners or customers, for which specific networking support programs were considered useful. But also the lack of opportunities to develop the venture was evident in a number of the portraits of entrepreneurs, as it was more difficult to get deals or contracts. One article stated, "If you look at the number of black-owned established businesses in the US, it is about a third of the percentage of other groups." "When we looked at entrepreneurs of all races from around the country, the likelihood of being refused for a loan is higher among African-American entrepreneurs" (Milwaukee, 4 October 2006, page D1). Getting the financing to take over an existing business or franchise was also presented as a challenge in several articles.

Reactions of minority entrepreneurs to these challenges were also described, such as attempts to make the business leaner and more profitable, including streamlining operations and the billing processes. To meet the challenge of expanding in a globalizing economy, involvement in joint ventures was presented as an avenue of one minority entrepreneur. The support during the start-up process by a mentor was described in several articles. In addition, a challenge perceived by several entrepreneurs was to persuade others that they were capable business people despite belonging to a certain religious or ethnic group. Finally, other reported challenges of ethnic minority entrepreneurs were not specific to this group of entrepreneurs, such as finding a work–life balance, dealing with increasing prices for supplies, establishing a firm position within the chosen niche, and optimizing the business model. This suggested positively that a few portraits of ethnic minority entrepreneurs actually do represent them in their everyday entrepreneurial activities, rather than with focus on what differentiates them from the "norm."

Performance

In entrepreneurship literature, an underperforming hypothesis of ethnic minority ventures is still common (Ndofor & Priem, 2011), but this image is not often conveyed by the newspaper articles. Only two ventures portrayed in the articles were run by individual entrepreneurs without employees. Only one article discussed an entrepreneur facing difficulties and having to lay off employees, while 19 articles described how the entrepreneur expanded the business by hiring new employees. Another 11 articles reported a stable situation for the venture regarding employees. Only two articles reported decreasing profitability of ventures and one financial losses, while five reported about increasing profitability. Other articles did not take up this issue. Only one article reported decreasing sales, while 26 reported increasing sales.

Discussion, recommendations, and conclusion

In summary, as shown by the overall small number of articles over the five-year span, ethnic minority entrepreneurs are largely absent from the public discourse as led by US newspapers. Because ethnic minority entrepreneurship is a positive phenomenon for the US economy, society, and community development, this lack of reporting is unfortunate. Role models, as created by media, have been found to be a source of identification that could contribute to a positive image of entrepreneurship and propensity of becoming entrepreneurially active (Achtenhagen & Welter, 2011). This clearly demonstrates that the topic of ethnic minority entrepreneurship is hardly considered worth reporting on in its own right, while the relevance given to it by spending government resources on fostering it attracts some very limited attention. However, the limited existing reporting had potential to create a positive image of ethnic minority entrepreneurship.

So what does this research mean for community development? Community leaders can help their economies and encourage ethnic minority entrepreneurship in the following ways.

Help ethnic minority entrepreneurs believe they can start businesses

The Small Business Administration (SBA) (2010) has shown that minority people have higher rates of job creation. The newspapers related many positives of entrepreneurship and how entrepreneurs sought opportunities, even after starting businesses out of necessity. The articles showed that the often-used dichotomy with the opposing poles of opportunity-necessity in entrepreneurship (Smallbone & Welter, 2006) does not appear to reflect reality. Thus, the image created in the articles does not show this type of endeavor as being worthless due to their limited business models (Shane, 2009); rather it is illustrated that ethnic minority entrepreneurs can expand their ventures and provide employment. The articles had a mainly positive representation of ethnic minority entrepreneurs of both genders and many races. They mostly avoided stereotypes found in previous research (Achtenhagen & Welter, 2011; Light, 2007). This should be mirrored in communication efforts by community development officials through promoting successful role models through different media channels, while avoiding stereotypes and showing that many types of people can create successful businesses.

Continue creating or publicizing programs to help ethnic minority entrepreneurs

Although ethnic minority entrepreneurs start businesses more frequently, they are more likely to fail because of lack of access to financing and other aspects that are necessary to keep a business going (Small Business Administration, 2010). Many local and national programs have been created to assist minority entrepreneurs and the articles reviewed highlighted many formal and informal programs. However, more needs to be done for minority entrepreneurs to become aware of and use these programs. For example, the articles showed that most businesses had no succession plans, but research shows that more than half a million US family businesses are facing succession through 2016 (Shanker & Astrachan, 1996). The articles also said that minority entrepreneurs need more information to grow beyond a sole proprietorship and that mentors help their business development. A clear implication for community leaders is to enhance the visibility of ethnic minority entrepreneurs by publicizing information about programs, mentoring opportunities, and business development classes or workshops. Also, as pointed out by Waldinger et al. (1990), public policy measures to support ethnic minority entrepreneurs often receive too little money to be able to have major impact. Thus, another implication is to review the budgeting for policies in relation to their goals and previous achievements.

Work with newspapers to show the benefits of promoting ethnic minority entrepreneurship

As stated previously, minority-owned businesses contributed more than $1 trillion in annual economic output (MBDA Annual Performance Report, 2012). Given that many minority groups live in declining urban centers, the conditions of the communities can be enhanced by improved conditions for ethnic minority entrepreneurs. Now that many newspapers are more involved in community journalism (Nip, 2006), some have made a strong commitment to the topic. For example, the *Milwaukee Journal Sentinel* had a reporter specifically covering minority and entrepreneurial issues and, therefore, had the most articles during the five-year time frame. While Bruni et al. (2004) pointed out that the role of media is very important for the social construction of the image of entrepreneurship, in the study some articles demarcated ethnic minority entrepreneurship by delimiting it from the "other," "normal" entrepreneurship and positioning it as an inferior, less desirable form of entrepreneurship. Still, most articles painted a positive image of it. Therefore, community development officials and newspaper reporters need to work together to show how minority entrepreneurship is desirable and not "out of the norm." As Nip (2006) explained, newspapers can choose frames that help citizens discuss issues, and help the community deliberate and search for solutions. Both leaders and newspapers need to be realistic about the challenges for ethnic minority entrepreneurs, but do what is needed to help them face the challenges. Community leaders could write articles or public opinion pieces about ethnic minority entrepreneurship and help create the positive frame.

To date, little to no community development literature has been published about how newspapers frame ethnic minority entrepreneurs and how that might affect the community. Our study found that the majority of the articles about ethnic minority entrepreneurship published in US newspapers between 2003 and 2008 portrayed the occurrence in its different facets and thereby its heterogeneity (see Ram et al., 2000) – providing a rather positive image of these entrepreneurs, but also accurately pointing out the challenges and struggles faced. However, two critical aspects emerge from our analyses. First, ethnic minority entrepreneurship is largely absent from the public discourse transmitted in US newspapers. Considering not only its economic relevance, but also the policy attention it has received through the amount of public resources invested in encouraging ethnic minority entrepreneurship, this is highly surprising. An accurate representation of what it means to be an ethnic minority entrepreneur, i.e. its positive aspects as well as its challenges, could help to encourage more people to consider entrepreneurship as a viable career and/or investment option, making a positive impact on community development. Second, there is a tendency in a number of articles to portray ethnic minority entrepreneurship as the deviation to the rule – in contrast to the norm of entrepreneurship of white, middle-aged men. Thus, we conclude that ethnic minority entrepreneurship has not yet significantly found its way into the public discourse and that its invisibility hinders not only a process of social construction about the phenomenon to take place, but also fails to provide a source of identification and inspiration that could encourage ethnic minority people to consider this career option.

This should not be misinterpreted to mean that only reporting about successful entrepreneurs should be in focus or that only the positive aspects of being entrepreneurially active should be stressed. If people have the chance to learn more about all aspects of entrepreneurial life, to identify with role models and build an opinion on entrepreneurship through the process of social construction as discussed above, they might feel attracted to the option of becoming self-employed, and it is important that they do not get attracted by wrong promises. Even for a broader audience, it would be interesting to find out more about the fascinating business activities of ethnic minority individuals, and these accounts could positively contribute to the social construction of the phenomenon of ethnic minority entrepreneurship and the role these people can play for revitalizing declined urban centers.

Skeptics could argue that much more reporting on ethnic minority entrepreneurs takes place, but that we did not capture this because our choice of key words restricted to this group of entrepreneurs only. When examining the same time frame for the key words, "minority business owners," we did find 120 more articles. However, while journalists may not differentiate between entrepreneurs and business owners, the notions used in this study are the ones typically used by both academic scholars and policy makers. Future research could include the broader term to see if it would affect the representation of ethnic minority entrepreneurs. Future research could also investigate what importance newspaper editors feel should be given to writing about ethnic minority entrepreneurs, including a comparison between more conservative and liberal newspapers, the size of the cities, and the ethnic makeup within them. With the advent of community journalism, more editors could feel a strong connection to enhancing the economic viability of their communities. Now that social media has exploded in popularity, especially after the time period of this study, future research needs to explore the role that it could have in enhancing the image or recruitment of ethnic minority entrepreneurs.

As ethnic minority entrepreneurs face more challenges than those faced by entrepreneurs in general and, nonetheless, make a valuable contribution to economic development, we argue that they deserve to be seen in the public discourse. Even though several policy programs exist to help foster ethnic minority entrepreneurship, these receive little media coverage. Higher visibility of ethnic minority entrepreneurs in media outlets could also help to increase awareness of issues, such as their difficulties of receiving financing, and thus eventually contribute to reducing the challenges of such activities. This is specifically important for community development officials because economic development often rides on "locally groomed entrepreneurs" making an investment in the community (Korsching et al., 2007, p. 40). As the MBDA implied, when public and private sectors work together, more ethnic minority individuals will consider becoming entrepreneurs, because they will feel supported, both through programs to help them and through the positive construction of entrepreneurship in their communities. That can be the turning point when their invisible struggles become known and changed into success. The focus of this article is on ethnic minority entrepreneurs in their own right. A more detailed comparison of their situation with that of mainstream entrepreneurship would be an interesting topic for future research.

Disclosure statement

No potential conflict of interest was reported by the authors.

Notes

1. Because this study's purpose is examining how US newspapers covered ethnic minority entrepreneurs, the terms "business owner," "businessman," "businesswoman," or "business person" were not included in the search.
2. Because some of the newspapers cover the same cities, they potentially had access to the same entrepreneurs; therefore, the article is about newspaper coverage of ethnic minority entrepreneurship in each city. Also, because of the relatively few articles about ethnic minority entrepreneurs, there would not have been enough data to do a valid comparison between differing types of newspapers in the same city.
3. The full codebook is available from the authors upon request.
4. Future research should examine if minority business owners are thought of as entrepreneurs for a longer time period than white business owners. The terms entrepreneurs and entrepreneurship were examined including white entrepreneurs, but not just the phrase "business owners" without the terms "minority" or "ethnic".

References

Achtenhagen, L., & Welter, F. (2007). Entrepreneurship discourse in the media. In H. Neergaard & J. Parm Ulhoi (Eds.), *Handbook of qualitative research methods in entrepreneurship* (pp. 193–215). Cheltenham: Edward Elgar.

Achtenhagen, L., & Welter, F. (2011). Surfing on the ironing board: The representation of women's entrepreneurship in German newspapers. *Entrepreneurship & Regional Development, 23*, 763–786.

Acs, Z. (2006). How is entrepreneurship good for economic growth? *Innovations: Technology, Governance, Globalization, 1*, 97–107.

Acs, Z. A., & Varga, A. (2005). Entrepreneurship, agglomeration and technological change. *Small Business Economics, 24*, 323–334.

Bagwell, S. (2008). Transnational family networks and ethnic minority business development: The case of Vietnamese nail-shops in the UK. *Journal of Entrepreneurial Behavior and Research, 14*, 377–394.

Baran, S. J., & Davis, D. K. (2012). *Mass communication theory: Foundations, ferment, and future* (6th ed.). Boston, MA: Wadsworth Cengage Learning.

Bisk, L. (2002). Formal entrepreneurial mentoring: The efficacy of third party managed programs. *Career Development International, 7*, 262–270.

Bosma, N., & Harding, R. (2006). *Global entrepreneurship monitor: GEM 2006 summary results*. London: Babson College and London Business School.

Bruni, A., Gherardi, S., & Poggio, L. (2004). Entrepreneur-mentality, gender and the study of women entrepreneurs. *Journal of Organizational Change Management, 17*, 256–268.

Dascher, P. E., & Jens, W. G. (1999). Family business succession planning. *Business Horizons, 42*, 2–4.

Deakins, D., Ishaq, M., Smallbone, D., Whittam, G., & Wyper, J. (2007). Ethnic minority businesses in Scotland and the role of social capital. *International Small Business Journal, 25*, 307–326.

Edelman, L. F., Brush, C. G., Manolova, T. S., & Greene, P. G. (2010). Start-up motivations and growth intentions of minority nascent entrepreneurs. *Journal of Small Business Management, 48*, 174–196.

Fouhy, E. (1994, Summer-Fall). The dawn of public journalism. *National Civic Review, 83*, 259–266.

Fregetto, E. (2004). Immigrant and ethnic entrepreneurship: A US perspective. In H. P. Welsch (Ed.), *Entrepreneurship: The way ahead* (pp. 253–268). New York, NY: Routledge.

Goffman, E. (1986). *Frame analysis: An essay on the organization of experience*. Boston, MA: Northeastern University Press.

Habermas, J. (1991). *The structural transformation of the public sphere: An inquiry into a category of bourgeois society*. Boston, MA: MIT Press.

Hisrich, R. D. (1985). The women entrepreneur in the United States and Puerto Rico: A comparative study. *Leadership and Organizational Development Journal, 5*, 3–8.

Hustedde, R. J., & Ganowicz, J. (2002). The basics: What's essential about theory for community development practice? *Journal of the Community Development Society, 33*(1), 1–19.

Korsching, P. F., Allen, J. C., Vogt, R., & Sapp, S. G. (2007). Community leaders, business ownership, and support of entrepreneurship development: The role of macroentrepreneurs. *Community Development, 38*, 28–45.

Langowitz, N., & Morgan, C. (2003). Women entrepreneurs: Breaking through the glass barrier. In J. Butler (Ed.), *New perspectives on women entrepreneurs* (pp. 101–119). Greenwich, CT: Information Age Publishing.

Levenson, A. R., & Willard, K. L. (2000). Do firms get the financing they want? Measuring credit rationing experienced by small businesses in the US. *Small Business Economics, 14*, 83–94.

Lichtenstein, G. A., Lyons, T. S., & Kutzhanova, N. (2004). Building entrepreneurial communities: The appropriate role of enterprise development activities. *Journal of the Community Development Society, 35*, 5–24.

Light, I. (1972). *Ethnic enterprise in America*. Berkeley: University of California Press.

Light, I. (2007). Women's economic niches and earnings inferiority: The view from the ethnic economy. *Journal of Ethnic and Migration Studies, 33*, 541–557.

Lippmann, W. (1922). Public opinion. Reprinted in H. Tumber (Ed.), (1999). *News: A reader* (pp. 5–10). Oxford: Oxford University Press.

Little, C. (2014, November). Contrary to stereotypes, millennials rely on newspaper media to be engaged and informed. *Newspaper Association of America*. Retrieved from http://www.naa.org/News-and-Media/CEO-Update/2014-Millennialsaspx

MBDA Annual Performance Report. (2012). *A catalyst for global business expansion*. Minority Business Development Agency, US Department of Commerce. Retrieved from http://www.mbda.gov/sites/default/files/APR2012pdf

Mitchell, L. (2011). *Overcoming the gender gap: Women entrepreneurs as economic drivers* (Ewing Marion Kauffman Foundation Report). Retrieved from http://www.kauffman.org/uploadedFiles/Growing_the_Economy_Women_Entrepreneurspdf

Muske, G., & Woods, M. (2004). Micro business as an economic development tool: What they bring and what they need. *Journal of the Community Development Society, 35*, 97–116.

Ndofor, H. A., & Priem, R. L. (2011). Immigrant entrepreneurs, the ethnic enclave strategy, and venture performance. *Journal of Management, 37*, 740–818.

Nip, J. Y. M. (2006). Exploring the second phase of public journalism. *Journalism Studies, 7*, 212–236. doi:10.1080/14616700500533528

Ojo, T. (2006). Ethnic print media in the multicultural nation of Canada: A case study of the black newspaper in Montreal. *Journalism, 7*, 343–361.

Park, R. E. (1940). News as a form of knowledge: A chapter in the sociology of knowledge. Reprinted in H. Tumber (Ed.), (1999), *News: A reader* (pp. 11–15). Oxford: Oxford University Press (Originally published in American Journal of Sociology, 1940, 669–686).

Procter, D. E. (2004). Building community through communication: The case for civic communion. *Journal of the Community Development Society, 35*, 53–72.

Radu, M., & Redien-Collot, R. (2008). The social representation of entrepreneurs in the French press: Desirable and feasible models? *International Small Business Journal, 26*, 259–298.

Ram, M. (1994). Unravelling social networks in ethnic minority firms. *International Small Business Journal, 12*, 42–53.

Ram, M., Sanghera, B., Abbas, T., Barlow, G., & Jones, T. (2000). Ethnic minority business in comparative perspective: The case of the independent restaurant sector. *Journal of Ethnic and Migration Studies, 26*, 495–510.

Ram, M., Smallbone, D., Deakins, D., & Jones, T. (2003). Banking on 'break-out': Finance and the development of ethnic minority businesses. *Journal of Ethnic and Migration Studies, 29*, 663–681.

Reynolds, P., Bosma, N., Autio, E., Hunt, S., De Bono, N., Servais, I., & Lopez-Garcia, P. (2005). Global entrepreneurship monitor: Data collection design and implementation 1998–2003. *Small Business Economics, 24*, 205–231.

Rindova, V., Pollock, T., & Hayward, M. (2006). Celebrity firms: The social construction of market popularity. *Academy of Management Review, 31*, 50–71.

Rogers, T. (2010). Most news still comes from newspapers, study finds. *Journalism*. Retrieved from http://journalism.about.com/b/2010/01/12/most-news-still-comes-fron-newspapers-study-findshtm

Rosenthal, S. S. (2008). Old homes, externalities, and poor neighborhoods: A model of urban decline and renewal. *Journal of Urban Economics, 63*, 816–840.

Shane, S. (2009). Why encouraging more people to become entrepreneurs is bad public policy. *Small Business Economics, 33*, 141–149.

Shanker, M. C., & Astrachan, J. H. (1996). Myths and realities: Family businesses' contribution to the US economy – A framework for assessing family business statistics. *Family Business Review, 9*, 107–123.

Small Business Administration. (2010). *The small business economy: A report to the president*. Washington, DC: The United States Government Printing Office.

Small Business Association Office of Advocacy. (2010). *The small business economy: A report to the president*. Washington, DC: United States Government Printing Office. Retrieved from http://www.sba.gov/sites/default/files/sb_econ2010pdf

Smallbone, D., & Welter, F. (2006). Conceptualising entrepreneurship in a transition context. *International Journal of Entrepreneurship and Small Business, 3*, 190–206.

Soloski, J. (1989). News reporting and professionalism: Some constraints on the reporting of the news. *Media, Culture, & Society, 11*, 207–228.

Sriram, V., Mersha, T., & Herron, L. (2007). Drivers of urban entrepreneurship: An integrative model. *International Journal of Entrepreneurial Behaviour & Research, 13*, 235–251.

US International Trade Commission. (2010). *Small and medium-sized enterprises: US and EU export activities, and barriers and opportunities perceived by US firms* (Investigation No. 332-509, USITC Publication 4169). DIANE Publishing. Retrieved from http://www.usitc.gov/secretary/fed_reg_notices/332/332_509_institution11252009sgl.pdf

Valdez, Z. (2008). The effect of social capital on white, Korean, Mexican and Black business owners' earnings in the US. *Journal of Ethnic and Migration Studies, 34*, 955–973.

Waldinger, R. (2001). *Strangers at the gate: New immigrants in urban America*. Berkeley: University of California Press.

Waldinger, R., Aldrich, H., Bradford, W. D., Boissevain, J., Chen, G., Kerte, H., … Wilsen, P. (1990). Conclusions and policy implications. In R. Waldinger, H. Aldrich, & R. Ward (Eds.), *Ethnic entrepreneurs: Immigrant business in industrial societies* (pp. 177–197). Newbury Park, CA: Sage.

Wallace, S. L. (1999). Life on "EZ" street: Linking community economic development to the empowerment zones and enterprise community policy goals. *Journal of the Community Development Society, 30*, 154–177.

Welter, F. (2011). Contextualizing entrepreneurship: Conceptual challenges and ways forward. *Entrepreneurship Theory & Practice, 35*, 165–184.

Zonta, M. M. (2012). The continuing significance of ethnic resources: Korean-owned banks in Los Angeles, New York and Washington, DC. *Journal of Ethnic and Migration Studies, 38*, 463–484.

Constructing a multi-dimensional measure of local entrepreneurial culture

Nicole Breazeale, Michael W.-P. Fortunato, James E. Allen IV, Ronald J. Hustedde and Helen Pushkarskaya

This article proposes a scale that measures the local entrepreneurial culture of a place based on residents' perceptions. The initial 36-item pool was developed through semi-structured interviews with entrepreneurs and non-entrepreneurs in Kentucky (USA) and then reviewed by a focus group composed of entrepreneurship coaches. These items were included in an extensive survey of rural and urban Kentuckians. Factor analysis resulted in a 17-item scale with four major components. To ascertain the predictive validity of the subscales, a series of analysis of covariance (ANCOVA) models evaluated their correlations with county-level rates of entrepreneurship obtained from an independent data set. The analysis confirmed that perceptions of the local entrepreneurial culture *do* correlate with entrepreneurial activity. In line with the theoretical model presented in this article, the ANCOVAs also controlled for the modulating effect of important individual-level characteristics and regional factors. The proposed scale is recommended for use by entrepreneurship support programs that provide one-on-one assistance for small businesses, yet seldom assess nor consider how they might improve the entrepreneurial culture of the place where these businesses operate. Furthermore, this measure is an important contribution to entrepreneurship research. Existing measures of entrepreneurial culture focus mostly on the regional and national levels, overlooking the role of local cultural characteristics; they also tend to focus on general cultural attributes rather than on residents' perceptions of the entrepreneurial climate. This entrepreneurship culture scale opens the door to new directions in research.

Introduction

The beating heart of the social sciences is the question of how culture and values develop over time, eventually becoming institutionalized, creating patterns of social behavior, and forming norms, rules, laws, and mores that nuance and influence how people think about the world around them. Research on entrepreneurship has only recently recognized that the entrepreneurial act cannot be understood apart from the society that contains it, that the role of the entrepreneur must be situated in a social context, and that this social context is a product of national, regional, and local culture (Julien, 2007).

Studies of entrepreneurial culture focus primarily on the impact of national and regional characteristics on entrepreneurship, despite the fact that the vast majority of firms are small, local entities that are highly embedded in their communities, relying on their local roots for start-up, survival, and development (Julien, 2007). The few studies that have examined the effects of local characteristics on entrepreneurial activity in the USA have found wide variation in entrepreneurship rates across counties (Acs & Armington, 2006; Low, Henderson, & Weiler, 2005), and county types (Rupasingha & Goetz, 2013). Interestingly, regions with high levels of entrepreneurship continue to remain highly entrepreneurial even following major social and political shifts (Fritsch & Wyrwich, 2012). By contrast, localities such as "company towns" exhibit a strong cultural preference for wage employment over self-employment long after the decline of the primary industry in that town (Fortunato & McLaughlin, 2012), sometimes creating an embedded legacy of economic disempowerment or disaffection that outlasts the primary industry (Gaventa, 1982; Luloff & Bridger, 2003). These studies suggest it is important to consider local cultural factors when trying to understand why some localities seem to flourish with entrepreneurial activity, while other regions do not (Julien, 2007).

The primary goal of this research is to explore how perceptions of local culture affect entrepreneurial activity. This research agenda fills a gap in the literature dominated by macro-level approaches to investigating the impact of culture on entrepreneurship. It also makes an important contribution by focusing on perceptions of the entrepreneurial climate rather than relying solely on objective measures that seek to capture general cultural attributes.

Making the empirical link between local culture and entrepreneurial action is complicated. A first step is to construct a valid measure of local cultural characteristics that impede or facilitate entrepreneurship, which is the specific objective of this article. Building on the work of other scholars who have examined local entrepreneurial culture (Frazier, Stoel, Niehm, & Eckerson, 2013), the scale presented here: (1) results from a mixed method approach to data collection; (2) is multi-dimensional; (3) is based on the perceptions of residents, rather than on objective measures of culture, since individuals have discordant views of objective reality and are motivated to act based on their perceptions; (4) it has significant predictive power as shown by correlating the subscales with county-level rates of entrepreneurship, obtained from an independent data set; (5) its predictive power has been tested within a conceptual framework that recognizes modulating effects of individual and regional factors on the relationship between local culture and aggregate business activity; and (6) the scale was examined separately for rural and urban areas, and revealed significant yet different results in each location category.

Scale development began with 23 semi-structured interviews of entrepreneurs and non-entrepreneurs around the state of Kentucky (USA), focusing mainly on rural areas. Interview prompts uncovered several elements of the local culture that are themes commonly found throughout the entrepreneurship literature. The results were used to construct an initial pool of 36 items, which were refined by a focus group of eight Kentucky entrepreneurs before being included in a comprehensive survey on entrepreneurship completed by 1481 Kentuckians. Items addressed a respondent's perception of their local community culture, including questions such as: "Overall, my county has a can-do attitude" or "My county has a powerful elite that blocks change."

Using the survey data, factor analysis was used to identify four underlying dimensions of local entrepreneurial culture, producing subscales that were titled: "Diversity and Change Climate" (DCC), "Business Promotion Climate" (BPC), "Business Discouragement Climate" (BDC), and a community-wide "Focus on Local" (FLC). The refined scale included a total of 17 items across these four factors, although there was a difference in items that loaded for the fourth factor across the rural and urban subsamples.

This article begins by presenting a review of the entrepreneurial culture literature, in which the operationalized definitions of both "entrepreneurship" and "entrepreneurial culture" used to guide the research are presented. The conceptual model is then presented, followed by the specific research questions that drive this article. Each step of the scale development process is then described, including the results of the factor analyses, each step of the scales' development, and predictive validity testing. The article concludes by discussing the value of the measure and study findings for community development practice and entrepreneurship research.

Review of the literature

A particular challenge of the research on entrepreneurial culture is that the entrepreneurship field has not converged on a consistent definition for either entrepreneurship or culture (Davidsson, 2009; Shane, 2003). The following review of the literature contextualizes and presents an operationalized definition of entrepreneurship. It then goes on to discuss different scholarly treatments of "entrepreneurial culture," and describes how the research advances upon this small, but important body of work.

Defining and measuring entrepreneurship

Entrepreneurship is a notoriously difficult concept to define and measure, as it blends elements of an observable behavior (launching a venture) with a value judgment about the contribution and innovativeness of that venture (Davidsson, 2009). This activity differs widely across different social and cultural contexts, and motivations for becoming an entrepreneur (and what type of entrepreneur one becomes) are culturally influenced and exceptionally diverse (Dana, 1995; Julien, 2007). The role of the entrepreneur as a tireless innovator and "creative destroyer" who facilitates economic development was recognized and appreciated by the likes of Schumpeter (1934) and many who followed in his wake. This heroic notion of the entrepreneur par excellence persists even though most new businesses stay small over time and tend to replicate existing ideas (Julien, 2007).

Shane (2003) provides a more commonly accepted and applied definition of entrepreneurship as "an activity that involves the discovery, evaluation, and exploitation of opportunities to introduce new goods and services, ways of organizing, markets, process, and raw materials through organizing efforts that previously had not existed" (p. 4, originally in Shane & Venkataraman, 2000; Venkataraman, 1997). Many scholars debate this definition. Common critiques include the contested nature through which entrepreneurs act on opportunities (Alvarez & Barney, 2007; Sarasvathy, 2009), the extent to which culture influences entrepreneurial ambition, and how opportunities are perceived in the first place (Dana, 1995; Julien, 2007). Despite these debates, there exists a strong consensus around the idea that entrepreneurship generally refers to the act of launching a new venture based upon the identification or creation of a novel opportunity, which requires some degree of personal or financial risk on the part of the entrepreneur (Davidsson, 2009; Gartner, 1988; Shane & Venkataraman, 2000).

Practically speaking, the risk-bearing, opportunity-seeking behavior of entrepreneurs is inherently subjective and very challenging to measure empirically. Low et al. (2005) recommend the use of self-employment ("non-farm proprietorship") as a reasonable proxy for entrepreneurship analyses at the regional level due to the availability of these data. While Schumpeter (1934) might cringe at the idea of using "self-employment" as a replacement for truly innovative entrepreneurship, other authors have made the reasonable assumption that areas with higher self-employment are also more likely to contain more entrepreneurs, who are themselves self-employed proprietors (Fortunato & McLaughlin, 2012; Rupasingha & Goetz, 2013). Low et al. (2005) also underscore the need to differentiate "high entrepreneurship" areas along two dimensions: self-employment *breadth* and *depth*. Self-employment breadth examines the number of self-employed individuals as a share of the total population; these measures are commonly derived from occupational data. Self-employment depth examines the income generated by non-farm proprietors, generally as compared to wage-earning employees in the same region. Personal income is a common way to measure depth, although revenue capture, or the amount of business revenue taken by the proprietor as profit, is another common proxy for the relative "success" of businesses in a region (Low et al., 2005). Since we are comparing unlike areas in this study (rural and urban), and because incomes tend to be higher in urban areas, we focus on entrepreneurial breadth – the share of self-employment in a given county – as our primary measure of entrepreneurial activity in an area.

Defining and measuring local entrepreneurial culture

The idea of an entrepreneurial culture is employed and measured in many different ways in the literature, although scholars in this camp all emphasize its critical importance. Julien (2007) stresses that an innovative "social milieu" is a fundamental precondition for high rates of entrepreneurial action. Shane (2003) refers to this as the "entrepreneurial environment," and also stresses its role in facilitating or inhibiting entrepreneurship.

In the realm of entrepreneurial culture, most major studies examine cultural and institutional differences across national and regional borders. Perhaps most notably, the Global Entrepreneurship Monitor (GEM) tracks "entrepreneurial attitudes and perceptions" from a massive survey administered across 70 participating nations at various stages of development (Amorós & Bosma, 2014). The GEM examines perceived opportunities, perceived capabilities, fear of failure, entrepreneurial intentions, entrepreneurship as a good career choice, high status to successful entrepreneurs, and media attention to successful entrepreneurs as indicators of the importance and viability of entrepreneurship in the national culture. Sometimes, culture is measured by some particular cultural norm, such as whether or not the culture is performance-based (Hopp & Stephan, 2012) or if the culture perceives entrepreneurship as a legitimate enterprise (Klyver & Thornton, 2010). Examining slightly different cultural elements, Wennberg, Pathak, and Autio (2013) instead look at the effects of regional attitudes toward institutional collectivism, assertiveness, performance orientation, and uncertainty avoidance on individual self-efficacy and fear of entrepreneurial failure. Beugelsdijk (2007) constructs a measure of entrepreneurial culture that incorporates views on individual effort, government ownership, state responsibility, unemployment, and long-term success.

The measure was then found to have a significant correlation with economic growth in 54 European regions. Similarly, Dimitratos, Voudouris, Plakoyiannaki, and Nakos (2012) designed a six-dimension scale of international entrepreneurial culture that included measures for motivation, networking, and entrepreneurial, market, and learning orientation that explained some international variation in entrepreneurship across the USA and the UK. Taken together, this group of studies provides excellent insights about some of the central cultural elements influencing entrepreneurship, but demonstrates a large range of cultural components and provides less information about how local dynamics can influence small business behavior.

The idea of a "local culture" assumes that people in a particular place view themselves as a collective, sharing common experiences, traits, values, attitudes, traditions, and institutions distinguishing them from other people. Overall, examinations of local culture go beyond rational, firm-centric approaches to understanding entrepreneurial action and underscore the fundamental role of the local society in shaping entrepreneurial values, possibilities, and outcomes (Dana, 1995; Julien, 2007). Specific definitions of a local entrepreneurial culture in the literature have included community social capital (Besser & Miller, 2013; Kwon, Heflin, & Ruef, 2013; Roxas & Azmat, 2014), community entrepreneurial climate (Chatman, Altman, & Johnson, 2008; Goetz & Freshwater, 2001), the institutional environment (Fortunato & McLaughlin, 2012; Frazier et al., 2013; Kibler, 2013), or a set of social norms (Hopp & Stephan, 2012; Klyver & Thornton, 2010). While each study recognizes and examines an important aspect of a local entrepreneurial culture, none of them fully encompass the inherent richness of the concept. There is a need to develop a valid, multi-dimensional measure that deeply examines many facets of this broad concept.

There have been some notable attempts to quantify and examine these various dimensions of a local entrepreneurial culture. In one example, Frazier et al. (2013) surveyed 1161 residents and business owners across 32 rural US communities, investigating community-wide attitudes and norms related to the local business sector. Their data-driven, multi-dimensional measure of institutional norms included openness to change, community performance actions, community symbolic actions, retailer symbolic actions, and retailer performance actions. They correlated this measure with residents' and business owners' optimism about the prospects of new businesses' success, which were found to be positively related. Similarly, Fortunato and McLaughlin (2012) examined cultural differences across high- and low-entrepreneurship rural communities, finding that high levels of interaction among entrepreneurs, a collaborative mentality, and cultural openness to change and diversity were critical to building a more entrepreneurial culture.

This research builds on the insights from these and other studies, but enhances the measurement of entrepreneurial culture in several ways. First of all, the majority of literature on entrepreneurial culture focuses on "objective" measures, such as individual values, social capital, and so forth. Yet, theoretical and empirical evidence from social psychology indicates that it is not the objective environment, but rather the subjective perception of this environment that serves as a significant moderator of individual behavior (Armitage & Conner, 2001). Exceptions in the entrepreneurial culture literature include GEM-based studies (Amorós & Bosma, 2014) that measure the importance of individual perceptions of the social environment for entrepreneurship. Importantly, however, this type of data from the GEM is only available at the national level. Building on this approach, this research examines individual perceptions of the local cultural environment.

Since measures of people's perceptions are highly subjective, an important focus of this research is to explore the predictive validity of a local entrepreneurial culture scale. This is accomplished by correlating a (subjective) measure with an objective measure of entrepreneurship (self-employment breadth, controlling for income and prior business experience) to determine if a significant relationship exists between the two. This is an important step in scale development (Clark & Watson, 1995) that strengthens the approach presented here.

Finally, the scale measure and overall approach to the research question at hand takes into account a key geographical variable, namely whether a locality is rural or urban. In states like Kentucky (the focus of this study), discriminating between rural and urban areas is critical. While high levels of innovative entrepreneurship often occur close to major cities (Acs & Armington, 2006) and research universities (Audretsch, Lehmann, & Warning, 2005), rural entrepreneurship presents a different set of entrepreneurial motivations, mix of industries, startup needs, opportunities, risks, and small business culture (Fortunato, 2014; Henderson, 2002; Stathopoulou, Psaltopoulos, & Skuras, 2004). One might expect that the relevant characteristics of a local entrepreneurial culture would vary across these types of counties. Thus, the scale's structure and predictive validity was examined separately for rural and urban areas.

A conceptual model: Linking entrepreneurial culture to entrepreneurial action

How do perceptions of the local entrepreneurial culture relate to entrepreneurial behavior? This research borrows from social psychology – combining research on planned behavior (Ajzen, 1991; Ajzen & Fishbein, 1980; Fishbein & Ajzen, 1975) and research on environmental perception (Kautonen, van Gelderen, & Tornikoski, 2013; Sheppard, Hartwick, & Warshaw, 1988). Such theories propose that behavior is influenced not only by personal characteristics, but also by the individual's perception of cultural norms relevant to the behavior, which in turn are influenced by personal experience in this objective environment.

With respect to entrepreneurship, these theories suggest that individual perceptions about the local entrepreneurial culture, modulated by personal experience, influence individual's propensity to act entrepreneurially. Since each locality has a different culture, and a different mix of citizens with entrepreneurial experience or proclivity, these factors aggregate to the local and regional levels to partially explain differences in entrepreneurship rates. As discussed in the previous section, all of this is bounded by

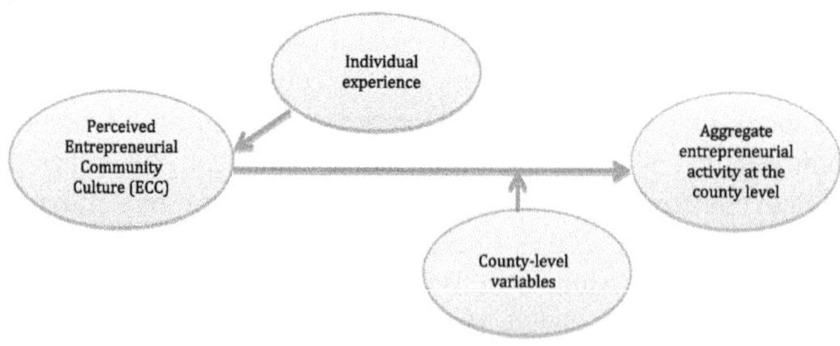

Figure 1. Conceptual model: Relationship between perceived ECC and aggregate entrepreneurial activity at the county level.

the broader context – in this case, whether the county is rural or urban. Figure 1 depicts this relationship.

Before this model can be tested, valid measures of perceptions of local entrepreneurial culture must be developed. That said, this model is used to guide scale development and statistical analyses in this article.

Study goals

This article has two primary goals:

(1) To construct a scale that measures the Entrepreneurial Community Culture (ECC) of a place, based on resident perceptions.
(2) To examine the predictive validity of the scale within the conceptual model described above.

Methods

Scale development

Qualitative data collection and construction of the initial pool of items

To construct a quantitative measure of local entrepreneurial culture, data collection began by conducting semi-structured interviews with entrepreneurs and non-entrepreneurs around Kentucky.[1] Three-hour interviews were conducted with 23 individuals with diverse individual entrepreneurial experiences from counties with diverse levels of entrepreneurial activity. Half of the targeted counties had experienced a significant increase in entrepreneurship over the last decade, while the other half had not. Eight of the 23 respondents had entrepreneurial intentions back in 2005, and all eight followed through with their business idea to some extent. Most of the 23 interview participants had some personal experience with self-employment (for many this was farming). A few of the individuals became high-profile entrepreneurs, while a couple had limited success or their business failed. The sample included one-third women, two-thirds men. All but two considered themselves "insiders" to their community (i.e. either grew up in the county or had been there for 20 years or more). All but two of the entrepreneurs interviewed had opened their businesses in rural parts of Kentucky, which was intentional since it was hypothesized that the perceived entrepreneurial culture was likely to be particularly consequential in rural areas.

The section of the interview that discussed perceptions of the local entrepreneurial culture began with the following prompt: "Just going with your gut instinct, would you say this community generally values entrepreneurship and local people who start their own businesses? Why or why not?" Additional prompts included questions such as:

> For the sake of discussion, can you tell me about one or two well-known entrepreneurs in your community (someone who starts innovative businesses)? What do they do? What do others think of this person? Has the entrepreneur ever failed at a new business activity? How did the community respond? and Do elected officials celebrate entrepreneurship through public awards that recognize the successes and contributions of local innovators?

These prompts were identified based on an extensive literature review and in consultation with entrepreneurial support groups.

Comparing the answers to these and other questions between rural and urban counties revealed the main sources of similarity and difference in respondents' perceptions of their community culture, as well as pinpointed some components of the local culture that seemed particularly important to their overall assessment of the entrepreneurial culture in their county. From this analysis, a multi-dimensional scale was constructed to measure the local entrepreneurial culture.

A focus group was then conducted with eight members of the Kentucky Entrepreneurial Coaches Institute. The group reviewed the pool of questions and helped finalize the wording and selection of 36 initial items that were included in the survey. The items were framed in the form of positive or negative statements that describe the respondent's county. For instance, "My county appreciates unique perspectives." Respondents were asked to rate how strongly they agreed or disagreed with these 36 statements. The final version of the 36 items can be found in the Appendix 1.

Survey data collection

The next component of the scale development process involved conducting an extensive mail survey that included the 36 initial items. The goal was to survey half entrepreneurs and half non-entrepreneurs in a wide variety of rural and urban Kentucky counties. Addresses were purchased from USADATA, which allowed the research team to target households based on the occupation of the household head and the county of residence.

The sample area consisted of 79 of Kentucky's 120 counties – 56 rural farming counties, 12 rural mining counties, and 11 urban counties, stratified in order to obtain data from a representative number of residents living in Kentucky's rural and urban economies. The US Department of Agriculture's Rural-Urban Continuum Codes were used to classify counties in Kentucky as rural or urban, and the share of county employment in agriculture and mining were used to further classify the rural counties. For each occupation category of interest (self-employed, farming, neither self-employed nor farming), USADATA generated a random address list for the sample area; entries per county were proportional to the number of available addresses for each occupation category. In total, surveys were mailed to 12,000 households, of which 5693 had a household head who was self-employed, 2000 had a household head in farming, and 4307 had a household head who was neither self-employed nor a farmer.

The Western Kentucky University Social Science Research Center (WKU SSRC) was contracted to distribute the surveys and input/clean the data. Use of a mail survey was intentional, as some have found that mail surveys yield a higher response rate relative to other survey methods (Dillman et al., 2009). This is especially true in rural areas where Internet access and phone coverage is limited. To improve the response rate (Yammarino, Skinner, & Childers, 1991), all mailings included a pre-paid business reply envelope; reminder postcards were sent to all addresses one month after the initial mailing; a second full mailing was sent three weeks after the postcard to the 11,065 households who had not yet responded to the first mailing; respondents who completed and returned the survey received a $10 check; and the study got permission to waive documentation of informed consent to reduce burdensome paperwork. The eight-page survey asked questions (229 in total) about the respondents' entrepreneurial background, their perceptions of their county and its culture, their perceptions of their own skills and abilities, their farming experience (if applicable), and their household demographic characteristics.

Completed surveys were returned by 1481 residents, which yielded a response rate of 12.3% (similar to Pushkarskaya, 2006). This response rate can be considered a major shortcoming of the research. The research team addressed non-response error post hoc by comparing the sample with population sociodemographic characteristics. In comparison to the 2012 American Community Survey for Kentucky, the sample was older, more educated, wealthier, and included fewer minorities than the state as a whole. Specifically, the median age of survey respondents was 56 compared to the median age of Kentuckians at 38, which is explained by the fact that the study does not include individuals under the age 18. Of the respondents, 16.7% had obtained a graduate degree compared to 8.5% of the Kentucky population, and the sample also included more wealthy households and fewer low-income families than the state as a whole. Additionally, 95% of respondents were white compared to 88.1% of Kentuckians. Based on this comparison, one would not expect any major non-response distortions other than age and socioeconomic status. However, readers are asked to keep this limitation in mind when interpreting the findings from the study.

The final sample did capture the diversity of occupational experiences and county types that were intended. In the sample, 45% had started a business at some point in their lives, and 20% of respondents were currently self-employed. A little over one-fourth of the surveys came from individuals living in Louisville or Lexington – major population centers in Kentucky – but no other county had more than 5% of the total respondents. Rural areas were oversampled, producing 100 completed questionnaires from rural mining counties, 574 questionnaires from rural faming counties, and 756 questionnaires from urban counties. Since few surveys were received from individuals in mining counties, these respondents were excluded from further analysis.

Refining and validating the measure (statistical analyses of survey data)[2]

Factor analysis procedure

Exploratory factor analysis was used to identify the interrelated subcomponents of local entrepreneurial culture, as perceived by survey respondents. All 36 items were included in the analysis. Rural and urban subsamples were analyzed separately. A confirmatory maximum likelihood factor analysis with oblimax rotation and Keiser normalization was then performed on the refined scale, again treating rural and urban subsamples independently. The results of these two statistical tests are presented below.

Analysis of covariance procedure

To examine the predictive validity of the local entrepreneurial culture scale, survey data were correlated with an entirely independent data set that estimated county-level rates of entrepreneurship. The proxy for aggregate rates of "entrepreneurship" was a county-level measure of total non-farm proprietorship/total non-farm employment, which was constructed using the most recent Bureau of Economic Analysis data. Later, a more in-depth measure was incorporated based on 2011 microbusiness statistics, which broke down the number of businesses by those without employees, those with one to four employees, and those with more than four employees. This data set was compiled by the Association for Enterprise Opportunity using publicly available data from the US Census Bureau's County Business Patterns.

A series of analysis of covariance (ANCOVA) models were employed, incorporating additional variables as specified in the conceptual model presented above (Figure 1).

Personal income was included, because earnings can be an important predictor of entrepreneurial outcomes and perceptions. In particular, *opportunity* entrepreneurship tends to be focused among higher income individuals who employ business strategy to uncover profitable opportunities. By contrast, *necessity* entrepreneurship tends to be focused among lower income individuals who use whatever skills they possess to survive month-to-month (Acs, 2006). Additionally, a history of self-employment indicates prior experiential knowledge about entrepreneurship, which can have an important effect on the perception of opportunities (Shane, 2000). Taken together, personal income and history of self-employment thus serve as proxies for individual experience in the local community. Rural/urban classifications were used as a proxy for county economic and geographic characteristics. The focus of the G2 statistic is the external validity of the ECC scale; thus, the list of the remaining variables was not meant to be complete.

ANCOVAs were conducted separately on rural and urban subsamples, with aggregate entrepreneurial activity serving as the dependent variable. Covariates included components of the ECC (derived via factor analysis, as described above) and two groups of interaction variables to account for the modulating effects of individual experience. One group included interaction between ECC subscales and INCOME (ECC × INCOME); INCOME was defined as equal to "1" if the respondent was from a household with an income level less than $40,000 a year, and "0" otherwise ($40,000 was selected as it is the approximate median household income across most communities in the sample). Another group included interaction between ECC subscales and BUSINESS (ECC × BUSINESS); BUSINESS was defined as equal to "1" if the respondent had started his or her own business at some point prior to the survey, and "0" otherwise. The conceptual model predicts that the effects of ECC, ECC × INCOME, and ECC × BUSINESS variables on county aggregate entrepreneurial activity will be significant and will differ between urban and rural counties.

Findings

Exploratory factor analysis

Factor analysis was used to identify the subcomponents of local entrepreneurial culture, and rural and urban subsamples were analyzed separately. For the urban subsample, the factor analysis produced acceptable Cronbach's alpha internal reliability statistics between .70 and .88 for each factor and individual factor loadings above .40 (or below −.40). The overall model had a Chi-Square of 427.104 (df = 149) and was statistically significant ($p < .001$). For the rural subsample, the factor analysis produced acceptable Cronbach's alpha statistics between .66 and .86 for each factor and individual factor loadings above .44 (or below −.44). The overall model had a Chi-Square of 151.507 (df = 101) and was statistically significant ($p < .01$). The urban and rural factor loadings can be seen in Tables 1 and 2, respectively.

For both subsamples, four factors had eigenvalues higher than 1.00, accounting for 54.4 and 56.4% of the variance in the urban and rural subsamples, respectively. Note that the items in three of the factors largely overlap between rural and urban subsamples. These three factors were given the following names: DCC, BPC, and BDC. However, items from the fourth factor were very different for rural and urban subsamples. Even though items from this factor in both subsamples seem to be related to some notion of valuing local, the specific items did not overlap. This result is consistent with the idea that culture impacts entrepreneurship differently in urban and rural settings.

Table 1. Factor analysis – Rotated factor matrix for ECC items, urban subsample, $n = 764$.

Item #	Entrepreneurial Community Culture (ECC) items	Diversity and Change	Focus on Local	Business Promotion	Business Discouragements
21	My county is fairly innovative	**.766**	.042	.048	−.019
22	My county is relatively forward-looking	**.762**	−.085	.108	.027
20	My county has a lot of citizens who are working hard to develop the region	**.672**	−.062	.000	−.023
27	My county appreciates unique perspectives	**.661**	−.054	.007	.041
24	My county has change-makers who are highly respected	**.624**	−.073	−.104	−.005
26	My county is open to supporting outsiders	**.585**	.079	−.055	.029
25	Local government tries to reach out to a diverse group of individuals	**.562**	−.076	−.002	.026
28	My county supports musicians, artists, and craftspeople	**.527**	.042	−.077	.049
19	There are very active civic groups in my county	**.470**	.005	−.108	−.039
16	The county and city work together to promote a common strategy for economic development and job creation	**.442**	−.127	−.172	.014
34	My county is becoming more supportive of small, locally owned business	.096	**−.808**	−.081	−.003
36	Overall, my county is quite friendly to entrepreneurs and small businesses	.317	**−.500**	−.060	.129
35	Things are now looking up for small, local businesses in my county	.190	**−.443**	−.079	.130
29	Local elected officials work closely with the Chamber of Commerce	−.055	.000	**−.853**	−.012
30	The local Chamber of Commerce is a strong and powerful force in my county	.092	.032	**−.639**	−.016
31	The local Chamber of Commerce works hard to support, promote, and encourage local businesses and entrepreneurs	.090	−.109	**−.560**	.131
8	Established businesses in my county actively discourage new business start-ups	−.037	−.029	−.006	**.518**
14	My county has a powerful elite that blocks change	.246	.040	.032	**.482**
18	People in my county chose self-employment only when there is no other option	−.003	.088	.006	**.478**
33	Small, local businesses don't appear to have much of a place in my county	.019	−.273	−.105	**.464**

(Continued)

Table 1. (*Continued*).

Item #	Entrepreneurial Community Culture (ECC) items	Diversity and Change	Focus on Local	Business Promotion	Business Discouragements
12	Local government is focused on supporting large industries more than supporting local start-ups	−.052	−.215	−.013	**.445**
7	People in my county have little faith in one another	.061	−.059	−.088	**.405**
	Variance	6.74	4.20	4.62	3.63
	Cronbach's alpha	.88	.83	.77	.70
	Goodness of fit statistics				
	Chi-square (149)	427.104			
	p-value	.00001			

Since a goal of the research was to develop a scale that could be used in both rural and urban areas, all items that loaded in both subsamples for the first three factors were retained. This left six items in the DCC factor, three items in the BPC factor, and four items in the BDC factor. Because the fourth factor did not have any common items between rural and urban subsamples, both groups of questions were kept for the next set of analyses and were named "Focus on Local in an Urban Setting" (FLC-Urban, four items) and "Focus on Local in a Rural Setting" (FLC-Rural, four items). These specific items can be found in Tables 1 and 2, respectively.

Confirmatory factor analysis

A confirmatory maximum likelihood factor analysis with oblimax rotation and Keiser normalization was performed on the refined pool of items, treating rural and urban subsamples independently. For both subsamples, four factors had eigenvalues higher than 1.00, accounting for more than 54% of the variance in each subsample. Items in three factors: "DCC" (alpha = .84 for urban subsample, alpha = .86 for rural subsample), "BPC" (alpha = .77 for urban subsample, alpha = .76 for rural subsample), and "BDC" (alpha = .70 for urban subsample, alpha = .75 for rural subsample) had robust loadings greater than .40 for both subsamples. This suggests that these three subscales capture perceived cultural characteristics of the locality that are similar in rural and urban settings.

The items from FLC-Urban did not have strong loadings for the rural subsample, and items from FLC-Rural did not have strong loadings in the urban subsample, as expected. This result confirms the notion that some components of an entrepreneurial culture differ significantly between rural and urban communities. The alpha statistics on FLC-Urban were sufficiently high (alpha = .83 for urban subsample, alpha = .83 for rural subsample), while the alpha statistics on FLC-Rural were relatively low (alpha = .53 for urban subsample, alpha = .67 for rural subsample). Keeping both subscales in the analysis, it should be noted that due to low reliability, results associated with FLC-Rural should be treated with caution. Results from this simple comparison can be seen in Table 3.

All five scales moderately correlated with each other in Table 3, suggesting that they reflect different features of the same construct: a local entrepreneurial culture. Ratings

Table 2. Factor analysis – Rotated factor matrix for ECC items, rural subsample, $n = 580$.

Item #	Entrepreneurial Community Culture (ECC) items	Diversity and Change (DCC)	Business Discouragements (BDC)	Focus on Local (FLC)	Business Promotion (BPC)
22	My county is relatively forward-looking	**.867**	.013	−.018	.014
20	My county has a lot of citizens who are working hard to develop the region	**.743**	−.178	.069	−.131
24	My county has change-makers who are highly respected	**.643**	.061	−.029	−.169
21	My county is fairly innovative	**.596**	.097	.086	−.026
26	My county is open to supporting outsiders	**.562**	.088	−.006	−.033
16	The county and city work together to promote a common strategy for economic development and job creation	**.497**	.099	.031	−.145
14	My county has a powerful elite that blocks change	.252	**.616**	−.012	.075
18	People in my county chose self-employment only when there is no other option	−.078	**.556**	−.062	−.071
33	Small, local businesses don't appear to have much of a place in my county	.123	**.530**	.171	−.079
8	Established businesses in my county actively discourage new business start-ups	.184	**.472**	.089	.073
12	Local government is focused on supporting large industries more than supporting local start-ups	−.100	**.464**	−.014	−.121
7	People in my county have little faith in one another	.204	**.460**	.129	−.018
1	Most people in my county think that local, small business is valuable	−.097	.122	**.806**	.077
5	Local entrepreneurs are generally respected county members	−.012	.026	**.539**	−.055
9	Owning one's own business is a desirable goal among most people in this county	.026	−.157	**.453**	−.108
2	Most people in my county try to buy from local businesses when they can	.230	.031	**.440**	.012
29	Local elected officials work closely with the Chamber of Commerce	.035	.064	.099	**−.663**
30	The local Chamber of Commerce is a strong and powerful force in my county	.138	−.003	−.004	**−.595**

(Continued)

Table 2. (*Continued*).

Item #	Entrepreneurial Community Culture (ECC) items	Diversity and Change (DCC)	Business Discouragements (BDC)	Focus on Local (FLC)	Business Promotion (BPC)
31	The local Chamber of Commerce works hard to support, promote, and encourage local businesses and entrepreneurs	.132	.199	.040	**−.573**
	Variance	4.96	3.08	2.81	3.36
	Cronbach's alpha	.86	.75	.66	.71
	Goodness of fit statistics				
	Chi-square (101)	151.507			
	p-value	.001			

on all five scales were also significantly different between people with and without prior business experience, which is consistent with the conceptual model. To avoid multicollinearity, the relationship between perceived entrepreneurial culture and aggregate entrepreneurial activities at the county level were examined by including each of the five variables (unstandardized, since all of them are ratings on the same 1–5 scale) in the ANCOVAs as a covariate one at a time in stepwise fashion.

Analysis of covariance

Finally, the predictive validity of the ECC scale was examined within the conceptual model presented earlier (Figure 1). To that end, analyses examined whether or not subjective perceptions of the local entrepreneurial culture are related to objective entrepreneurial activity in the region, keeping in mind the hypothesized modulating effects of individual experience, and the county's economic and geographical characteristics. Results of the ANCOVA analyses validate the multi-dimensional ECC scale and are consistent with predictions of the conceptual model.

Most importantly, the "DCC" subscale emerged as the strongest and the most consistent cultural predictor of entrepreneurial activity in both rural and urban counties (see Table 4), which is consistent with prior literature (Amorós & Bosma, 2014; Hustedde, 2007). The "BPC" subscale is also significant as well, but it is not as strong a predictor. The complete results can be seen in Table 4.

Table 4 illustrates a number of main and interactive effects of the scale factors on local entrepreneurial activity. Beginning with "DCC", this scale differs interactively with business size. Overall, correlation of perceptions of DCC with aggregate entrepreneurial activity was negative and significant for all individuals surveyed ($\beta = -.72$ for urban, $\beta = -1.05$ for rural, both $p < .01$), with no significant effects across entrepreneurs and non-entrepreneurs. This is an interesting finding, as it indicates that higher entrepreneurship rates were observed in counties where residents were more *pessimistic* about the local culture's openness to diversity and change.

However, further analyses revealed that this effect is modulated by business size. The overall negative correlation was driven by a correlation with local levels of self-employment (i.e. businesses that have no employees). Thus, in counties where people tend to be more pessimistic about their local culture and the extent to which

Table 3. Cronbach's alpha reliability scores and Pearson correlations of ECC subscales.

		Cronbach's alpha urban subsample ($n = 764$)	Cronbach's alpha rural subsample ($n = 580$)	Correlation ($p < .001$ for all values)	DCC	FLC-Rural	FLC-Urban	BPC	BDC
DCC	(6 items)	.84	.86		–				
FLC-Rural	(4 items)	.53[a]	.67		.423	–			
FLC-Urban	(3 items)	.83	.83		.676	.478	–		
BPC	(3 items)	.77	.76		.576	.379	.598	–	
BDC	(6 items)	.70	.75		−.501	−.324	−.574	−.434	–

	DCC (6 items)	FLC-Rural (4 items)	FLC-Urban (3 items)	BPC (3 items)	BDC (6 items)
Urban subsample ($n = 764$)	.84	.53[a]	.83	.77	.70
Rural subsample ($n = 580$)	.86	.67	.83	.76	.75

[a]Indicate that the reliability score is very low.

Table 4. Correlation of measures of the ECC and aggregate entrepreneurial activities at the community level.

A. Overall non-farm proprietorship

	Non-farm businesses, % of all businesses			
	Urban		Rural	
Sample average	14.99		24.56	
	β	*F(3712)*	β	*F(3539)*
Diversity and change				
DCC	**−.72*****	*12.05*	**−1.05*****	*10.13*
DCC × Business	.02	*.1*	−.09	*.35*
DCC × Income	.06	*.41*	**.27***	*3.06*
Focus on local (rural)				
FLCr			−.11	*.08*
FLCr × Business			−.03	*.04*
FLCr × Income			**.26****	*3.73*
Focus on local (urban)				
FLCu	−.25	*1.68*		
FLCu × Business	.02	*.04*		
FLCu × Income	.08	*.91*		
Business promotion				
BPC	**−.64*****	*10.01*	**−.93*****	*7.79*
BPC × Business	.04	*.28*	−.09	*.36*
BPC × Income	.06	*.44*	.23	*2.46*
Business discouragements				
BDC	−.11	*.19*	.05	*.02*
BDC × Business	.04	*.17*	.06	*.12*
BDC × Income	.05	*.2*	**.31***	*3.25*

B. Non-farm proprietorship by business size

	Businesses with no employees, % of all non-farm businesses				Businesses with 1–4 employees, % of all non-farm businesses				Businesses with more than 4 employees, % of all non-farm businesses			
	Urban		Rural		Urban		Rural		Urban		Rural	
Sample average	72.58		80.42		13.24		10.7		14.19		8.88	
	β	*F(3712)*	β	*F(3539)*	β	*F(3712)*	β	*F(3539)*	β	*F(3712)*	β	*F(3539)*
Diversity and change												
DCC	−**.26***	*2.7*	−**.92*****	*13.39*	**.14*****	*6.21*	**.36*****	*8.11*	.12	*1.27*	**.54*****	*15.53*
DCC × Business	.03	*.32*	−.04	*.14*	−.01	*.32*	.03	*.23*	−.02	*.29*	.02	*.06*
DCC × Income	.04	*.34*	**.42*****	*12.87*	−.01	*.11*	−**.20*****	*11.32*	−.03	*.46*	−**.22*****	*11.16*
Focus on local (rural)												
FLCr			−.05	*.03*			0	*0*			.05	*.09*
FLCr × Business			0	*0*			.01	*.01*			−.01	*.03*
FLCr × Income			**.41*****	*16.35*			−**.19*****	*14.22*			−**.21*****	*14.34*
Focus on local (urban)												
FLCu	−.09	*.38*			.04	*.7*			.05	*.22*		
FLCu × Business	.02	*.14*			−.01	*.26*			−.01	*.09*		
FLCu × Income	.04	*.44*			−.01	*.17*			−.03	*.57*		
Business promotion												
BPC	−.14	*.86*	−**.84*****	*11.54*	.06	*1.11*	**.35*****	*7.86*	.08	*.66*	**.49*****	*12.32*
BPC × Business	.04	*.37*	−.03	*.06*	−.02	*.51*	.03	*.21*	−.02	*.72*	0	*0*
BPC × Income	.03	*.16*	**.36*****	*10.79*	0	*.03*	−**.17*****	*9.61*	−.02	*.25*	−**.19*****	*9.24*
Business discouragements												
BDC	−.19	*.96*	.27	*.85*	.05	*.6*	−.2	*1.88*	.14	*1.07*	−.07	*.16*
BDC × Business	0	*0*	.05	*.14*	0	*.02*	−.01	*.01*	0	*0*	−.04	*.34*
BDC × Income	0	*0*	**.45*****	*12.28*	.01	*.03*	−**.21*****	*10.55*	−.01	*.02*	−**.24*****	*10.89*

*Significance at $p \leq .10$ level.
**Significance at $p \leq .05$ level.
***Significance at $p \leq .01$ level.

diversity and change is welcomed, there is a higher proportion of self-employed individuals, and this holds in both urban ($\beta = -.26$, $p < .10$) and rural ($\beta = -.92$, $p < .01$) settings. For counties with a greater share of larger businesses (i.e. those that hire at least one employee), the opposite was true. Perception of openness to diversity and change was positively and significantly correlated with rates of businesses with between one and four employees ($\beta = .14$ urban, $\beta = .36$ rural, both $p < .01$) and over four employees (non-significant for urban, $\beta = .54$ rural, $p < .01$).

Regardless of the direction of the correlation, the effect of DCC was always stronger in rural areas. Interestingly, a significant interactive effect of income on the DCC factor also exists only in rural areas. However, this effect was not linear, but attenuating. Finally, it is worth noting that the correlation between DCC and aggregate entrepreneurial activity was always weaker for respondents earning less than $40,000 a year.

The binary "FLC" factor, calculated separately for rural and urban areas, was found to have only moderate effects in rural areas, where it was only significant for low earners ($\beta = .26$, $p < .05$). Further analyses revealed that perceptions of FLC were more optimistic among low-earners in counties with higher proportions of self-employment (no employees, $\beta = .41$, $p < .01$), but less optimistic in counties with higher proportions of larger businesses ($\beta = -.19$ for 1–4 employees, and $\beta = -.21$ for more than four employees, both $p < .01$). In contrast, while FLC-Urban factors loaded significantly in the factor analysis (indicating that survey items act together to explain one underlying concept), this factor did not have any significant results on urban entrepreneurship rates – neither for main or interactive effects.

Perceptions of "BPC" were found to be strongly and significantly correlated with aggregate entrepreneurial levels in rural areas, but much less so in urban areas. In urban areas, perception of BPC correlated negatively with entrepreneurship rates ($\beta = -.64$, $p < .01$), although this effect disappeared when examining different business size categories independently or when controlling for the effects of business experience and income. In rural areas, perception of BPC correlated more strongly with aggregate entrepreneurial activity. Similarly to the effect of DCC, the correlation was also negative ($\beta = -.93$, $p < .01$). Examining across business size categories, one sees the same picture emerge that was explained for DCC. Perception of BPC was more pessimistic in counties with higher proportions of self-employment ($\beta = -.84$, $p < .01$), but more optimistic in counties with higher rates of businesses with 1–4 employees ($\beta = .35$, $p < .01$) and more than four employees ($\beta = .49$, $p < .01$). When controlling for participant income, an interactive effect also emerges, with the direction of the relationship reversing and weakening for individuals earning less than $40,000. Above this income threshold, perception of BPC was more optimistic in counties with higher proportions of self-employment ($\beta = .36$, $p < .01$), but more pessimistic in counties with higher rates of businesses with 1–4 employees ($\beta = -.17$, $p < .01$) and more than four employees ($\beta = -.19$, $p < .01$).

Finally, perceptions of "BDC" only produced significant correlations in rural areas among low-earners. Since "discouragements" are a negative/pessimistic sentiment, a positive correlation implies higher levels of pessimism. Participants earning less than $40,000 were slightly more likely to view their local culture as discouraging business development ($\beta = .31$, $p < .10$) in counties with higher levels of entrepreneurial activity. Again, when business activity is broken down by size, a more complex picture emerges. This effect was driven by a correlation with rates of self-employment ($\beta = .45$, $p < .01$). In keeping with previous results, the relationship was negative when FCC was correlated with rates of business activity by larger establishments (for businesses with 1–4 employees $\beta = -.21$, $p < .01$, for businesses with more than four employees $\beta = -.24$, $p < .01$). When controlling for participant income, an interactive effect also emerges, as these correlations weaken for individuals earning less than $40,000. No significant effects of BDC were found in urban areas.

Discussion and implications for further research and action

This article describes the development of a multi-dimensional scale that measures the perceived entrepreneurial culture of a specific locality. Factor analysis of the survey data lead to a 17-item scale with four distinct dimensions of local entrepreneurial culture: DCC, BPC, BDC, and a FLC. The predictive validity of the scale was evaluated by correlating the survey results (perceptions of local entrepreneurial culture) with county-level rates of self-employment, controlling for important individual-level factors and whether the county is rural or urban. It was found that the measure does predict entrepreneurial activity, and would therefore be useful as a tool for evaluating entrepreneurial culture in other contexts.

Arguably, the most notable finding in the research is the fact that the correlation between perceived entrepreneurial culture and actual entrepreneurship rates was much stronger in rural than in urban areas. In fact, the BPC, BDC, and FLC-rural factors were nearly exclusively correlated with entrepreneurship rates in rural areas. It is possible that this finding could potentially reflect a bias in the initial data-gathering stage (the original pool of questions was derived primarily from interviews with rural residents). However, it is more likely to indicate that perceptions of the local entrepreneurial culture are particularly consequential in rural areas, since factor analysis revealed three out of four components being identical in urban and rural settings. This is in line with a longstanding body of literature. Rural communities are often characterized by stronger community social ties (Wilkinson, 1991), so individual behavior may be more influenced by perceived cultural norms and attributes in this context. This is an idea dating back to the Gemeinschaft community framework proposed by Tönnies (1955) or the mechanical solidarity of Durkheim (1897/1951), where rural areas serve as repositories of a more traditional culture (even in business) that is grounded more strongly in interpersonal relationships and reputations, rather than in functional, role-based transactions. Naturally, both reputational and transactional frames of action exist in both the city and country, although the small population size and relatively close-knit nature of many rural communities allows local cultural norms to transcend more impersonal and decentralized ways of doing business. By contrast, urban individuals may take a more traditional view of the entrepreneur as a highly transactional *homo œconomicus*, combining resources creatively to take advantage of an economic opportunity à la Kirzner (1978).

Also of particular importance is the fact that the DCC subscale was the strongest predictor of entrepreneurial activity. This finding is also consistent with much of the entrepreneurial culture scholarship, which consistently points to this particular aspect of an entrepreneurial environment (Frazier et al., 2013; Hustedde, 2007). These findings are similar to those presented in Fortunato and McLaughlin (2012), who found a history of primary industry turnover and a predominance of entrepreneurs open to diversity in high entrepreneurship rural communities. If researchers can only include a few items in their questionnaires, the six questions included in this subscale would be a good choice. Given that the items that loaded on the fourth subscale (FLC) were different across rural and urban areas, researchers would need to select the appropriate subset of questions based on their research site.

Another finding worth mentioning is that the ANCOVAs confirmed modulating effect of income suggested by the conceptual model. The effect was not linear, but attenuating; correlations (both negative and positive) were stronger for individuals with higher incomes than for individuals with lower incomes. One explanation might be that individuals of high socioeconomic status are more involved in professional organizations, clubs, and informal social circles that give them privileged access to what is happening behind the scenes in their community, thus giving these individuals a different perspective on local entrepreneurial opportunities. Indeed there was some evidence for this contention in the qualitative interviews that were conducted, but this matter is clearly one that requires further research.

Finally, it is fascinating that the correlation between perceptions of entrepreneurial culture (how "friendly" or "open" the local culture was) and rates of entrepreneurial activity was *negative*. In other words, in counties where people tend to be more *pessimistic* about the local culture, there are *higher* rates of self-employment. That said, for counties with a greater share of *larger* businesses (i.e. those who hire employees rather than merely providing income for a sole proprietor), the opposite is true. One possible explanation for this finding may be the dissatisfaction hypothesis put forth by Hofstede et al. (2004) which found that overall life satisfaction was negatively correlated with the likelihood that one would become self-employed. In other words, in places where lots of people were generally dissatisfied with life, there were higher rates of self-employment. Perhaps, one sees a similar trend in localities where people are generally more pessimistic about the local culture. This too is clearly an area that requires further research.

The scale (along with the results from the ANCOVA) can be used to inform community development practice. In particular, the measure is recommended for use by entrepreneurship support programs that provide one-on-one assistance for small businesses, yet seldom assess or consider how they might improve the entrepreneurial culture of the place where their businesses operate. This is especially true for those programs operating in rural areas. For example, the US Small Business Administration's Small Business Development Centers (SBDCs) provide aspiring and current business owners with free consulting and low-cost training services around the country (there are 14 locations in Kentucky alone), but they do little to address the entrepreneurial culture of the places they serve. It may be that these centers and other similar organizations are not aware that local culture plays a role in business development. Or perhaps they believe that the local culture is a contextual variable that is out of their control. The work of the Kentucky Entrepreneurial Coaches Institute (Scorsone & Powers, 2005) provides an example of how an entrepreneurial support program can work towards improving the local culture. The issue can be studied and discussed with local business owners, and they can be trained in how to engage local policy-makers on the topic. Working towards a culture that embraces diversity and change is a goal that the research certainly supports.

Practitioners may also learn from this research that a negative cultural environment appears to be a significant barrier to business expansion and growth (i.e. hiring employees, etc.). Thus, programs that work with small businesses poised for growth (e.g. Economic Gardening) need to be particularly vigilant about assessing and trying to improve the local entrepreneurial culture. These programs may want to partner with Business Retention and Expansion programs, which do currently get community leaders involved in discussing the local entrepreneurial climate. Another option might be to support programs such as Junior Achievement, which promote youth education in entrepreneurship and may eventually contribute to an improved entrepreneurial culture.

Besides contributing to better entrepreneurial culture assessment in community development practice, this scale measure contributes to future entrepreneurship research. Existing measures of entrepreneurial culture focus mostly on the regional and national levels, overlooking the role of local cultural characteristics; they also tend to focus on general cultural attributes rather than on residents' perceptions of the entrepreneurial climate. This measure provides a validated scale that assesses the local entrepreneurial climate, which can be included in future questionnaires and used to test more culturally focused theories of entrepreneurship that are emerging in the literature (Julien, 2007). In future studies, the research team will continue this line of research, using the scale to test the conceptual model presented earlier. Further research is also needed to test the measure for reliability and adapt/refine/validate it for specialized contexts, such as mega-cities, cultural enclaves (e.g. Chinatowns and new immigrant neighborhoods), and other cultural regions – both international and domestic.

Acknowledgments

The authors also extend sincere thanks to key members of the research team who were essential to the completion of this study, most especially Principal Investigator Alison Davis of the Community and Economic Development Initiative of Kentucky (CEDIK) and Co-Principal Investigator Ellen Usher at the University of Kentucky. Critical graduate student support was provided by Cami Bush at Western Kentucky University (WKU) and Shaheer Burney of CEDIK. WKU undergraduates Spencer Walters and Stephen Gibbons also contributed to this project.

Disclosure statement

No potential conflict of interest was reported by the authors.

Funding

The authors are deeply indebted to the USDA National Institute of Food and Agriculture (NIFA) for funding the Kentucky Entrepreneurship Survey, and thus this research project [grant number 2011-68006-30807].

Notes

1. To identify participants for the qualitative interviews, the research team followed up with residents who had been surveyed in a 2005–2006 study of rural entrepreneurship in the context of the tobacco buyout (Pushkarskaya, 2006, survey of rural Kentucky residents, 2005–2006). Among other things, the survey asked whether people intended to start a new business or not. Overall, 702 surveys were completed and 335 of these respondents agreed to be re-contacted at a later date.
2. Statistical analyses were conducted using IBM SPSS Statistics 21 statistical package.

References

Acs, Z. (2006). How is entrepreneurship good for economic growth? *Innovations: Technology, Governance, Globalization, 1*, 97–107.

Acs, Z. J., & Armington, C. (2006). *Entrepreneurship, geography, and American economic growth*. Cambridge: Cambridge University Press.

Ajzen, I. (1991). The theory of planned behavior. *Organizational Behavior and Human Decision Processes, 50*, 179–211.

Ajzen, I., & Fishbein, M. (1980). *Understanding attitudes and predicting social behaviour*. Englewood Cliffs, NJ: Prentice-Hall.

Alvarez, S. A., & Barney, J. B. (2007). Discovery and creation: Alternative theories of entrepreneurial action. *Strategic Entrepreneurship Journal, 1*, 11–26.

Amorós, J. E., & Bosma, N. (2014). *Global entrepreneurship monitor 2013 global report*. Recovered on February 28, 2014, from http://www.gemconsortium.org/docs/download/3106

Armitage, C. J., & Conner, M. (2001). Efficacy of the theory of planned behaviour: A meta-analytic review. *British Journal of Social Psychology, 40*, 471–499.

Audretsch, D. B., Lehmann, E. E., & Warning, S. (2005). University spillovers and new firm location. *Research Policy, 34*, 1113–1122.

Besser, T. L., & Miller, N. J. (2013). Community matters: Successful entrepreneurship in remote rural US locations. *The International Journal of Entrepreneurship and Innovation, 14*, 15–27.

Beugelsdijk, S. (2007). Entrepreneurial culture, regional innovativeness and economic growth. *Journal of Evolutionary Economics, 17*, 187–210.

Chatman, D., Altman, I., & Johnson, T. (2008). Community entrepreneurial climate: An analysis of small business owners' perspectives in 12 small towns in Missouri, USA. *Journal of Rural and Community Development, 3*, 60–77.

Clark, L. A., & Watson, D. (1995). Constructing validity: Basic issues in objective scale development. *Psychological Assessment, 7*, 309–319.

Dana, L. P. (1995). Entrepreneurship in a remote sub-Arctic community. *Entrepreneurship Theory and Practice, 20*, 57–72.

Davidsson, P. (2009). *The entrepreneurship research challenge*. Cheltenham: Edward Elgar Publishing.

Dillman, D. A., Phelps, G., Tortora, R., Swift, K., Kohrell, J., Berck, J., & Messer, B. L. (2009). Response rate and measurement differences in mixed-mode surveys using mail, telephone, interactive voice response (IVR) and the Internet. *Social Science Research, 38*(1), 1–18.

Dimitratos, P., Voudouris, I., Plakoyiannaki, E., & Nakos, G. (2012). International entrepreneurial culture – Toward a comprehensive opportunity-based operationalization of international entrepreneurship. *International Business Review, 21*, 708–721.

Durkheim, E. (1897/1951). *Suicide: A study in sociology* (J. A. Spaulding & G. Simpson, Trans.). Glencoe, IL: Free Press.

Fishbein, M., & Ajzen, I. (1975). *Belief, attitude, intention and behavior: An introduction to theory and research*. Reading, MA: Addison-Wesley.

Fortunato, M. W., & McLaughlin, D. K. (2012). Interaction and purpose in highly entrepreneurial communities. *Entrepreneurship Research Journal, 2*(1), 1–34, Article 6.

Fortunato, M. W. P. (2014). Supporting rural entrepreneurship: A review of conceptual developments from research to practice. *Community Development, 45*, 387–408.

Frazier, B., Stoel, L., Niehm, L., & Eckerson, N. (2013). Optimism for new business survival in rural communities: An institutional perspective. *Journal of Small Business & Entrepreneurship, 26*, 443–462.

Fritsch, M., & Wyrwich, M. (2012). *The long persistence of regional entrepreneurship culture: Germany 1925–2005* (Discussion papers). Berlin: German Institute for Economic Research. Retrieved from http://www.econstor.eu/handle/10419/61329

Gartner, W. (1988). Who is an entrepreneur? Is the wrong question, American. *Journal of Small Business Spring, 12*, 11–31.

Gaventa, J. (1982). *Power and powerlessness: Quiescence and rebellion in an Appalachian valley*. Champaign: University of Illinois Press.

Goetz, S., & Freshwater, D. (2001). State-level determinants of entrepreneurship and a preliminary measure of entrepreneurial climate. *Economic Development Quarterly, 15*, 58–70.

Henderson, J. (2002). Building the rural economy with high-growth entrepreneurs. *Economic Review-Federal Reserve Bank of Kansas City, 87*, 45–75.

Hofstede, G., Noorderhaven, N. G., Thurik, A. R., Uhlaner, L. M., Wennekers, A. R., & Wildeman, R. E. (2004). Culture's role in entrepreneurship: Self-employment out of dissatisfaction. In T. E. Brown & J. Ulijn (Eds.), *Innovation, entrepreneurship and culture: The interaction between technology, progress and economic growth* (pp. 162–203). Northampton, MA: Edward Elgar Publisher. ISBN: 9781843763468.

Hopp, C., & Stephan, U. (2012). The influence of socio-cultural environments on the performance of nascent entrepreneurs: Community culture, motivation, self-efficacy and start-up success. *Entrepreneurship & Regional Development, 24*, 917–945.

Hustedde, R. (2007). What's culture got to do with it? Strategies for strengthening an entrepreneurial culture. In N. Walzer (Ed.), *Entrepreneurship and local economic development* (pp. 39–58). New York, NY: Rowman & Littlefield Publishers.

Julien, P.-A. (2007). *A theory of local entrepreneurship in the knowledge economy.* Cheltenham: Edward Elgar Publishing.

Kautonen, T., van Gelderen, M., & Tornikoski, E. T. (2013). Predicting entrepreneurial behaviour: A test of the theory of planned behaviour. *Applied Economics, 45*, 697–707.

Kibler, E. (2013). Formation of entrepreneurial intentions in a regional context. *Entrepreneurship & Regional Development, 25*, 293–323.

Kirzner, I. M. (1978). *Competition and entrepreneurship.* Chicago, IL: University of Chicago Press.

Klyver, K., & Thornton, P. H. (2010). *The cultural embeddedness of entrepreneurial self-efficacy and intentions: A cross-national comparison.* Paper presented at Fourth Global Entrepreneurship Monitor Research Conference, London, UK.

Kwon, S.-W., Heflin, C., & Ruef, M. (2013). Community social capital and entrepreneurship. *American Sociological Review, 78*, 980–1008.

Low, S., Henderson, J., & Weiler, S. (2005). Gauging a region's entrepreneurial potential. *Economic Review – Federal Reserve Bank of Kansas, 90*, 61–89.

Luloff, A. E., & Bridger, J. (2003). Community agency and local development. In D. Brown & L. Swanson (Eds.), *Challenges for rural America in the twenty-first century* (pp. 203–213). University Park, PA: Pennsylvania State University Press.

Pushkarskaya, H. N. (2006). Schemes to regulate non-point water pollution: Making sense of experimental results. *Available at SSRN 906138.* Retrieved from http://papers.ssrn.com/sol3/papers.cfm?abstract_id=906138.

Roxas, H. B., & Azmat, F. (2014). Community social capital and entrepreneurship: Analyzing the links. *Community Development, 45*, 134–149.

Rupasingha, A., & Goetz, S. J. (2013). Self-employment and local economic performance: Evidence from us counties. *Papers in Regional Science, 92*, 141–161.

Sarasvathy, S. D. (2009). *Effectuation: Elements of entrepreneurial expertise.* Cheltenham: Edward Elgar Publishing.

Schumpeter, J. A. (1934). *The theory of economic development: An inquiry into profits, capital, credit, interest, and the business cycle.* New York, NY: Transaction Publishers.

Scorsone, E. A., & Powers, K. (2005). Entrepreneurial facilitation: 'Approaches to boosting entrepreneurship in local economic development'. *Community Development Society, CD Practice Issue No. 10,* 1–19.

Shane, S. (2000). Prior knowledge and the discovery of entrepreneurial opportunities. *Organization Science, 11*, 448–469.

Shane, S. (2003). The environmental context of entrepreneurship. In S. Shane (Ed.), *A general theory of entrepreneurship* (pp. 145–160). Northampton, MA: Edward Elgar Publishing.

Shane, S., & Venkataraman, S. (2000). The promise of entrepreneurship as a field of research. *Academy of Management Review, 25*, 217–226.

Sheppard, B. H., Hartwick, J., & Warshaw, P. R. (1988). The theory of reasoned action: A meta-analysis of past research with recommendations for modifications and future research. *Journal of Consumer Research, 15*, 325–343.

Stathopoulou, S., Psaltopoulos, D., & Skuras, D. (2004). Rural entrepreneurship in Europe: A research framework and agenda. *International Journal of Entrepreneurial Behavior & Research, 10*, 404–425.

Tönnies, F. (1955). *Gemeinschaft und gesellschaft* [Community and association]. London: Routledge & Paul.

Venkataraman, S. (1997). The distinctive domain of entrepreneurship research. *Advances in Entrepreneurship, Firm Emergence and Growth, 3*, 119–138.

Wennberg, K., Pathak, S., & Autio, E. (2013). How culture moulds the effects of self-efficacy and fear of failure on entrepreneurship. *Entrepreneurship & Regional Development, 25*, 756–780.

Wilkinson, K. P. (1991). *The community in rural America.* Appleton, WI: Social Ecology Press.

Yammarino, F. J., Skinner, S. J., & Childers, T. L. (1991). Understanding mail survey response behavior: A meta-analysis. *Public Opinion Quarterly, 55*, 613–639.

Appendix 1. Questions on Entrepreneurial Culture from Kentucky Entrepreneurship Survey.

People have different views about their county and how supportive it is of small business and local entrepreneurship. Using the rating scale below, please tell us how strongly you agree or disagree with each of the following statements about the *county in which you currently live*:

1 Strongly disagree	2 Disagree	3 Neutral	4 Agree	5 Strongly agree	? Don't know

1. Most people in my county think that local, small business is valuable	2. Most people in my county try to buy from local businesses when they can
3. My county is fairly negative about its economic future	4. Overall, my county has a can-do attitude
5. Local entrepreneurs are generally respected county members	6. People in my county recognize that some change can be good
7. People in my county have little faith in one another	8. Established businesses in my county actively discourage new business start-ups
9. Owning one's own business is a desirable goal among most people in this county	10. People in my county generally do not kick each other when business is down
11. Local government does its best to support small, local business through financial assistance and encouragement	12. Local government is focused on supporting large industries more than supporting local start-ups
13. Bankers and investors go out of their way to help local businesses get started	14. My county has a powerful elite that blocks change
15. Small, locally-owned businesses are publicly celebrated with awards, ribbon cuttings, etc.	16. The county and city work together to promote a common strategy for economic development and job creation
17. Most of the leaders in this county are people who own their own businesses	18. People in my county choose self-employment only when there is no other option
19. There are very active civic groups in my county	20. My county has lot of citizens who are working hard to develop the region
21. My county is fairly innovative	22. My county is relatively forward-looking
23. The local media do a good job of covering local business news	24. My county has change-makers who are highly respected
25. Local government tries to reach out to a diverse group of individuals	26. My county is open to supporting outsiders
27. My county appreciates unique perspectives	28. My county supports musicians, artists, and craftspeople
29. Local elected officials work closely with the Chamber of Commerce	30. The local Chamber of Commerce is a strong and powerful force in my county

(*Continued*)

Appendix 1. (*Continued*).

1 Strongly disagree	2 Disagree	3 Neutral	4 Agree	5 Strongly agree	? Don't know

31. The local Chamber of Commerce works hard to support, promote, and encourage local businesses and entrepreneurs
32. My county does not work with surrounding counties to promote county and economic development
33. Small, local businesses don't appear to have much of a place in my county
34. My county is becoming more supportive of small, locally-owned business
35. Things are now looking up for small, local businesses in my county
36. Overall, my county is quite friendly to entrepreneurs and small businesses

Government and the entrepreneurial ecology: The case of Halifax, Nova Scotia

Bruce Dye[1] and Theodore R. Alter

Entrepreneurship promotion and support is an integral component of an economic development strategy. The state of a community's entrepreneurial ecology impacts the volume and success rates of new ventures. Building a better understanding of a community's entrepreneurial ecology will facilitate better policy and program interventions for the purpose of economic development. This research endeavors to build a better understanding of the entrepreneurial ecology of Halifax, Nova Scotia, Canada. In particular, the primary focus is the impact of government policy and practice on the entrepreneurial ecology. The research determines that according to key informants, municipal, provincial, and federal government supports for entrepreneurs in Halifax are helpful but may have an unduly bad reputation. Additionally, business registration and reporting processes have been successfully streamlined, government supports often involve removing risk from entrepreneurs with potential unintended consequences, and secondary government interactions may be undermining encouragement and support for entrepreneurship.

Introduction

An entrepreneurial ecology is the combination of socio-political-cultural influences on entrepreneurship within a community's local economy. Given the important role of entrepreneurial activity in the growth of local economies, understanding the entrepreneurial ecology of communities and how it supports or inhibits entrepreneurial action is central to fostering sustainable community economic development (Morris, 2001). The right, community-specific mix of these influences will positively impact the volume and success rate of entrepreneurial ventures (Griffiths, Gundry, Kickul, & Muñoz Fernandez, 2009). Therefore, it is important to better understand these influences, thus allowing more successful policy and program interventions. Without this understanding, policies and programs aimed at shaping the entrepreneurial ecology may be created and implemented indiscriminately and without recognition of their likely consequences (Dye, 2014). In addition, interventions directed toward non-economic issues may have unintended consequences with respect to entrepreneurial activity. A better understanding of the entrepreneurial ecology of communities is useful for informing policy and program

---

[1]This research was undertaken as part of the Master of Professional Studies in Community and Economic Development Program at The Pennsylvania State University.

decisions directed toward the local economy and other public issues regarding their likely impacts on entrepreneurial action.

The goal of this research is to increase understanding of the entrepreneurial ecology of Halifax, Nova Scotia, Canada. This increased understanding can then be used to effectively shape this community's entrepreneurial ecology for the purpose of economic development. Government is the primary focus of this research because it plays such a central and critical role in the creation and maintenance of the entrepreneurial ecology. Government creates and enforces rules related to business creation, registration, and reporting and, therefore, is the gatekeeper of formal entrepreneurial activity. This research focuses on the following questions:

(1) How do government policies, programs, and activities impact how entrepreneurs start, operate, and grow businesses in Halifax?
(2) Overall, what is the impact of government on entrepreneurial activity in Halifax?

These questions are rooted in the assumption that the collective sum of how entrepreneurs in Halifax order, classify, and interpret their entrepreneurial ecology becomes the reality that is Halifax's entrepreneurial ecology. To distinguish itself from other studies and indexes of entrepreneurial environments or climates (Fisher, 2005; Neumark, Kolko, & Mejia, 2012), this research goes beyond the mere identification of the presence or absence of policies, programs, and activities of government. Instead, the objective is to understand, by talking to those who function within the ecology, what impact government has on them and, in their perception, on their entrepreneurial ecology.

There are two primary benefits derived from this inquiry. First, it offers insights with respect to how the policies, programs, and activities of government impact the entrepreneurial ecology in Halifax, and how these might be shaped to encourage positive impacts and discourage negative impacts. Second, while the focus of this research is limited to Halifax, the findings will be useful in suggesting directions and questions for further inquiry with respect to Halifax's entrepreneurial ecology as well as those of other communities'.

Understanding the entrepreneurial ecology

This research is rooted in an attempt to understand the entrepreneurial ecology of Halifax and not simply the entrepreneurial environment in Halifax. This distinction is consistent with the movement within the entrepreneurship and economic development literature from the concept of the entrepreneurial *environment* (De Hoyos-Ruperto, Romaguera, Carlsson, & Perelli, 2012; Fogel, 2001) to that of the entrepreneurial *ecology* (Busenitz et al., 2003; Fortunato, 2011). Both the entrepreneurial environment and entrepreneurial ecology concepts focus on the complex set of social-political-cultural surroundings in which entrepreneurs function.

The difference, though, is more than semantic. The entrepreneurial environment concept recognizes the various individual influences upon entrepreneurship, but the entrepreneurial ecology concept also recognizes that these influences are necessarily connected, interactive, fluid, and dependent upon each other. Micklin and Sly (1998) refer to the social ecological perspective as "a method for classifying and organizing specific sets of ecosystem variables to facilitate more detailed analyses of the full range of empirical relationships" (p. 53). They also suggest that a change in any one of the variables necessarily "implies change in each of the others" (1998, p. 54).

Extant research suggests that the state of the entrepreneurial ecology influences the volume of innovative and entrepreneurial activity and the likelihood of success of entrepreneurial ventures (Griffiths et al., 2009). Additionally, there is a reciprocal relationship. That is, benefits derived from entrepreneurial activity can extend beyond the individual entrepreneur to also benefit the community (Kao, 2006). For example, entrepreneurial activity contributes to sustainable community and economic development by creating new jobs, stimulating new spending, offering import substitutions, offering new goods and services, alleviating poverty (Servon & Bates, 1998), improving political and social networks, and offering benefits derived from innovation (Acs & Storey, 2004; De Forest, 1965).

Mai and Gan (2007) surveyed the various discussions of economic, political, and social factors that influence entrepreneurship by Fogel (1994), Gartner (1985), Zapalska and Zapalska (1999), Davidsson (1991), Dana (1987, 1990), and Pennings (1982), and created a comprehensive list of such factors that they believe are most central to the entrepreneurial ecology. These include market mechanisms, accessibility to markets, accessibility to financing, government policies, regulations, incentives, administrative rigidities, taxation, accessibility of training, innovation, propensity to accept risk, perceptions of entrepreneurial failure, perceptions of entrepreneurship as a career, and availability of entrepreneurial role models (Mai & Gan, 2007).

Fortunato (2011) built upon the model developed by Busenitz et al. (2003), citing Amit, Glosten, and Muller (1990), Shane and Venkataraman (2000), and Venkataraman (1997), and presented the framework in Figure 1 for understanding the ecology within which entrepreneurial activity functions.

The "individuals and teams of individuals" component of this entrepreneurial ecology model encompasses individuals' personal entrepreneurial characteristics, the comparison of these characteristics between individual entrepreneurs as well as between entrepreneurs and non-entrepreneurs, and the dynamic processes through which individuals create intellectual and human capital (Busenitz et al., 2003). The "culture"

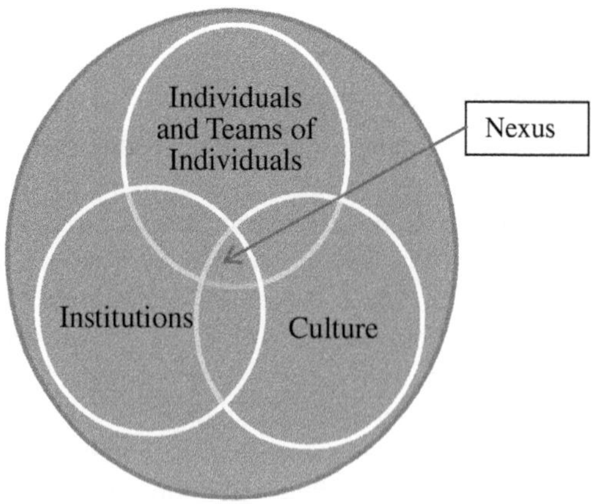

Figure 1. The entrepreneurial ecology model.
Source: Adapted from Busenitz et al., 2003; Fortunato, 2011.

component considers social influences on entrepreneurship that support or deter the identification, creation, and exploitation of opportunities (Busenitz et al., 2003). It also considers that social networks and social embeddedness play a role in the choice to become an entrepreneur (Reynolds, 1991), and that these social connections are likely visible within an entrepreneur's successful employment history (Buss, 1995).

The "institutions" component of the entrepreneurial ecology considers the modes of organizing for the purpose of entrepreneurial activity (Busenitz et al., 2003). The institutional context in which entrepreneurs function has a direct impact on many of the decisions they make, the way they perceive opportunities (Acs, Desai, & Hessels, 2008), and the way they are forced to adapt to their institutional surroundings. It is crucial to recognize that these impacts will vary within and between countries (Acs et al., 2008) and are not evenly distributed among all entrepreneurs (Estrin & Mickiewicz, 2011). For example, Estrin & Mickiewicz, 2011 conclude that the effects of institutional rules and rigidity are sometimes felt more acutely by female entrepreneurs than by their male counterparts.

Formal institutions that impact the entrepreneurial ecology include government, banks, and non-government organizations (Busenitz et al., 2003). There is significant literature, including the work of Bates (1995), about the attempts by government to positively impact the entrepreneurial ecology for purposes of economic development. There are a variety of ways to do this, including offering business financing and consulting services, operating incubators, instituting policies that are favorable to entrepreneurial activity, and assuming some of the risk associated with entrepreneurship (Paulson, Townsend, & Karaivanov, 2006). However, not all literature agrees that governments should promote and support entrepreneurs. Critics such as Brockett (1992) and Shane (2003) question government policies that promote and support entrepreneurs and offer a discussion of the appropriateness of this type of government intervention in a market economy.

A second way government impacts the institutional component is through its approach to the business registration process. Some governments recognize that there is a correlation between ease of registration and volume of formal entrepreneurial activity and, as a result, have lessened restrictions, difficulty, and rigidity (Kamleitner, Korunka, & Kirchler, 2012).

A third impact of governments on the entrepreneurial ecology is through their responsibility for creating and enforcing small business taxation laws. Many jurisdictions have recognized the burden taxation can have on entrepreneurs (Gill & Biger, 2012) and, in an attempt to encourage entrepreneurship, have lessened that burden (Kamleitner et al., 2012).

The "nexus" of the entrepreneurial ecology model is where the individual, cultural, and institutional components of the entrepreneurial ecology overlap, and where the collective impact of the individuals, culture, and institutions components of a community's entrepreneurial ecology manifests itself (Fortunato, 2011). At the nexus, the effects of the three components of an entrepreneurial ecology have contributing, compounding, and/or negating effects on entrepreneur behavior.

This research focuses on the "institutions" component of the model and, in particular, within that component, the formal institution of government. However, this research is seated within the context of the entire entrepreneurial ecology model and the entrepreneurial ecology of Halifax.

Research context

While the entrepreneurial ecology model provides a framework to study community entrepreneurial conditions, it is necessary to recognize that entrepreneurial ecologies will differ from community to community. It is, therefore, necessary to situate research on the entrepreneurial ecology in a particular local context.

This research is situated within the context of Halifax, Nova Scotia, Canada. Canada has experienced a modest population growth of just 1.2% per year between the census periods of 2006 and 2011 (Statistics Canada, 2006, 2011). Citizens enjoy a relatively low unemployment rate of just 6.6% and of those who work full time, the average income is $41,400. The economy and labor force are service driven, as evidenced by 76% of those employed working in the service sector (Statistics Canada, 2006, 2011).

Halifax has a population of 390,096 and serves as the provincial capital of Nova Scotia. Halifax is also the unofficial regional capital as it is the largest city within the surrounding provinces. The city has experienced a steady population growth over the past decade, averaging 4% per year (Statistics Canada, 2006, 2011, 2013).

Halifax has a relatively young population with a median age of 39.9 years (Statistics Canada, 2011). This is due to the large number of post-secondary institutions located in the city. The city remains relatively homogeneous as is evidenced by the fact that those who self-identify as immigrants constitute only 7.42% of the population, and only 5.59% report being a visual minority[1] (Statistics Canada, 2006).

The workforce is relatively highly educated, with 57.05% of the population having participated in some post-secondary education (Statistics Canada, 2006). Halifax has an unemployment rate of just 6.4% (Statistics Canada, 2013). Income levels are also relatively high with a median income for those 15 years and older who are employed of $27,193 (Statistics Canada, 2006). More than 64% of the workforce is involved in service provision (Statistics Canada, 2006). Another 22% are engaged in quasi-service endeavors such as retailing, wholesale, and financial and real estate sales (Statistics Canada, 2006). The remaining 12% provide some type of production, such as manufacturing, construction, agriculture, or resource extraction and processing (Statistics Canada, 2006).

This research uses a case study approach wherein Halifax's entrepreneurial ecology is of interest. Although this method is not conducive to producing generalizable results, this approach provides insight into the phenomenon of the entrepreneurial ecology in Halifax. Additionally, Halifax is reasonably representative of Canadian cities of similar size, especially in Eastern Canada, in terms of demographic characteristics, employment composition, and economic status. Findings may be suggestive of conditions in similar Canadian cities and can provide direction for further research and policy development.

In Halifax, all three levels of government – federal, provincial, and municipal – appear very active in promoting and supporting entrepreneurial activity. The primary municipal government entity for entrepreneurship promotion is The Greater Halifax Partnership. This entity offers assistance to entrepreneurs in the form of training, consulting, and financing (Greater Halifax Partnership, 2014). Provincially, Nova Scotia Business Inc. (NSBI) offers consulting services to entrepreneurs and financing in the form of loans, loan guarantees, payroll rebates, and venture capital (Nova Scotia Business Inc., 2014).

The Atlantic Canada Opportunity Agency (ACOA) is a federal entity that operates only in the Atlantic Region of Canada. ACOA offers consulting services related to business planning and marketing planning as well as offering loans and financing (Atlantic Canada Opportunity Agency, 2014).

The Business Development Bank of Canada is a federal entity operating in all provinces of Canada. It offers consulting services as well as financing, venture capital, and securitization (Business Development Bank of Canada, 2014). While the name of the entity implies it is a "bank," it does not actually function like a traditional commercial bank. It does not offer bank account services or investment services. It is solely in existence to assist businesses, especially small businesses, with problems they face related to accessing capital and growing and managing their businesses (Business Development Bank of Canada, 2014).

Research methods

A qualitative approach was used for this research because it is the most appropriate approach for understanding how informants interpret the world in which they live (McBurney & White, 2007). Qualitative methods are rooted in the interpretive tradition, making the assumption that "what is of paramount importance is how we order, classify, structure, and interpret our world" (Prasad, 2005, p. 13). It is not uncommon for initial forays into understanding a phenomenon of interest, such as the entrepreneurial ecology, that is relatively understudied to look to qualitative methods to provide direction for future research (Stoecker, 2005).

A case study method was used and, according to Yin (2013), "the classic case study consists of an in-depth inquiry into a specific and complex phenomenon (the 'case'), set within its real-world context" (p. 321). The case in question is Halifax's entrepreneurial ecology. Some argue that the primary limitation of this method is the lack of the ability to generalize (Stoecker, 2005). However, it is not our intent to pursue sample-to-population generalization (Yin, 2013), but, instead, to explore the specific case that is Halifax's entrepreneurial ecology. At this stage in our understanding of the entrepreneurial ecology concept, the tensions between an in-depth understanding and generalizability (Small, 2009) weigh more heavily on the need for richness of data and suggest that a 'small-*n* study' study is appropriate, rather than problematic (Small, 2009).

The research questions were designed to garner insight into how government can impact the entrepreneurial ecology, according to the entrepreneurs working within it. These methods allowed the presentation of open-ended questions and the probing of informants (McBurney & White, 2007). It is possible that until they were probed, the informants may not have realized what impact government has on their entrepreneurial activity.

A quantitative instrument such as a survey would not have captured the richness, complexity, and subtle nuances associated with the impact of government on the informants' behaviors and activities. This research is not primarily concerned with only "counting characteristics of something and then conducting a statistical analysis to see if there are any patterns" (Stoecker, 2005, p. 6); the concern, rather, is with understanding these complexities and nuances.

The researcher identified potential informants using his professional network. Informants were chosen using a purposeful sampling method. The researcher identified potential informants using word of mouth. Purposeful sampling identifies informants based on them having "the characteristics ... necessary to answer questions about a certain matter" (Koerber, 2008, p. 495). In this case, entrepreneurs in Halifax have the characteristics necessary to talk about the impact of government on their behaviors and businesses, and, in their perception, the entrepreneurial ecology in Halifax. Although informants were chosen to represent all major economic sectors, the sampling was not done randomly and there were no further attempts to ensure that the sample was representative of the population of entrepreneurs in Halifax. This was not necessary because the intent of the study was to explore the ecology through individual experiences, not to draw conclusions about all entrepreneurs in the population.

Key informant methodology has a history of use in studying elements of communities, such as the community of entrepreneurs in Halifax (Houston & Sudman, 1975). Houston specifically suggests that key informant methodology is an effective tool for the study of the "ecology of local institutions" (Houston & Sudman, 1975, p. 151). It is appropriate for this research because the method allows "informants to report on various aspects of the social system in which they perform role functions" (Houston & Sudman, 1975, p. 151).

Of the ten informants interviewed, nine are male, one had immigrated to Canada within the past two years, education levels vary widely from high school to a master-level degree, and all would be considered to be mid-career with an estimated age range of 32–48 years old. Their length in business ranges from .5 to 20 years. Five have owned multiple businesses. There were two informants from each of the following employment sectors: business services, other services (consumer services), retail trade, construction, and manufacturing. Table 1 provides a description of each informant.

The interview method was chosen based on its ability to gather complex information about relatively understudied phenomena, the flexibility afforded the researcher in terms of asking probing questions and responding to non-verbal cues and informant characteristics, and the richness of data provided (Bryman & Bell, 2011). The crafting of the interview protocol (see Appendix 1) was influenced by tenets of MacCracken's Long Interview format (1988). The method includes grand tour and mini tour questions and

Table 1. Informant profiles.

Informant	Sector	Description
1	Manufacturing	Male, mid-forties, master's degree, second venture, in business 10 years
2	Business services	Male, mid-forties, professional degree, third venture, in business 2 years
3	Business services	Male, mid-forties, degree, first venture, in business 20 years
4	Manufacturing	Male, mid-forties, technical courses, second venture, in business 1.5 years
5	Other services (consumer services)	Male, mid-thirties, second venture (simultaneous), master's degree, venture 1 in business 5 years, venture 2 in business .5 years
6	Construction	Male, mid-forties, first venture, high school, in business 10 years
7	Retail trade	Female, early thirties, first venture, start-up/pre-revenue
8	Retail trade	Male, late forties, professional degree, second venture (simultaneous), venture 1 in business 1.5 years, venture 2 in business .5 years
9	Construction	Male, late forties, high school, second venture (simultaneous), venture 1 in business 10 years, venture 2 in business 4 years
10	Other services (consumer services)	Male, mid-forties, college, second venture, 18 years in business

provides structure and continuity while simultaneously allowing the researcher to probe and explore experiences with participants. Prior to the use of the interview guide, it was pre-tested by two entrepreneurs and two other individuals who reviewed the guide and offered insight and suggestions.

The interviews were conducted in February and March of 2014. With permission from informants, the interviews were recorded and transcribed. Using a process informed by Glaser and Strauss's (1967) constant comparison method, data were analyzed in an attempt to identify similarities, differences, and themes within and between the responses of the interviewees (Boeije, 2002). This method involves a comprehensive process of comparing within a single interview, comparing between individual interviews, pairing interviews, and then comparing them to other pairs (Boeije, 2002). This process facilitates a complete and comprehensive analysis of the interview data.

Findings

The analysis of the interview data yielded seven significant findings. They are each addressed in turn in the following subsections.

Government's overall impact on Halifax's entrepreneurial ecology is slightly positive

To initiate discussion related to research question one, "How do government policies, programs, and activities impact how entrepreneurs start, operate, and grow businesses in Halifax?" and, ultimately, what impact informants think government has on Halifax's entrepreneurial ecology, informants were asked the following question: "Overall, what is the government impact on entrepreneurial activity in Halifax?" Informants were asked to rate government impact on a scale from 1 (very discouraging) to 10 (very encouraging).

The interviewer did not distinguish between federal, provincial, and municipal government. All three are involved in entrepreneurship promotion and support, and the interviewer did not want to bias the conversation toward any particular level of government. The results from all ten informants are provided in Figure 2.

The average response is 5.1 with a median of 5, and a range of 1–10. Only two informants rate the government impact as very positive, in the 4th quartile. Six informants rate the impact at the median or above (5 or above out of 10). Four of the

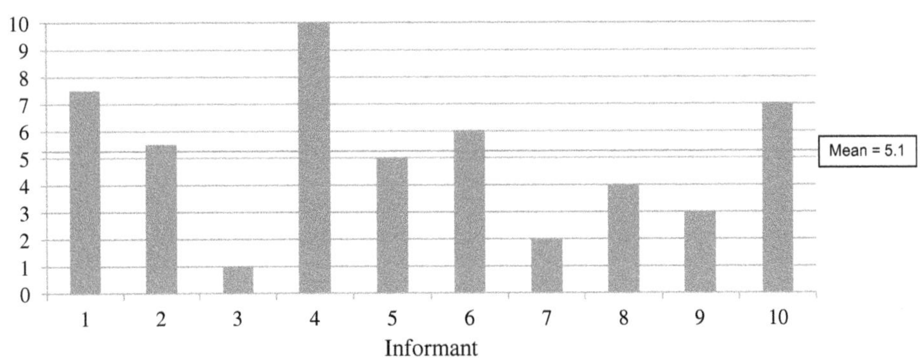

Figure 2. Government impact on entrepreneurial activity in Halifax according to all ten informants.
Note: 1 = very discouraging, 10 = very encouraging.

responses are below the median. These mixed responses are only slightly positive in aggregate. If the goal is for government to be extremely effective at encouraging and supporting entrepreneurs, in the opinion of the informants, government is falling short. Intended as a gage of overall impact, this question lent itself to a rating scale, and deeper interpretation is neither possible nor desired. The rest of the questions in the study were open-ended and elicited richer explanations and understandings of the entrepreneurial ecology.

Government departments and agencies tasked with supporting entrepreneurs are showing signs of success

Interaction between entrepreneurs and government in Halifax is typically with departments and agencies specifically charged with encouraging and supporting entrepreneurs. As detailed above, these typically include the ACOA, NSBI, the Business Development Corporation (BDC), and the Greater Halifax Partnership. Five informants reported interacting with such agencies and departments.

Of the informants who interacted with government support services, they described the experience as "fairly important," "beyond fantastic," and in one case reported that government made it possible to complete a project and that without that assistance, this project and informant would have failed. It was clear that several of the informants perceived government support to be a contributing factor to their success. Four of the ten informants specifically stated or implied that "they could not have done it without them [government]."

These five informants' perceptions of the impact that government has on entrepreneurs in Halifax is detailed in Figure 3.

It is important to note that informants were asked to rate government impact, in general, and not the impact of particular support services provided by government departments and agencies. The general opinion from these five informants who actually had contact with government departments and agencies was more positive than those of the entire group of ten informants. The mean response across the five informants was

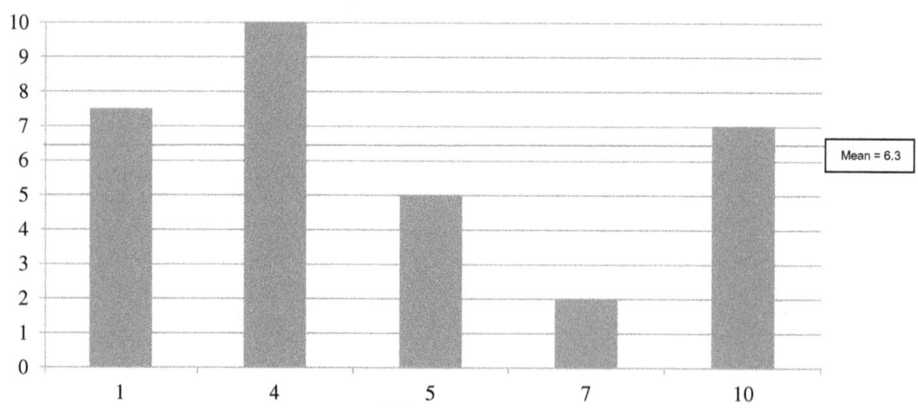

Figure 3. Government impact on entrepreneurial activity in Halifax according only to the five informants who interacted with government supports.
Note: 1 = very discouraging, 10 = very encouraging.

6.3 (median 7, range 2–10). Two of the five informants rated government impact as very positive (4th quartile). Four of the five rated government impact as above the median possible rating score.

One informant, who rated the government impact as 2, reported having very mixed experiences. This informant reported an extremely positive experience with government entrepreneurship support services, but a very negative experience with indirect interactions with zoning and permitting authorities. It appears that negative indirect interaction experiences with government resulted in this informant rating overall government interaction as only 2 out of 10.

Informants who did not interact with government supports hold a poor opinion of government supports for entrepreneurs

Among the five informants who did not interact with government support services, there was a common negative perception of government agencies and departments that aim to support entrepreneurs. These negative perceptions of government may have prevented some informants from initiating interaction with potentially beneficial government support services.

Five of the ten informants stated that they purposely did not initiate interaction with government entrepreneurial support services. There was an informant who specifically reported that he was "nervous" to approach the government because he generally viewed government as a policing entity that should be avoided if possible. Additionally, a different informant specifically stated that he purposely avoids agencies, such as ACOA and BDC, because he perceives that they cannot be of any help to him or his business. He felt that the bureaucratic processes would hinder rather than help. Other informants reported or insinuated that they believed government does not have the expertise necessary to understand their business or their industry. Still others reported that their perception is that government is only interested in supporting high-tech industries and research and development. In short, half of the informants did not view government as a potential partner in the success of their entrepreneurial venture and, as a result, purposefully avoided interaction with government departments or agencies.

Government efforts to support entrepreneurs often involves shifting risk from the entrepreneur to the government

A common response from the informants related to governmental impacts on the entrepreneurial ecology in Halifax pertains to government willingness to accept some of the risk that is normally present in entrepreneurial ventures. This is done in various ways, but the most obvious way is through lending and financing. The entrepreneur is often not held personally liable for part or all of a business loan in the event of business failure. This arrangement shifts the risk from the entrepreneur to the government. Informants one, two, and three operate in the technology industry, and they reported that government plays a very large role in their businesses in this regard. They noted that government has been willing to assume some of the risks associated with electronics research and development. Informant one suggests that one role of government, in support of entrepreneurs, is to "finance risky technology development." He clearly views the government as a stakeholder in his business and sees the government role of assuming risk as being "fairly important" to the success of his business. This is consistent with informant two, who suggested that it is a role of government to "lend to risky operations" and assume some of the risk associated with "developing new or risky products." Informant three echoed this theme and asserted that "government accepts risk" related to his business.

The business registration process is efficient and streamlined

There is consensus among the informants that the business registration process within Halifax's entrepreneurial ecology is streamlined, efficient, and not overly bureaucratic. Some of the informants are shareholders of incorporated entities, and some are sole proprietors. Regardless of the specific form of business organization, there is consensus that the government has been successful in its efforts to create a business registration process that is efficient and accessible. Specific comments from six of the informants concerning registration include: "not very burdensome," "registration process [is] reasonably simple," "registration system works pretty well," "registration [is] pretty easy," "registration pretty straight forward," and "registration is pretty easy actually." None of the informants reported that they experienced any onerous processes or other difficulties related to registering their business.

Business taxation and reporting requirements and processes are reasonable

Seven of the ten informants reported that the taxation and reporting processes for entrepreneurs are basically streamlined, non-bureaucratic, and efficient. Some of the informants' specific positive comments concerning taxation and reporting involved: "not very burdensome," "tax and reporting not onerous," "easy and not time consuming," "reporting not onerous," "I was amazed – I sent them papers they said ok and they sent the check – it is not as bureaucratic as it could be," and "taxation and reporting pretty good – online stuff helps."

Only three of the ten informants stated that the reporting and taxation requirements are overly time-consuming and therefore require too much effort on the part of the entrepreneur. Some of their negative comments included "taxation and reporting is cumbersome – I mean, the HST (sales tax) is just phenomenal – constant grind," "excessive – high amount of work and effort without compensation," and "so time consuming – it seems never ending – need less reporting."

Other government departments are creating barriers for entrepreneurs

A commonly held view among the informants is that interactions with other government departments and agencies that are not charged with encouraging and supporting entrepreneurs often had a negative impact on entrepreneurial activity. For example, informant five, who operates as a real estate developer, reported ongoing problems with zoning rules, stringent federal and provincial building codes, and building codes that can make houses cost more than the market will bear. He reported that these constraints have a major impact on how he runs his business. Despite acknowledging that workplace safety is of paramount importance, informant six discussed the overly onerous safety rules, the inflexible application of the rules, and the heavy-handed enforcement of the rules. Informant seven also ran into significant obstacles erected by government zoning and code departments when she was launching her business. She concluded that in her experience, government "processes and time are business killers," and that her start-up was "blocked by policies and processes" that delayed her opening by nearly six months.

Informant eight reported that his experiences with these same departments have cost him a great deal of money to ensure compliance. He reported that, on a particular project, code and zoning compliance cost him more than $25,000 on a $400,000 project, and the approval process took more than 60 days. He was also concerned that, in his opinion, "inspectors have a lot of authority and very little flexibility." Finally, informant nine reported his concern that when dealing with these government departments, entrepreneurs are viewed by the government as "guilty until proven innocent."

Despite the fact that departments, such as those responsible for zoning, codes, and building permits, are not tasked with supporting entrepreneurs, they have the potential to have a large impact on entrepreneurs and entrepreneurial activity. It appears that while government recognizes the importance of creating a positive environment for entrepreneurs by reducing the bureaucratic processes associated with departments and agencies that interact with entrepreneurs, agencies and regulators may have overlooked the impact that other departments have on entrepreneurs and entrepreneurial activity.

Discussion: themes, implications, and recommendations

Four themes have been identified across the interview findings that build on the understanding of entrepreneurs' perception of how government impacts them and their entrepreneurial ecology. Each theme has important implications for public policy.

Government supports are helpful, but may have an unduly bad reputation

As discussed in the findings, there were very positive responses from the five informants who interacted with government support services designed specifically to serve entrepreneurs. These positive responses suggest that entrepreneur-focused agencies and departments experience some success at creating an environment that encourages and supports entrepreneurship through activities, such as lending and other support services.

The remaining five informants purposely did not interact with government supports. Despite not having interaction with these agencies and departments, these informants reported negative perceptions of them. Considering that those informants who did interact with government reported them as being helpful and positive, it appears unfortunate these five informants did not interact with them. The resulting implication is troublesome. They are foregoing potentially beneficial services for reasons that appear to be rooted in preconceived negative impressions of government entrepreneurship supports and of government in general. It is also troubling because these departments and agencies are in existence solely to support entrepreneurs and to also yield the many benefits to society that can result from individuals' entrepreneurial activity (Acs et al., 2008; De Forest, 1965; Kao, 2006; Servon et al., 1998).

A recommendation stemming from this finding is that even though the government agencies and departments tasked with serving entrepreneurs in Halifax appear to be effective and efficient at doing so, they should pay closer attention to public perceptions and better manage their public messaging. They should do this in order to reduce or manage the negative public perception that some entrepreneurs have of them. It may be necessary for these departments and agencies to modify or reframe the visibility of their affiliation with traditional bureaucratic government processes in order to reach more entrepreneurs and potential entrepreneurs for the sake of encouraging economic development. For example, the agencies and departments could better brand themselves as entrepreneurial and entrepreneur-serving business units, separate and distinct from traditional government bureaucracy. They could actively attempt to combat what may be an unduly negative perception of them in the eyes of entrepreneurs. Further research, perhaps a qualitative analysis of the government employees' perceptions and knowledge of the impact they have on the entrepreneurial ecology, could provide insight with regard to this matter.

Business registration and reporting has been streamlined

A majority of informants consistently reported that government's mandatory reporting and registration processes for businesses are streamlined, efficient, and not overly burdensome. In particular, there was consensus that the business registration process in Halifax is efficient and non-burdensome.

The fact that the majority of informants agreed that little can be done to improve the reporting and registration processes is a testament to the efforts of government to encourage and support entrepreneurs. If we accept the claims from the literature such as those of Kamleitner et al. (2012) that there is a correlation between ease of registration and volume of entrepreneurial activity, the authorities in Halifax may well be boosting the volume of entrepreneurial activity by ensuring that the registration process is easy and efficient. Future research should further explore Halifax's success in this area with the promise that models such as those in play in Halifax might be replicated elsewhere.

Secondary government interactions with entrepreneurs create barriers

The aforementioned direct interactions between the informants and government were reported to be efficient and streamlined; however, informants also indicated that indirect interactions were far less than efficient and effective. In fact, informants specifically reported that interactions with government entities responsible for zoning and safety created obstacles and barriers to entrepreneurial activity.

The obvious implication is that while government has taken steps to make direct interactions with entrepreneurs, such as reporting and registration, efficient and effective, the same cannot be said for secondary interactions. It appears that government departments that happen to interact with entrepreneurs in an indirect way have not taken into consideration the impact their policies and bureaucratic processes have on entrepreneurs. The result could be that despite efforts by some government departments and agencies to encourage and support entrepreneurs, others are undermining those efforts by remaining overly bureaucratic and inefficient and therefore discouraging and being unsupportive of entrepreneurs.

Those individuals, departments, and agencies within Halifax's entrepreneurial ecology that are charged with encouraging and supporting entrepreneurs need to look beyond their own units' policies and practices and analyze and influence the impact that other government agencies and departments have on entrepreneurial activity.

Government support often means the removal of risk from entrepreneurs

A theme emerged related to government efforts to support entrepreneurs by facilitating business loans. This process often includes government not holding entrepreneurs personally liable for government-backed business loans. In the event of a business failure, the entrepreneur is only personally liable for a small portion of a government-backed loan, if any. The impact of financial risk distribution on entrepreneurs' behavior has implications for the scope and scale of economic activity in communities. In some scenarios, entrepreneurs may become more aggressive and engage in activities in which they would not normally engage if the consequences of risk were present. In other scenarios, entrepreneurs may become less aggressive when the risk is removed due to the decreased need to aggressively pursue opportunities in order to succeed. Better understanding of the relationship between financial risk distribution, entrepreneur behavior, business development, and economic growth in particular cultural and community contexts is central in designing effective public policy and programs to support entrepreneurs and their initiatives. Outright elimination of significant entrepreneurial risk via government policies and programs creates conditions that could result in moral hazard and contribute to unintended negative consequences, such as supporting the wrong individuals or supporting the right individuals in the wrong situations. Further research is required.

Conclusion: what has been accomplished and where to go from here

The goal of this research was to contribute to the understanding of Halifax's entrepreneurial ecology so it can be more effectively shaped for the purpose of economic development. The research was designed to probe beyond the mere presence or absence of government policy, programs, and activities and discern the impact government has according to entrepreneurs who function in Halifax. The study also offers important insight into the entrepreneurial ecology model. It became apparent when talking to the informants that government plays a significant role in determining Halifax's conditions for entrepreneurship. The stated goals of this research were achieved as evidenced in seven findings, four themes, and resulting implications and recommendations. These findings, themes, and recommendations also provide a platform of perspectives and questions useful in informing similar inquiries in other communities.

The richness of the qualitative research process facilitated the disclosure of a wide variety of the informants' personal circumstances and experiences. However, the detailed responses from informants and the themes that emerged from the data indicate that the collective perception of the informants is that the net effect of government impact on Halifax's entrepreneurial ecology is mixed. If the government wishes to develop Halifax's local economy by contributing to the creation and maintenance of an encouraging and supportive entrepreneurial ecology, it is imperative that agencies and regulators rely on research such as this to better understand how potential and actual practicing entrepreneurs perceive the state of the entrepreneurial ecology. This understanding will contribute to more effective crafting and monitoring of policies, programs, and activities that directly and indirectly impact the ability for entrepreneurs to grow and flourish.

Disclosure statement

No potential conflict of interest was reported by the authors.

Note

1. "Visible minority refers to whether a person belongs to a visible minority group as defined by the *Employment Equity Act* and, if so, the visible minority group to which the person belongs. The *Employment Equity Act* defines visible minorities as 'persons, other than Aboriginal

peoples, who are non-Caucasian in race or non-white in color.' The visible minority population consists mainly of the following groups: Chinese, South Asian, Black, Arab, West Asian, Filipino, Southeast Asian, Latin American, Japanese and Korean." http://www.statcan.gc.ca/eng//definitions/minority01.

References

Acs, Z., Desai, S., & Hessels, J. (2008). Entrepreneurship, economic development and institutions. *Small Business Economics, 31*, 219–234.

Acs, Z., & Storey, D. (2004). Introduction: Entrepreneurship and economic development. *Regional Studies, 38*, 871–877.

Amit, R., Glosten, L., & Muller, E. (1990). Does venture capital foster the most promising entrepreneurial firms? *California Management Review, 32*, 102–111.

Atlantic Canada Opportunity Agency. (2014). *Start a business*. Retrieved January 21, 2014, from http://www.acoa-apeca.gc.ca/eng/IWantTo/StartABusiness/Pages/Home.aspx

Bates, T. (1995). Small businesses appear to benefit from state or local government's economic development assistance. *Urban Affairs Review, 31*, 206–225.

Boeije, H. (2002). A purposeful approach to the constant comparative method in the analysis of qualitative interviews. *Quality and Quantity, 36*, 391–409.

Brockett, M. (1992). Struggling small businesses: Can (should) the community economic development profession help. *Small Business, 10*, 46–49.

Bryman, A., & Bell, E. (2011). *Business research methods, 3e*. Oxford: Oxford University Press.

Busenitz, L., West, G., Shepherd, D., Nelson, T., Chandler, G., & Zacharakis, A. (2003). Entrepreneurship research in emergence: Past trends and future directions. *Journal of Management, 29*, 285–308.

Business Development Bank of Canada. (2014). *Entrepreneurs first*. Retrieved January 21, 2014, from http://www.bdc.ca/EN/Pages/home.aspx

Buss, T. (1995). Displaced workers and rural entrepreneurship: A four-state study. *Economic Development Quarterly, 9*, 15–24.

Dana, L. (1987). Entrepreneurship and venture creation: An international comparison of five commonwealth nations. In N. Churchill, J. Hornaday, B. Kirchhoff, D. Krasner, & K. Vesper (Eds.), *Frontiers in entrepreneurship research* (pp. 91–98). Wellesley, MA: Babson College.

Dana, L. (1990). Saint Martin/Saint Maarten: A case study of the effects of culture on economic development. *Journal of Small Business Management, 28*, 91–98.

Davidsson, P. (1991). Continued entrepreneurship: Ability, need, and opportunity as determinants of small firm growth. *Journal of Business Venturing, 6*, 405–429.

De Forest, J. (1965). Entrepreneurship and economic development. *Challenge, 13*, 27–31.

De Hoyos-Ruperto, M., Romaguera, J., Carlsson, B., & Perelli, S. (2012). Entrepreneurial environment dilemma in Puerto Rico: A challenge of self and system. *Journal of Marketing Development and Competitiveness, 6*, 11–28.

Dye, B. (2014). *Gatekeepers of entrepreneurial activity: Formal institutions and the entrepreneurial ecology* (Unpublished master of professional studies paper). The Pennsylvania State University, State College, PA.

Estrin, S., & Mickiewicz, T. (2011). Institutions and female entrepreneurship. *Small Business Economics, 37*, 397–415.

Fisher, P. (2005). *Grading places: What do the business climate rankings really tell us?* Retrieved July 3, 2015, from http://s2.epi.org/files/page/-/old/books/grading_places/grading_places_(full_text).pdf

Fogel, G. (1994). Perceptions of small business owners: A study of the development of entrepreneurship in Hungary. *Midwest Review of Business Research, Academy of International Business, 3*, 89–99.

Fogel, G. (2001). An analysis of entrepreneurial environment and enterprise development in Hungary. *Journal of Small Business Management, 39*, 103–109.

Fortunato, M. (2011). *The individual-institutional-opportunity nexus: Examining interaction, purpose, and opportunity in rural entrepreneurship development* (Unpublished doctoral thesis). The Pennsylvania State University, State College, PA.

Gartner, W. (1985). A conceptual framework for describing the phenomenon of new venture creation. *Academy of Management Review, 10*, 696–703.

Gill, A., & Biger, N. (2012). Barriers to small business growth in Canada. *Journal of Small Business and Enterprise Development, 19*, 656–668.

Glaser, B., & Strauss, A. (1967). *The discovery of grounded theory: Strategies for qualitative research*. New York, NY: Aldine.

Greater Halifax Partnership. (2014). *Smart business*. Retrieved January 21, 2014, from http://www.greaterhalifax.com/en/home/ourprograms/smartbusiness/default.aspx

Griffiths, M., Gundry, L., Kickul, J., & Muñoz Fernandez, A. (2009). Innovation ecology as a precursor to entrepreneurial growth. *Journal of Small Business and Enterprise Development, 16*, 375–390.

Houston, M., & Sudman, S. (1975). A methodological assessment of the use of key informants. *Social Science Research, 4*, 151–164.

Kamleitner, B., Korunka, C., & Kirchler, E. (2012). Tax compliance of small business owners. *International Journal of Entrepreneurial Behaviour & Research, 18*, 330–351.

Kao, R. (2006). Defining entrepreneurship: Past, present and? *Creativity and Innovation Management, 2*, 69–70.

Koerber, A. (2008). Qualitative sampling methods: A primer for technical communicators. *Journal of Business and Technical Communication, 22*, 454–473.

Mai, Y., & Gan, Z. (2007). Entrepreneurial opportunities, capacities and entrepreneurial environments. *Chinese Management Studies, 1*, 216–224.

McBurney, D., & White, T. (2007). *Research methods*. Belmont, CA: Wadsworth.

McCracken, G. (1988). *The long interview*. Newbury Park, CA: Sage.

Micklin, M., & Sly, D. (1998). The ecology complex: A conceptual elaboration. In K. C. Land & M. Micklin (Eds.), *Communities in sociological human ecology* (pp. 51–66). New York, NY: Plenum.

Morris, M. (2001). From the editor: Entrepreneurship is economic development is entrepreneurship. *Journal of Developmental Entrepreneurship, 6*(3), 5–6.

Neumark, D., Kolko, J., & Mejia, M. (2012). *Assessing state business climate indices: Federal Reserve Bank of San Francisco economic letters*. Retrieved July 3, 2015, from http://www.frbsf.org/economic-research/publications/economic-letter/2012/september/state-business-cycle-index/

Nova Scotia Business Inc. (2014). *Nova Scotia, a hotbed of business brilliance*. Retrieved January 21, 2014, from http://www.novascotiabusiness.com/en/home/default.aspx

Paulson, A., Townsend, R., & Karaivanov, A. (2006). Distinguishing limited liability from moral hazard in a model of entrepreneurship. *Journal of Political Economy, 114*, 100–144.

Pennings, J. (1982). Organizational birth frequencies: An empirical investigation. *Administrative Science Quarterly, 27*, 120–144.

Prasad, P. (2005). *Crafting qualitative research: Working in the postpositivist tradition*. Armonk, NY: M.E. Sharpe.

Reynolds, P. (1991). Sociology of entrepreneurship: Concepts and contributions. *Entrepreneurship: Theory and Practice, 16*, 47–70.

Servon, L., & Bates, T. (1998). Microenterprise as an exit route from poverty: Recommendations for programs and policy makers. *Journal of Urban Affairs, 20*, 419–441.

Shane, S. (2003). Why encouraging more people to become entrepreneurs is bad public policy. *Small Business Economics, 33*, 141–149.

Shane, S., & Venkataraman, S. (2000). The promise of entrepreneurship as a field of research. *Academy of Management Review, 25*, 217–226.

Small, M. (2009). 'How many cases do I need?' On science and the logic of case selection in field-based research. *Ethnography, 10*, 5–38.

Statistics Canada. (2006). *Community profile 2006*. Retrieved January 17, 2014, from http://www12.statcan.gc.ca/census-recensement/2006/dp-pd/prof/92-591/details/page.cfm?Lang=E&Geo1=CSD&Code1=1209034&Geo2=PR&Code2=12&Data=Count&SearchText=halifax&SearchType=Begins&SearchPR=12&B1=All&Custom=

Statistics Canada. (2011). *Community profile 2011*. Retrieved January 17, 2014, from http://www12.statcan.gc.ca/census-recensement/2011/dp-pd/prof/details/page.cfm?Lang=E&Geo1=CSD&Code1=1209034&Geo2=CD&Code2=1209&Data=Count&SearchText=halifax&SearchType=Begins&SearchPR=12&B1=All&Custom=&TABID=1

Statistics Canada. (2013). *Labour force characteristics*. Retrieved January 21, 2014, from http://www.statcan.gc.ca/tables-tableaux/sum-som/l01/cst01/lfss04a-eng.htm

Stoecker, R. (2005). *Research methods for community change*. Thousands Oaks, CA: Sage Books.

Venkataraman, S. (1997). The distinctive domain of entrepreneurship research: An editor's perspective. In J. Katz & R. Brockhaus (Eds.), *Advances in entrepreneurship, firm emergence, and growth* (pp. 119–138). Greenwich, CT: JAI Press.

Yin, R. (2013). Validity and generalization in future case study evaluations. *Evaluation, 19*, 321–332.

Zapalska, A., & Zapalska, L. (1999). Small business ventures in post-communist Hungary. *Journal of East-West Business, 5*, 5–21.

Appendix 1. Interview guide for informants

(1) How do the policies, programs, and activities of the government impact your ability to start, maintain, and grow a business in Halifax?

Potential follow-up questions

(a) How does the government influence the business decisions you make as an entrepreneur?
(b) How do the government influence how you grow your business?
(c) How does the business registration process impact you?
(d) How do the taxation and reporting requirements impact you?
(e) How do the entrepreneurship support services offered by government impact you?

(2) How do the policies, programs, and activities of the banks impact your ability to start, maintain, and grow a business in Halifax? Please explain. Please provide some examples.

Potential follow-up questions

(a) How do the banks influence the business decisions you make as an entrepreneur?
(b) How do the banks influence how you grow your business?
(c) How do the banks' lending rules and regulations impact you?

(3) How do the policies, programs, and activities of entrepreneurial supporting NGOs impact your ability to start, maintain, and grow a business in Halifax?

Potential follow-up questions

(a) How do NGOs influence the business decisions you make as an entrepreneur?
(b) How do NGOs influence how you grow your business?
(c) How do entrepreneurship support services offered by NGOs impact your business activity?

(4) In your experience as an entrepreneur, do you think that governments, traditional banks, and NGOs together create positive, neutral, or negative conditions for entrepreneurship in Halifax?

Potential follow-up question

(a) Do governments, banks, and NGOs make it easier or more difficult for you to do business in Halifax?

(5) Overall, on a scale from one to ten, how would rate the governments', traditional banks', and non-governmental organizations' impact on entrepreneurial activity in Halifax? (1 being very negative impact/10 being very positive impact)

(6) Overall, on a scale of one to ten, how encouraging is Halifax in terms of entrepreneurs and entrepreneurship? (1 being not very encouraging/10 being very encouraging)

(7) Demographic Information

Annual sales/Number of full-time employees/Number of part-time employees/Years in business/Type of business/Business sector/Education level of entrepreneur/How many businesses have they owned

(8) Is there anything else you would like to add concerning the impact that governments, traditional banks, and NGOs have on entrepreneurial activity and the entrepreneurial ecology in Halifax?

Creating and sustaining a model of community-based enterprise learning: a participatory case study of ready hubs

Tim Vorley and Nick Williams

Entrepreneurship education has increased in prominence over the past decade yet somewhat paradoxically remains outside the statutory school curriculum in many places, including the UK. Despite this, there has been a growing movement to embed enterprise education widely, including supporting enterprise through community-based learning. This article is the output from a participatory action research case study which analyzes the implementation of community-based enterprise learning in Rotherham (UK) and examines the experiences of developing community-based enterprise learning and the challenges of creating a sustainable model. The article finds that such a model depends on creating an effective community of practice with distributed leadership that is able to co-produce community-based enterprise learning. The article concludes by reflecting on the emerging model and identifies recommendations for achieving sustainable community-based enterprise learning.

Introduction

Over the past few decades, policy makers and academics have emphasized the importance of entrepreneurship in contributing to economic development (Acs, Desai, & Hessels, 2008; Wright & Marlow, 2011; Wright & Stigliani, 2013). Research has focused on the conditions necessary for creating the conditions to foster more entrepreneurial ecosystems, examining a variety of policy interventions and mechanisms for start-up/business support. The question as to whether entrepreneurs are born or made is persistent. Yet a central tenet of entrepreneurship education is that entrepreneurial and enterprising skills can be taught (Henry, Medhurst, & Lyttle, 2005; Jack & Anderson, 1999). As Gibb (1993, 2000) states, enterprise skills such as these are not fixed personality traits but can be learned and developed through experience and have become an important dimension of contemporary education. The growth of entrepreneurship education has resulted in a growing body of literature on different approaches and best practice from educators and researchers alike. While Vesper and Gartner (1997) trace the origins of enterprise education in the United States back to 1947, its adoption in the UK only really began in the late 1970s, and in recent decades, the number of programs associated with it has grown (Jack & Anderson, 1999). Despite this growth, enterprise education is not statutory in UK schools, and approaches to it remain diverse.

Assuming a participatory action research case study, this article presents the case of an innovative hub-based model of community-based enterprise learning in Rotherham,

UK. The article explores how the model has evolved from a school-focused local-government-funded project to become a more comprehensive and inclusive model of community-based enterprise learning. As the hub-based model has evolved, the case study highlights how new stakeholders have been enrolled and how the scale of activities has increased. Reflecting on the challenges of establishing a sustainable model of community-based enterprise learning, the article asserts that there is a need to develop a sense of ownership among stakeholders by fostering a more active community of practice. In doing so, the article offers insights into an alternative sustainable approach to promoting enterprise learning at a community scale by working with a range of stakeholders in a collaborative way by promoting distributed leadership and shared ownership. The article highlights the importance of securing and leveraging stakeholder commitment in community-based initiatives if they are to be sustainable. Lastly, the article concludes by identifying lessons and recommendations for the development community-based entrepreneurship in other contexts.

Community-based enterprise learning

Entrepreneurship educators assume a multitude of pedagogic approaches and teaching methods (Jack & Anderson, 1999). These range from more process-led linear pedagogies, premised on business planning and case study methods, to more dynamic cognitive approaches that are premised on encouraging learners to think more entrepreneurially. Edelman, Manolova, and Brush (2008) have highlighted that there is a gap between what is taught in entrepreneurship and what entrepreneurs do, and as such, there is scope for greater variety in terms of delivery. The methods used to teach entrepreneurship range from didactic classes to interactive games and experiential practice-based learning. In reflecting on the "new frontiers" of entrepreneurship education, Neck and Greene (2011) propose teaching entrepreneurship as a way of thinking and acting, using a portfolio of practice-based pedagogies, as opposed to a single or static approach. As such, this section outlines the key literature concerned with fostering positive cultures of entrepreneurship through education, and identifies how community-based approaches may represent a fruitful avenue for further policy development in extending the portfolio.

For several decades, economic policy makers and academics have increasingly emphasized the importance of entrepreneurship to economic development in a post-industrial, knowledge-intensive, and digital economy (Acs et al., 2008). The prevailing argument is that entrepreneurship drives growth by creating more high-growth small and medium-sized enterprises (SMEs), which in turn creates more jobs and enhances both competitiveness and innovation (Acs, 2006). As such, public policy has tended to focus on creating healthy conditions for entrepreneurial start-ups and the growth of SMEs (Huggins & Williams, 2009). In the UK, government policy has fostered entrepreneurship and supported SME growth using market-steered instruments, although there is increasing recognition of the importance of developing a pro-enterprise culture (Jones & Iredale, 2010).

Central to nurturing an enterprising culture is recognizing the normative value of entrepreneurship as well as holding enterprising skills and entrepreneurs in higher esteem. The phenomenon of entrepreneurship is largely a phenomenon of the mind, concerning alertness to opportunity, perception, and imagination (Kirzner, 1973; Sautet & Kirzner, 2006; Yu, 2001). Culture shapes "what an individual perceives as opportunities and thus what he overlooks, as entrepreneurship is always embedded in a cultural context" (Sautet & Kirzner, 2006, p. 17). As such, culture plays a key role in fostering entrepreneurship (Bosma & Levie, 2009; Hofstede, 1991; Williams & McGuire, 2010). Cultural change can be fostered by targeting values, perceptions, rituals, and symbols; however, change is slow, and mental programs passed from one generation to another are resistant to change (Hofstede, 1980; Williams & Vorley, 2014). Yet change is possible, as culture is neither static nor deterministic and evolves over time, and while some cultures hinder the development of entrepreneurship to a greater degree than others, this does not always remain the case (Sautet & Kirzner, 2006).

In the UK, the recent focus of government thinking has sought to promote a culture of enterprise with young people, particularly through the education system (Athayde, 2009; Gibb, 2000). Such approaches were discussed in policy circles in the 1970s, and were again resurrected under the Labour government of 1997–2010 (Department for Education & Skills, 2002; Gibb, 2000). The Labour government commissioned the "Davies Review of Enterprise and the Economy in Education" (Department for Education & Skills, 2002), which found schools played a key role in developing attitudes toward careers and identified them providing enterprise education as part of the curriculum. Moreover, the Review found schools to play a critical role in turning positive attitudes into action, and thereby developing capabilities and skills of young people to be entrepreneurial. With an increasingly globalized economy, it is clear that there will be greater need for people to have entrepreneurial skills to deal with uncertainty (Henry, Hill, & Leitch, 2003), and as such the Review recommended that government provides guidance to schools to support the development of "enterprise capability," defined as the capability to handle uncertainty and respond positively to change, to create and implement new ideas and new ways of doing things, to make reasonable risk/reward assessments and act upon them in one's personal and working life. As Gibb (1993, 2000) states, enterprise skills such as these are not fixed personality traits but can be learned and developed through experience.

After the Davies Review, the government committed funding to schools and guidance on standardizing enterprise education (HM Treasury, 2002, 2008a). For example, it was announced that all secondary school pupils would receive at least five days of enterprise activity (HM Treasury, 2004), and that £210 m would be committed to promoting enterprise across primary, secondary, and further education (HM Treasury, 2008a). Successive budgets also laid out activities aimed at promoting good practice in enterprise education. This included a guide to the most enterprising schools entitled "Enterprising Heads, Enterprising Schools," as well as support for Young Chambers of Commerce, and a quality assurance scheme for the National Education Business Partnership network. These measures, together with the plan announced in the 2008 Budget to establish a National Enterprise Academy, sought to foster better relationships between schools and businesses and serve as catalyst to a more enterprising culture in the UK (HM Treasury, 2008a, 2008b).

Following the formation of a Conservative-Liberal Democrat coalition government in 2010, policy interest in and emphasis on enterprise education continued, albeit in the context of austerity, which has reduced its funding and scope. Continuing the emphasis of the previous government, the coalition government commissioned the Young Report "Enterprise for All," which sets out the importance of enterprise education (Department for Business, Innovation & Skills, 2014). The report outlines that enterprise means more than simply the ability to become an entrepreneur and is a valuable attribute throughout life, yet also states that it is "a quality many bring with them on starting primary school but far too many leave secondary school without" (Department for Business, Innovation

& Skills, 2014, p. 1). Consequently, the report states that more needs to be done in the education system to support the acquisition of enterprising skills, including flexibility, responsiveness to change, and the ability to spot opportunities and act upon them.

Clearly, establishing a more entrepreneurial culture through policy intervention is not simple and is very much a long-term process (Volkmann et al., 2009). In the UK, the government appears to have put in the foundations, primarily within the education system, to facilitate such change. To ensure the highest likelihood of policy success, and to convert attitudes into positive action, policies aimed at cultural improvement must be sustained for a considerable number of years (Huggins & Williams, 2009). They should not, as has been the case with other enterprise-related policies over the years, be at the mercy of political change and expediency. Indeed, the challenges and opportunities presented by continuing globalization reinforce the need for effective policy to foster a strong enterprise culture in the UK (Huggins & Williams, 2009). As part of ongoing commitment to enterprise education, it is important that new ways of facilitating skills among young people are devised and examined. To achieve this, schools are pivotal in promoting an enterprise culture in the UK by embedding entrepreneurial learning into curricula. However, enterprise education is not currently a statutory component of the national curriculum, and instead remains an *extra*-curricular, *non*-mandatory subject. As such, ensuring enterprise education in schools has become a case of good practice as opposed to compulsory practice. Where enterprise education does exist effectively, it is often dependent on innovative and collaborative provision that sees entrepreneurship embedded both within the curriculum and beyond it, through community learning.

Much of the research around developing enterprising cultures in communities demonstrates that numerous barriers exist in challenging environments (Williams & Williams, 2011). One of the most important characteristics of overcoming barriers is the nature of community. Every community contains an implicit understanding of the influence of status, and entitlements of its individual members should be understood in relation to the requirements of the community itself (Peterson, 1988). Indeed, the more community-orientated a society is, the more its members gain benefits, including the satisfaction of economic and social needs (Peredo & Chrisman, 2006). This community orientation does not conflict with entrepreneurship (Peterson, 1988) as successful entrepreneurial communities can be fostered in part by the interdependences among individuals, families, and relevant stakeholders (Holt, 1997), for example through the co-production of potential solutions. Through such interdependencies, scholars recognize the importance of entrepreneurship as building on collective processes (Peredo & Chrisman, 2006). For example, collective learning and community building solidarity can explain the growth and resilience of Silicon Valley (Granovetter, 1989; Swedberg, 1997) and the emergence of business districts in Europe (Johannisson & Monsted, 1997). Entrepreneurial accomplishment may not only be compatible with diverse social arrangements, but may benefit from the integration of community-based cultural values and norms (Anderson, 2002). As such, there appears to be a diverse set of environments in which entrepreneurial activity can flourish, and in many small communities, especially those lacking entrepreneurial activity, a variety of combinations that simultaneously provide space and opportunities for fostering more positive cultures have emerged (Peredo & Chrisman, 2006). While much of the entrepreneurship literature examines culture and communities that are "successful," the fostering of entrepreneurial activity and mindsets in communities that have previously lacked a critical mass of entrepreneurs is comparatively under-researched (Williams & Williams, 2011). A challenge here is that while culture can be an important engine for entrepreneurial activity, historical, social, and cultural factors can impede as well as facilitate cooperation and social cohesion. Overcoming these barriers and impediments is an important consideration for community-based entrepreneurial learning and development. The remainder of this article focuses on how entrepreneurial learning can be fostered in communities that have traditionally lacked entrepreneurial activity as well as positive cultures of entrepreneurship.

Empirical focus and method

The empirical focus of this article is a participatory action research case study. As Ram, Edwards, Jones, Kiselinchev, and Muchenje (2014, p. 7) note, "what constitutes 'valid' action research has always been a thorny issue," although it has come to be accepted in terms of what Sayer (2000) referred to in terms of "practical adequacy." The intention of this study was to provide critical reflection about the sustainability of community-based enterprise learning delivered through Ready Hubs. As such, the case study presented here is the outcome of participatory action research, which saw the staff actively involved in all aspects of the research process from establishing the research design through to analyzing and presenting the research findings. In this way, as highlighted by Greenwood, Whyte, and Harkavy (1993), the research process has enhanced learning and understanding of both the academic and participatory researchers involved.

Our study is focused on Rotherham, a town that lies in northern England within the Sheffield City Region (SCR), and forms part of a wider ongoing study of the entrepreneurial ecosystem. The case study and action research partner were Rotherham Ready, a public sector initiative established in 2005 by the local authority Rotherham Metropolitan Borough Council (RMBC). A central aspect of this co-produced work was to better understand and promote a culture of enterprise among young people. The initial objective was to develop an "enterprise entitlement" for young people aged 4–19 years, enabling them to learn about enterprise in real-world contexts. In 2011, the Rotherham Ready initiative was recognized by government as a successful example of an enterprise-focused school improvement program (OFSTED, 2011).

Rotherham Ready was supported under a "Creative Councils" program funded by the National Endowment for Science Technology and Arts (NESTA) and the Local Government Association (LGA) in the UK to extend and develop a new approach to socioeconomic community challenges through enterprise. In 2012, Rotherham Ready extended their activities beyond enterprise education with the creation of three so-called "Ready Hubs" in Rotherham. Ready Hubs aim to provide a more integrative and inclusive approach toward enterprise learning for young people, their families, and the wider community, premised on developing a range of enterprise learning activities and range of stakeholders. The Ready Hubs, which are school-based, serve as the focal point for community-based enterprise learning, with the aim of fostering a more enterprising culture. However, as a project with finite funding from NESTA and the LGA, Ready Hubs faced a number of strategic and operational challenges in terms of how to sustain their activities when the funding is exhausted.

Working in an "equitable partnership" on this project between mid-2012 and early 2014 meant that the authors as academic researchers were not privileged over the participatory researchers from the Ready Hub or other stakeholders (Harrison & Leitch, 2000; Rappaport, Alegria, Mulvaney-Day, & Boyle, 2008). Indeed, the nature of the research process was highly collaborative, with the knowledge informing the findings and recommendations co-produced by exploring the issues raised. This action research has culminated in strategic and operational improvements for Ready Hubs, in order to sustain the delivery of their enterprising activities. Indeed, for the academic researchers, the project provided an impetus to consider a broader question about developing a sustainable model of community-based enterprise learning.

As a methodological approach, the community-based nature of this participatory action research case study was deemed appropriate for four reasons. First, the basis of the research was initiated by the then Rotherham Ready project team, who were looking to the academic researchers for critical insight. Second, the research was co-funded by Rotherham Ready and the University of Sheffield, and as such was not consultancy or paid for expert advice. Third, the intended outcome in terms of promoting enterprise awareness through education *and* addressing socioeconomic challenges though enterprise are consistent with the ideologies of the academic researchers. Fourth, and finally, as noted above, the project contributed to the wider ongoing program of study in the SCR.

Given the prominent rise of the enterprise agenda in the UK as discussed in the previous section, the scope of the project was threefold. First, to examine the different activities delivered and facilitated through the Ready Hubs in Rotherham to empower young people and communities through enterprise learning. Second, to understand the nature and involvement of different stakeholder in fostering enterprise through the Ready Hubs. Third, to distill lessons for effectively promoting community-based enterprise learning within but also beyond the case study of Rotherham Ready.

Semi-structured interviews were conducted with the two members of the management team at Rotherham Ready, the Ready Hub coordinator, and the officers at RMBC involved with the Rotherham Ready project. The interviews explored the strategy and operational activity of Ready Hubs, and were used to map activities, stakeholders, and beneficiaries. The next stage saw eight stakeholders supporting delivery of the enterprise entitlement interviewed; in addition, sixteen beneficiaries (including young people and their families) were interviewed to understand the outcomes and impacts of the enterprising activities delivered through the Ready Hubs. The project incorporated two ethnographic methods: first drawing on reflections from the participatory research partner working at the Ready Hubs about their experiences in managing and delivering community-based enterprise learning; and second incorporating observations from the academic researchers about the enterprising activities at which we were present. This collaborative and participatory multi method approach has provided insights about community-based enterprise learning, which are written-up by the academic authors with the involvement of the research partner at Rotherham Ready.

Findings

The findings and reflections from the research are presented here in two parts. The first part presents an overview of how the Ready Hubs have developed and how they work, with a focus on the three core areas of training, facilitating, and network building. The second part addresses the sustainability of Ready Hubs as a model for delivering community-based enterprise learning and explores the underlying challenges this presents.

Building an enterprise entitlement

Ronstadt (1990) rightly noted that entrepreneurship education should not be viewed as mechanistic, but instead should be considered as holistic and integrated, and the design and delivery of the enterprise entitlement can be seen as testament to this. As noted above, enterprise education in the UK is not statutory but rather *extra*-curricular, which poses a number of challenges for positioning, prioritizing, and financing its delivery. Gibb (2002) argues for the need for a new paradigm in entrepreneurship education, as although the emphasis on entrepreneurship education has grown it still remains fragmented and reforms have been both slow and piecemeal. Following the creation of Rotherham Ready in 2005, the initiative implemented a series of enterprise education programs in schools across the town of Rotherham. The core activities primarily focused on training the teaching staff to develop and embed enterprising and entrepreneurial learning through the curriculum for all young people aged 4–19. However, with financial support of NESTA and the LGA in 2012 Rotherham Ready sought to scale its activities through the creation of the so-called "Ready Hubs." While educators have traditionally taken the lead in the design and delivery of enterprise education in schools, the premise of Ready Hub has been to pursue a more integrative and inclusive approach both in terms of the range of activities delivered and facilitated as well as the range of stakeholders and beneficiaries engaged. The Ready Hub model was launched and piloted as a new approach toward enterprise learning for young people that is both embedded in the curriculum and delivered through extracurricular activities both within schools and the wider community. The development of the three prototype Ready Hubs sought to reappraise and pioneer a more integrated approach toward enterprise learning in Rotherham.

The first fundamental difference between Ready Hubs compared to the activities of Rotherham Ready was the organization and scale of engagement. Instead of working with and supporting individual teaching staff at different schools, each of the Ready Hubs was centered on a particular "learning community" in Rotherham (i.e. a secondary school with a number of partner primary schools). In this way, the intention was to establish a critical mass of individuals and activities to promote, support, and deliver community-based enterprise learning, which Bonk, Wisher, and Nigrelli (2004) assert is integral to actively fostering an emotional connection with enterprise in this case. Additional funding from NESTA and the LGA enabled a full-time enterprise coordinator to be appointed, who worked across the three Ready Hubs. The coordinator was integral in setting up and operationalizing the Ready Hubs in each of the learning communities, despite having no official jurisdiction in the schools that comprise them. A key role of the coordinator has been to build the capacity of the Ready Hubs by engaging, leveraging, marshaling, and mobilizing resources to support the development of community-based enterprise learning. Notably, this meant engaging local entrepreneurs and businesses as well as enterprise stakeholders, such as the local chambers of commerce and universities, with a view to developing capacity through three domains that built on the core activities of Rotherham Ready, namely (1) delivering enterprise and leadership training (2) facilitating community-based enterprise learning, and (3) creating an enterprise network.

Delivering enterprise and leadership training

There are two strands to delivering training to foster enterprise learning: the first in schools and the second across the wider community in Rotherham. The first training program was a three-day continuing professional development (CPD) program aimed at supporting teaching staff responsible for leading on enterprise. Initially, the attendees were representatives from each school nominated by the head teacher, although subsequently over 30 teachers and support staff attended the training. The program highlighted synergies between enterprise education and the statutory curriculum, and also considered how enterprise might be embedded. The core elements of the CPD program are shown in Table 1. The program begins with an introduction to enterprise education and Ready Hubs before highlighting the importance of making links to business and the wider community. The two key aims of the CPD training are to raise awareness and support the design and planning of enterprise education within and across the Ready Hub schools. In addition to the training itself, the CPD event is important in creating a peer network of participating teachers and teaching assistants to promote good practice in enterprise learning by sharing knowledge and experience.

The second training program established through the Ready Hubs was the community leadership course (CLC). The CLC was established to promote and support community engagement in Ready Hubs, by empowering participants to support and develop enterprise education for young people and the community. The program was delivered as four sessions of three hours with the aim to raise participants' awareness of and enhance their personal and professional transferable skills. As shown in Table 2, the CLC program aims to provide participants with the key skills and competencies to be effective advocates, champions, and mentors in developing more enterprising communities.

The CLC is intended to empower members of the wider community to get involved in supporting community-based enterprise learning in different ways. Central to this is recognizing and valuing the respective contributions of volunteers, and empowering them as enterprise leaders. This is a key aim of the CLC, which connects them with existing enterprising activities (see below) or supports them to pursue their own projects, enhancing the capacity of the Ready Hubs. Of the three cohorts of the CLC program completed to date, one group of volunteers has gone on to set up an after-school enterprise club with the support of the Ready Hub, while others have supported the various activities described below. One participant in the CLC who went on to volunteer has since embarked on a career change as an enterprise and personal development trainer and continues to volunteer through the Ready Hub while running her own business.

Together, those who have completed the three-day CPD in schools and the community volunteers who have completed the CLC represent important ambassadors for the Ready Hubs. Not only are they important in facilitating community-based enterprise learning, they represent the core of the Ready Hub network as discussed below.

Table 1. Overview of the CPD program.

Day 1	Day 2	Day 3
• Introduction to enterprise education pedagogy • Ready Hubs introduction to co-producing enterprise • Team building and sharing current practice • Action planning (practical elements such as meeting dates, agendas, needs)	• Why does enterprise education matter • What enterprise education exists • Linking enterprise education with local business and communities • The future of enterprise education – long-term aims • Action planning (practical elements such as meeting dates, agendas, needs)	• Enterprise learning for school effectiveness and performance • Designing Ready Hubs goals – presentation and facilitated discussion • Action planning and setting medium- and long-term goal

Table 2. Key skills and competencies covered in the CLC.

• Understanding Ready Hubs (introduction)	• Listening skills
• Confidence building	• Good time management
• How to work with young people	• Making a difference
• Understanding community needs	• Conflict resolution
• Safeguarding and risk assessment	• Teamwork
• Effective communication	• Inclusion and inclusive working

Facilitating community-based enterprise learning

Originally, Rotherham Ready developed a range of enterprise learning resources for use in schools intended to make embedding enterprise into the curriculum more accessible and straightforward. The creation of the Ready Hubs has seen a series of new activities developed and introduced to enhance the enterprise entitlement and promote engagement with the learning communities through the Ready Hubs. The core enterprise-based learning activities summarized in Table 3 describe the activity, the beneficiaries, and the stakeholders involved. As Table 3 shows, the intention has been to engage young people through schools as well as their families and the wider community. All of the activities are non-curricular, although there is scope to integrate them with enterprise learning in the classroom with different areas of the curriculum for students. Indeed, a number of teachers and students referred to writing articles for the student magazine in English lessons and creating visuals for the magazine in art lessons.

In addition to the core program, a series of further enterprise activities was developed in partnership between the Ready Hub and members of the Ready Hub community (i.e. teachers, parents, volunteers, etc.). These co-produced enterprising activities include a number of student-led initiatives, some of which are school-specific activities (i.e. a student cinema club), while others have been developed across different schools within a learning community (i.e. funding and producing an enterprise-focused student magazine). There have been activities established through the Ready Hubs where young people are not direct beneficiaries, such as the Fair Share Social Enterprise Group, which was created by former members of the CLC to support other members of the community with an interest in developing a social enterprise. These activities are premised around embedded enterprise skills and entrepreneurial learning for the different beneficiaries to develop Rotherham as a more enterprising community. There is also some evidence of stakeholders and partners leading different activities, which we refer to as self-organized, although these activities are in the minority at this point. The two main self-organized activities are (1) the creation of a peer network of teachers and teaching assistants to undertake cross-school enterprise planning meetings and share good practice in supporting the enterprise entitlement and (2) the student cinema club established by young people for their fellow students and families. These self-organized activities represent an important phase in the development of Ready Hubs, as those involve taking a lead in organizing and undertaking activities without the support of the Ready Hub coordinator.

The core, co-produced, and self-organized activities comprising the portfolio of Ready Hub activities shown in Table 3 assume different formats, although all shared values around action and practice learning. For example, "Make £5 Blossom" is an action learning-based activity that seeks to engage participants in real-world projects and challenges. As a part of Make £5 Blossom, the participants were loaned start-up capital and mentored in groups with the goal of establishing a return themselves. This

Table 3. Ready hub activities (beneficiaries and stakeholders).

Activity Name		Nature of Activity	Beneficiaries (Benefit)	Supporting Stakeholders/Partners (Contribution)
Make £5 Blossom	Core	A venture-based learning activity in which each child/group of children is given a loan of £150 to pursue an enterprising activity and work to turn a profit on the original investment before paying back the loan	• Young people (enterprising skills) • Initial Teacher Training students (work experience) • Regional University (placing students) • Schools (embedding enterprise)	• CLC Volunteers (mentoring) • Initial Teacher Training students (facilitating and mentoring) • Local businesses (loan capital) • Local entrepreneurs/business owners (mentoring) • Regional University (placing students) • Rotherham Ready (facilitate and support schools) • Schools (facilitating)
Family Money Tree	Core	A 5-week-long activity which brings parents/carers and schoolchildren together and engages them in an enterprising activities – including conducting market research, product development, and making sales	• Young people (enterprising skills) • Families (enterprising skills)	• CLC Volunteers (facilitating) • Rotherham Ready (facilitating and admin support) • Schools and Children's Centers (host venue)
Enterprise Market	Core	Planning and producing a range of activities and products for sale at the event hosted by Ready Hub schools as a part of Rotherham Children's Festival	• Young people (enterprising skills) • Families (enterprising skills) • Local Community (attending event)	• CLC Volunteers (facilitate and event support) • Local businesses (support) • Local Council (promotion and event management) • Ready Hub (facilitating and admin support) • Schools (facilitating)

Enterprise-focused student magazine	Co-produced	Across six Ready Hub schools, a student-led magazine is coordinated centrally by young people at the secondary and primaries. It is contributed by children across the RH schools	• Young people (enterprising skills) • Schools (developing child literacy, embedding enterprise)	• High-achieving students (inspiration/leadership) • Local businesses (purchase advertising space) • Local Journalists (critical friend/mentor) • Ready Hub (supervising)
Enterprise bridging placements	Co-produced	A 10-week summer placement for school leavers interested in a career in retail	• Young People (work experience) • Retail stores (work experience) • School (enhanced capacity)	• Retailers (Hosting placement student) • Rotherham Ready (facilitating and admin support) • Teachers/Teaching assistants (supervising)
Parents Enterprise Forum	Co-produced	A parent–teacher forum was established to support the development of enterprise-led extracurricular activities as well as promoting better parent–teacher communication	• Young people (enterprising skills) • Schools (embedding enterprise)	• Parents (championing enterprise/ representing parent interest) • Community members (setting up social • Teachers/Teaching assistants (coordinating) • Ready Hub (facilitating and admin support) • Schools (facilitating)
After-School Enterprise Club	Co-produced	A parent that attended the CLC program set up an after-school and lunch time enterprise club	• Young people (enterprising skills) • Schools (enhanced capacity, embedded enterprise) • Parents (after-school care provision)	• CLC Volunteer (supervising) • Ready Hub (facilitate and support event) • School (host venue) • Teachers/Teaching assistants (supervising)

(*Continued*)

Table 3. (*Continued*).

Activity Name		Nature of Activity	Beneficiaries (Benefit)	Supporting Stakeholders/Partners (Contribution)
Fair Share Social Enterprise Group	Co-produced	A group that met to support parents and members of the community interested in setting up a social enterprise	• Parents (setting up social enterprises) • Community members (setting up social enterprises)	• Parents (championing social enterprise) • Ready Hub (facilitate and support event) • School (host venue) Regional University (advisory)
Enterprise Teaching Group	Self-Organized	Peer-learning network to share good practice in embedding enterprise	• Teachers/Teaching assistants (sharing good practice) • Schools (enhanced capacity)	• Teachers/Teaching assistants (coordinating)
Enterprise placement students	Self-Organized	Placements for university students in Ready Hub schools to support enterprise	• Initial Teacher Training students (work experience) • Schools (enhanced capacity) • Regional University (placing students)	• Regional University (placing students) • Schools (Hosting placement student)
Student Cinema Club	Self-Organized	Year 9 pupils set up and delivered an after-school cinema club	• Young people (attendees) • Families (attendees) • Young people running cinema (enterprising skills) • Primary Schools (social activity)	• Parents (supervising) • Schools (facilitating and hosting) • Teachers (supervising) • Young people running cinema (coordinator)

activity supports developing enterprising and entrepreneurial skills, as well as team working and problem-solving skills. Through the Ready Hub schools, the Make £5 Blossom activity provided learning that would not have otherwise been available to participating students. Another example is the peer-learning facilitated through the Enterprise Teaching Group, which the participants found to be an effective way of sharing ideas and consequently increasing the motivation of teachers and teaching assistants to participate. By embedding enterprise in this way, enterprise has been incorporated into lesson planning in a way that would not have otherwise been the case unless it was a statutory part of the curriculum.

Beyond the classroom, the same action learning approach has been critical to the success and take-up of activities through the Ready Hubs that have supported community-based enterprise learning. The commitment of local retailers and Ready Hub schools to develop a 10-week summer placement for school students interested in a career in retail has been successful in developing enterprise skills and employability. Such practice placements provide a way for learners to gain relevant real-world experience with continuous feedback as opposed to simply undertaking classroom-based tasks. This and other activities, such as the student magazine, provide valuable opportunities to enhance the development of enterprising skills, as they are purposeful. In summary, the activities delivered and facilitated through the Ready Hubs provide what McGill and Beaty (1995, p. 21) describe as "a continuous process of learning and reflection … with the intention of getting things done," or otherwise serve to support such activities.

Creating an enterprise network

In addition to the CPD and enterprise learning activities delivered by the Ready Hubs, they have also sought to build a network of partners and stakeholders. The Ready Hub coordinator has been instrumental in setting up, facilitating, and supporting many of the different enterprise learning and CPD activities. An important aspect of this has been engaging a range of stakeholders, starting with the peer network of teaching staff involved at the Ready Hub schools, and community volunteers who had completed the CPD activities. Through the school-based activities, a number of participating parents became affiliated with Ready Hubs, presenting in the schools about their experiences in enterprise or as entrepreneurs. At the same time, the Ready Hub coordinator was critical in engaging a wider range of entrepreneurs, businesses, and enterprise stakeholders to support the enterprise entitlement through their involvement. In some instances, this was in the form of funding (e.g. for the Make £5 Blossom initiative) and infrastructure (e.g. the venue for the enterprise market), while other entrepreneurs, businesses, and enterprise stakeholders provided mentoring and in-kind support. Partnerships were also developed with regional universities, establishing student placements in schools that are part of the Ready Hubs with an enterprising focus and working with enterprise educators to develop funding proposals with other community-based enterprise programs.

The strategy to engage partners and develop a network has therefore in one sense been a success. Indeed, Table 3 shows the number of stakeholders and partners involved in supporting the various enterprising activities. However, beyond the existence of the network, there is a need to consider the nature of involvement and commitment of the members of the network to the Ready Hubs. While there has been a willingness to support the enterprise entitlement in Rotherham, it has proved more difficult to engage stakeholders in developing the Ready Hubs and to take responsibility for leading the different enterprising activities. Arguably the biggest challenge for the Ready Hubs has been to engender greater commitment and a sense of ownership beyond the activities themselves, which is ultimately necessary in order to sustain and scale their activities. While Ready Hubs have sought to engage partners through steering groups, town hall style forums as well as direct approaches, they have not as yet galvanized the network. Given that Ready Hubs were only recently established, this is somewhat understandable. However, it also highlights the need to develop an identity and values around fostering community-based enterprise learning which partners and stakeholders both relate to and are invested. It is the ability to establish a strong identity and sense of shared values which marks the difference between the existence of an informal network and the creation of a community of practice. If Ready Hubs can foster a stronger identity and sense of purpose around community-based enterprise learning, it is more likely to engender commitment to the community as a whole as opposed to a few partners and stakeholders linked to individual activities, as is currently the case.

A sustainable model through active engagement

Since the formation of Ready Hubs in 2012, they have served to increase the critical mass of enterprising activities in Rotherham. Unequivocally, Ready Hubs have been facilitated by the coordinator, who has supported a growing range of activities as well as enrolling a wider network of participants and stakeholders. Over a comparatively short period this represents a significant achievement, yet the coordinator-led model is not sustainable in the absence of funding from NESTA and the LGA. Given the limited resources available for coordinating Ready Hubs, securing a leadership commitment from partners and stakeholders is necessary to ensure their impact and longevity. Therefore, the challenge facing Ready Hubs is to sustain these achievements, by reflecting on the underlying model to promote, support, deliver, and ultimately (co-)lead community-based enterprise learning.

The coordinator has performed an integral role in facilitating the different training and enterprise learning activities as well as serving as a hub for the network of stakeholders. However, as funding awarded by NESTA and the LGA enabled the appointment of the coordinator comes to an end, Ready Hubs need to become self-sustaining if they are to build on their current achievements. While some grant funding is awarded to projects on a one-off basis, the Creative Councils funding was awarded to develop the scale and scope of Rotherham Ready's activities with the creation of Ready Hubs. The expectation, therefore, is that the Ready Hubs would continue after the original awards were expended.

As exemplified in the discussion above, Ready Hubs have developed an extended network although this has not yet evolved to become a functional community of practice. Whereas communities of practice are mostly self-sufficient, the current Ready Hubs network is not yet sufficiently engaged or proactive to be self-sustaining. Encouraging partners and stakeholders to become more actively engaged is critical to the sustainability of Ready Hubs, as communities of practice typically develop around things that matter to those involved. For this reason, it is imperative that the Ready Hubs can clearly articulate what they do and why it matters. It is also important that partners and stakeholders both see how their contribution matters and appreciate why the development of Rotherham as a more enterprising place is beneficial.

Having built the network, the challenge facing Ready Hubs is to move beyond a set of relationships to increase engagement and commitment of the both the stakeholders and beneficiaries. The critical next step in forging what Wenger (1998) describes as an active community of practice is to see the stakeholders and beneficiaries taking ownership and lead in the activities. This is where a strong shared vision and common values about the virtues of communities are more likely to galvanize those engaged with the Ready Hubs, which in turn is likely to increase their impact in terms of supporting community-based enterprise learning. To achieve this, the Ready Hubs can be seen to have various stages of development characterized by different levels of interaction among the members as well as a range of activities.

Understanding and fostering engagement is important to developing a (more) active community of practice as a means of sustaining the Ready Hub model. Table 4 provides an overview of the different levels of engagement that stakeholders/partners and beneficiaries/participants can encounter as they become more active in the Ready Hubs. The first critical step in sustaining Ready Hubs is to connect with and engage different stakeholders/partners and beneficiaries/participants. This is an awareness raising exercise, but more than that, it is about getting others to recognize the importance of developing Rotherham as a more enterprising place by supporting community-based enterprise learning. The benefits of creating more enterprising places are well documented (Audretsch, 2003). However, mustering the support and input of individuals and organizations who are not necessarily likely to benefit directly from their participation in Ready Hubs-specific activities makes the case for support more difficult. For Rotherham, the school-centered Ready Hubs, with their emphasis on young people, families, and the wider community, along with the backing of RMBC represented important aspects of getting buy-in external partner. Likewise, the Ready Hubs needed to be of interest to the different groups they seek to engage, while retaining a central focus on making the participant more enterprising and Rotherham a more enterprising place.

As shown in the Table 4, the first level of engagement is often indirect or passive. In practice, this means that stakeholders and partners may contribute in the form of financial support such as that for Make £5 Blossom. Other forms of in-kind support offered included the use of venues as well as providing access to promotional materials, printing, and other resources. As acknowledged by the Ready Hub coordinator and Rotherham Ready management team, such contributions are essential to developing the capacity and capabilities of Ready Hubs. However, those partners and stakeholders contributing in this way are often not directly involved with or privy to the range of community-based enterprise learning activities. Increasing the engagement of these partners and stakeholders represents an important aspect of growing the community of practice by getting them more active and directly involved in supporting community-based enterprise learning.

To achieve this, the Ready Hub coordinator has performed an important role as an intermediary in supporting the emerging community of practice, by sharing information about the importance and value of the contribution and the difference it makes. For example, getting sponsors to share their experience or act as judges on particular activities can be an important stepping-stone to them becoming more involved in the future. Ultimately, it is about fostering greater understanding of the community of practice and engendering a genuine commitment to community-based enterprise learning, while recognizing the value of their common endeavors. Indeed, the same principle applies to all those participating in the community-based enterprise learning activities. By increasing the interest and engagement of participants, they are more likely to become committed to Ready Hubs, and act as advocates and ambassadors of community-based enterprise learning in the future. Akin to this, there have also been a number of parents who initially accompanied their child, but have since gone on to assume an active role in supporting and facilitating different community-based enterprise learning activities.

Table 4. Levels of engagement in ready hubs.

Level of Engagement	Stakeholders/Partners		Beneficiary/Participant	
	Description	Example	Description	Example
Leader/ Champion	Assumes an active role in the leadership of Ready Hubs as well as developing Ready Hub activities; Activities led by the stakeholders or partner with little or no direct support from the Ready Hub coordinator	• Teachers organizing a peer network focused on enterprise education	Advocate for Ready Hub activities who actively engages others and also benefits through their own participation	• Young people actively promoting (championing) the Ready Hubs to others • The student cinema club established by young people for young people
Active/Direct Engagement	Coordinates activities with a leading role in delivery/facilitation; Activities co-led by stakeholders or partner with support from the Ready Hub coordinator	• The Fair Share Social Enterprise Group was created by former members of the CLC supported by the regional university and Ready Hub • The local journalists acting as mentors to the student magazine	Active participant in Ready Hub activities who also benefits through their own participation.	• Parents supporting the afterschool club with an enterprise focus • Taking the lead in organizing peer activities such as the student magazine
Passive/ Indirect Engagement	Contribute to Ready Hub activities indirectly or have a background/secondary role in delivery/ facilitation; Activities led by the Ready Hub coordinator	• Providing capital funding to students for the "Making £5 Blossom" challenge	Attends Ready Hub activities although engagement is peripheral	• Young people and families attending Family Money Tree events on a weekly basis
None	Pre engagement		Pre participation	

As well as increasing the level of engagement of those stakeholders and participants, the Ready Hubs have also attracted a growing number of partners who are actively engaged. The CPD and CLC have provided an important means of engaging participants to become involved in Ready Hubs. For teachers, the CPD program represented an important step in understanding enterprise education and becoming more engaged with Ready Hubs as enterprise educators. Similarly, the CLC brought together like-minded and engaged members of the community with an interest in enterprise and/or an interest in supporting community-based enterprise learning. The strategy of Ready Hubs has increasingly been one of "co-production," which Boyle and Harris (2009) assert can be more effective in fostering change and ultimately, in this case, the uptake of community-based enterprise learning. In co-producing many of the activities, the Ready Hubs have served critical roles in maintaining the cohesion of the community of practice as it has developed. In particular, the Ready Hub coordinator has performed an integral role in forging the makings of a community of practice by fostering the vision and values associated with community-based enterprise learning.

Arguably, the success of Ready Hubs in nurturing a community of practice to this point can be attributed to the ability of the Ready Hub coordinator, who has been central in enrolling and securing the buy-in and contribution of different stakeholders. However, the sustainability of Ready Hubs now depends on identifying how existing activities relate to the shared values of the stakeholders as well as meeting the needs (and wants) of participants. As the vision around community-based enterprise learning, originally upheld by Ready Hubs, is negotiated and consolidated, so it becomes more embedded. The prevailing commitment to mutual engagement with a mutual understanding is critical to partners and participants becoming leaders and champions within the Ready Hubs, as shown in Table 4. In keeping with Malhotra (2000), the success of Ready Hub depends on sharing if not shifting the locus of control to stakeholders and partners. With no single obvious (or willing) leader among the existing stakeholders, as is often the case in communities of practice, then a more distributed form of leadership is appropriate (Gronn, 2002; Spillane, 2005). Over a comparatively short period, the Ready Hubs have seen a number of possible leaders and champions emerge, although this has not yet resulted in those members of the community taking responsibility for the organization of enterprise learning independently of the Ready Hub.

Ready Hubs have evolved from simply being an organizational vehicle to become the basis of a community of practice, with shared values around community-based enterprise. As the shared values become stronger and clearer, stakeholders and partners are more likely to commit and sustain their activities, which in turn is more likely to increase the on-the-ground impact and longevity of community-based enterprise learning. Clearly this takes time, but Love and Ellis (2009) also highlight the importance of what they term "champions of practice," who are members of the community who work across organizational boundaries to examine and support specific community-based enterprise learning projects and activities.

The empirical project has highlighted that stakeholders are beginning to demonstrate increased commitment to Ready Hubs, with a shared vision and common values around the importance of community-based enterprise learning. For the objectives of Ready Hubs to become self-sustaining, the community of practice needs to be consolidated. However, as Fallah (2011) asserts, this cannot happen by decree but demands substantial effort in this case from the Ready Hub coordinator as the formal leader. An important aspect of this effort is in affirming the legitimacy of the stakeholders and their activities as a part of the community of practice. In this way, those stakeholders and partners involved have come to assume more active roles in the leadership of Ready Hubs at different times and in different situations. While substantial progress has been made, Ready Hubs are not in a position to be sustained by the activities of partners and beneficiaries alone.

Conclusions

Building on the foundation of Rotherham Ready, the creation of Ready Hubs sought to create a step change in developing community-based enterprise learning. The intention of the Ready Hubs was to serve as the focal point for a more comprehensive and inclusive form of enterprise education, delivered through a community of practice. Over a comparatively short period, and facilitated by the Ready Hub coordinator, a portfolio of community-based enterprise activities have developed, which are supported by a growing range of stakeholders. While the funding awarded by NESTA and the LGA under the Creative Council's program has been a catalyst to the achievements of Ready Hubs, the real challenge is in sustaining the legacy. There is evidence of an emerging community of practice, although this is not sufficiently mature to be self-sustaining. The Ready Hub coordinator has served an important form of leadership in the formative stage, as well as providing the structure and management for other partners who have supported community enterprise learning activities. That being said, there are a number of community members who have become more engaged and taken on greater leadership and ownership of specific learning activities. However, although Ready Hubs have not yet become self-sustaining, they have shown the potential to do so. Now that Ready Hubs have reached the end of their funding period, as an interim measure, the local authority (RMBC) has continued to provide limited financial support. In keeping with the objective of the Creative Council's funding and the long-standing strategy of Rotherham Ready, the intention remains for Ready Hubs to establish themselves as a self-sustaining model of community-based enterprise learning.

Developing a community of practice around enterprise learning takes time. However, in fostering community-based enterprise learning, there are three lessons that can be distilled from the experience of Ready Hubs that are relevant both within the UK and beyond. First, the importance of a strong identity, clear purpose, and shared values are critical to developing a community of practice. While Rotherham Ready established the original vision for the Ready Hubs, this has necessarily come to be negotiated as more partners and stakeholders have become involved. This also highlights the importance of the Ready Hub coordinator in establishing and brokering the foundations to foster the community of practice by ensuring the community is sufficiently balanced and focused. Second, while Ready Hubs have been effective in enrolling stakeholders, the challenge has been in increasing the engagement. Recognizing the contributions of those involved is important in terms of their own legitimization and the strength of the community as a whole. The number of co-produced and increasingly self-organized community-based enterprise learning activities is testament to this. However, this is not a process that can be forced, with members of the community of practice needing time to find their place. As such, sufficient time is required to allow this to occur. Third, as well as developing a more negotiated and co-produced model of community-based enterprise learning, there is a need to develop a more distributed form of leadership. Extending the responsibility for leadership beyond the Ready Hub coordinator means looking to others who have an intrinsic legitimacy in the community. Therefore, developing future leaders needs to be a priority, as it is only in this way that the onus on the Ready Hub coordinator will be reduced and the community of practice become self-organizing.

This article has highlighted Ready Hubs as a new model of community-based enterprise learning as well as the challenges associated with securing the sustainability of such a model. At the core of the Ready Hub model recognizes the variety and breadth of enterprise learning opportunities that span the pedagogic portfolio (see Neck & Greene, 2011). While Ready Hubs have been primarily aimed at developing the enterprise skills of young people, the importance of engaging families and the wider community has been a key aspect of the Ready Hub model. In this context, the core purpose of the Ready Hubs has been to empower communities to find resources and make connections in partnership with them as opposed to on their behalf. In this way, Ready Hubs and the activities of Rotherham Ready serve an important role in brokering a better social and economic future by transforming lives through enterprise. The lessons from the case study provide insights about the process of establishing and sustaining community of practice for others interested in community-based enterprise learning. In countries where enterprise education is not statutory, the study highlights the value of engaging the wider community, as enterprise education is not confined to schools and classrooms. The community approach has brought together a range of organizations and individuals who share common values about the importance of fostering enterprise in their local community, the benefits of which will be reaped by those engaged as well as the local economy more generally. Although the future sustainability of such Hubs remains to be seen, they have been successful in creating the foundations of an effective community of practice, and if this article encourages further exploration of community-based enterprise learning in other locations around the world, then it will have achieved its objective.

Disclosure statement

No potential conflict of interest was reported by the authors.

References

Acs, Z. J. (2006). How is entrepreneurship good for economic growth? *Innovations: Technology, Governance, Globalization, 1*, 97–107.

Acs, Z. J., Desai, S., & Hessels, J. (2008). Entrepreneurship, economic development and institutions. *Small Business Economics, 31*, 219–234.

Anderson, R. (2002). Entrepreneurship and aboriginal Canadians: A case study in economic development. *Journal of Development Entrepreneurship, 7*, 45–66.

Athayde, R. (2009). Measuring enterprise potential in young people. *Entrepreneurship Theory and Practice, 33*, 481–500.

Audretsch, D. (2003). Entrepreneurship policy and the strategic management of places. In D. M. Hart (Ed.), *The emergence of entrepreneurship policy: Governance, start-ups, and growth* (pp. 20–38). Cambridge: Cambridge University Press.

Bonk, C. J., Wisher, R., & Nigrelli, M. (2004). Learning communities, communities of practices: Principles, technologies and examples. In K. Littlton, D. Miell, & D. Faulkner (Eds.), *Learning to collaborate* (pp. 199–219). Hauppage, NY: Nova Science.

Bosma, N., & Levie, J. (2009). *Global entrepreneurship monitor: 2009 global report.* London: Global Entrepreneurship Monitor Consortium.

Boyle, D., & Harris, T. (2009). *The challenge of co-production.* London: NESTA.

Department for Business, Innovation and Skills. (2014). *Enterprise for all: The relevance of enterprise in education.* London: BIS.

Department for Education and Skills. (2002). *Davies review: A review of enterprise and the economy in education*. London: HMSO.

Edelman, L. F., Manolova, T. S., & Brush, C. G. (2008). Entrepreneurship education: Correspondence practices of nascent entrepreneurs and textbook prescriptions for success. *Academy of Management Learning and Education, 7*, 56–70.

Fallah, N. (2011). Distributed form of leadership in communities of practice (CoPs). *International Journal of Emerging Sciences, 1*, 357–370.

Gibb, A. A. (1993). The enterprise culture and education. *International Small Business Journal, 11*, 11–34.

Gibb, A. A. (2000). SME policy, academic research and the growth of ignorance, mythical concepts, myths, assumptions, rituals and confusions. *International Small Business Journal, 18*, 13–35.

Gibb, A. A. (2002). Creating conducive environments for learning and entrepreneurship; living with, dealing with, creating and enjoying uncertainty and complexity. *Industry and Higher Education, 16*, 135–148.

Granovetter, M. (1989). *Entrepreneurship, development and the emergence of the firms*. Wissenschaftszentreum Berlin: Sozialforschung and State University of New York.

Greenwood, D. J., Whyte, W. F., & Harkavy, I. (1993). Participatory action research as a process and as a goal. *Human Relations, 46*, 175–192.

Gronn, P. (2002). Distributed leadership as a unit of analysis. *The Leadership Quarterly, 13*, 423–451.

Harrison, R., & Leitch, C. (2000). Learning and organization in the knowledge-based information economy: Initial findings from a participatory action research case study. *British Journal of Management, 11*, 103–119.

Henry, C., Hill, F., & Leitch, C. (2003). Developing a coherent enterprise support policy: A new challenge for governments. *Environment and Planning C: Government and Policy, 21*, 3–19.

Henry, N., Medhurst, J., & Lyttle, J. (2005). *Review of the social enterprise strategy*. London: GHK Consulting.

HM Treasury. (2002). *Enterprise Britain: A modern approach to meeting the enterprise challenge*. London: HM Treasury. Retrieved from http://www.hm-treasury.gov.uk/d/adentbrit02part1-373 kb.pdf

HM Treasury. (2004). *Creating an enterprise culture: Discussion paper advancing enterprise, Britain in a global economy*. London: HM Treasury. Retrieved from http://www.hm-treasury.gov.uk/d/ent_paper_0104.pdf

HM Treasury. (2008a). *Enterprise: Unlocking the UK's talent*. London: HM Treasury. Retrieved from http://www.berr.gov.uk/files/file44992.pdf

HM Treasury. (2008b). *Budget 2008: Stability and opportunity*. London: HM Treasury. Retrieved from http://www.hm-treasury.gov.uk/d/bud08_completereport.pdf

Hofstede, G. (1980). *Culture's consequences: International differences in work-related values*. Beverly Hills, CA: Sage.

Hofstede, G. (1991). *Cultures and organizations: Software of the mind*. London: McGraw-Hill.

Holt, D. H. (1997). A comparative study of values among Chinese and U.S. entrepreneurs: Pragmatic convergence between contrasting cultures. *Journal of Business Venturing, 12*, 483–505.

Huggins, R., & Williams, N. (2009). Enterprise and public policy: A review of labour government intervention in the United Kingdom. *Environment and Planning C: Government and Policy, 27*, 19–41.

Jack, S. L., & Anderson, A. R. (1999). Entrepreneurship education within the enterprise culture: Producing reflective practitioners. *International Journal of Entrepreneurial Behaviour & Research, 5*, 110–125.

Johannisson, B., & Monsted, M. (1997). Contextualizing entrepreneurial networking. *International Studies of Management & Organization, 27*, 109–137.

Jones, B., & Iredale, N. (2010). Enterprise education as pedagogy. *Education + Training, 52*, 7–19.

Kirzner, I. M. (1973). *Competition and entrepreneurship*. Chicago, IL: University of Chicago Press.

Love, P., & Ellis, J. (2009). *Knowledge sharing, learning and situated practice: Communities of practice for projects*. European and Mediterranean Conference on Information Systems, 2009 (EMCIS2009). July 13–14, Imzir.

Malhotra, Y. (2000). Role of organizational controls in knowledge management: Is knowledge management really an "oxymoron"? In D. White (Ed.), *Knowledge mapping and management* (pp. 1–13). Hershey: Idea Group.

McGill, I., & Beaty, L. (1995). *Action learning*. London: Kogan Page.

Neck, H. M., & Greene, P. G. (2011). Entrepreneurship education: Known worlds and new frontiers. *Journal of Small Business Management, 49*, 55–70.

OFSTED. (2011). *Economics, business and enterprise education, a summary of inspection evidence April 2007 to March 2010*. London: Ofsted.

Peredo, A. M., & Chrisman, J. J. (2006). Toward a theory of community-based enterprise. *Academy of Management Review, 31*, 309–328.

Peterson, R. (1988). Understanding and encouraging entrepreneurship internationally. *Journal of Small Business Management, 26*, 1–8.

Ram, M., Edwards, P., Jones, T., Kiselinchev, A., & Muchenje, L. (2014). Getting your hands dirty: Critical action research in a state agency. *Work Employment & Society, 29*, 462–478.

Rappaport, N., Alegria, M., Mulvaney-Day, N., & Boyle, B. (2008). Staying at the table: Building sustainable community–research partnerships. *Journal of Community Psychology, 36*, 693–701.

Ronstadt, R. (1990). The educated entrepreneurs: A new era of entrepreneurial education is beginning. *American Journal of Small Business, 11*, 37–53.

Sautet, F., & Kirzner, I. (2006). *The nature and role of entrepreneurship in markets: Implications for policy*. Policy Primer No. 4, Mercatus Policy Series. Fairfax, VA: George Mason University.

Sayer, A. (2000). *Realism and social science*. London: Sage.

Spillane, J. (2005). Distributed leadership. *The Educational Forum, 69*, 143–150.

Swedberg, R. (1997). New economic sociology: What has been accomplished, what is ahead? *Acta Sociologica, 40*, 161–182.

Vesper, K., & Gartner, W. (1997). Measuring progress in entrepreneurship education. *Journal of Business Venturing, 12*, 403–421.

Volkmann, C., Wilson, K. E., Mariotti, S., Rabuzzi, D., Vyakarnam, S., & Sepulveda, A. (2009). *Educating the next wave of entrepreneurs: Unlocking entrepreneurial capabilities to meet the global challenges of the 21st century*. Geneva: World Economic Forum.

Wenger, E. (1998). *Communities of practice: Learning, meaning, and identity*. Cambridge: Cambridge University Press.

Williams, L. K., & McGuire, S. J. (2010). Economic creativity and innovation implementation: The entrepreneurial drivers of growth? Evidence from 63 countries. *Small Business Economics, 34*, 391–412.

Williams, N., & Vorley, T. (2014). Institutional asymmetry: How formal and informal institutions affect entrepreneurship in Bulgaria. *International Small Business Journal*. doi:10.1177/0266242614534280

Williams, N., & Williams, C. C. (2011). Tackling barriers to entrepreneurship in a deprived urban neighbourhood. *Local Economy, 26*, 30–42.

Wright, M., & Marlow, S. (2011). Entrepreneurial activity in the venture creation and development process. *International Small Business Journal, 30*, 107–114.

Wright, M., & Stigliani, I. (2013). Entrepreneurship and growth. *International Small Business Journal, 31*, 3–22.

Yu, T. F.-L. (2001). Entrepreneurial alertness and discovery. *The Review of Austrian Economics, 14*, 47–63.

Creating entrepreneurial communities: building community capacity for ecosystem development

Deborah M. Markley, Thomas S. Lyons and Donald W. Macke

Research on the economic impact of entrepreneurship makes the case for entrepreneur-focused economic development. Community economic development practitioners and policy-makers face the challenge of identifying and implementing the most promising strategies. Some community development researchers have argued effectively for an entrepreneurial development system, or ecosystem, approach as a way to build and grow a pipeline of entrepreneurial talent. Others document the importance of building community capacity as a prerequisite for the establishment of an effective ecosystem. This paper draws on field-based learning, primarily in Kansas and Australia, to develop the conceptual underpinnings for an approach to creating entrepreneurial communities that builds: (1) the capacity of the community to host and support an entrepreneurial ecosystem and (2) the capacity of entrepreneurs to grow themselves and their businesses in support of community economic development.

Introduction

Building a community's capacity to engage in entrepreneur-focused economic development in combination with a systems approach to developing entrepreneurs creates more sustainable community economic development outcomes. This notion recognizes that entrepreneur development is a place-based activity and that the community is an active participant in establishing the community milieu within which the development of entrepreneurial talent takes place.

Current approaches tend to be fragmented; the rationale for taking a more systems approach to entrepreneurial development arises from this failure and addresses the problem by providing a bridge between a business development approach, focusing exclusively on agency (the individual entrepreneur) and a community development approach that focuses on context (place) (Lichtenstein & Lyons, 2001). In this article, such a systems approach provides a bridge between a business development approach that focuses exclusively on agency (the individual entrepreneur) and a community development approach that focuses on context (place). We argue that a focus on both agency *and* context (individual entrepreneurship *and* community entrepreneurship) is needed (Granovetter, 1985). In this way, we present a theory of entrepreneurial community building that connects community development practice with entrepreneur development practice in an integrative and reinforcing way. The current and future development of such a systems approach should provide a valuable tool for both community and economic development practitioners.

The rest of this section further develops the systemic frame, defines "entrepreneurship" as we use it in this paper, and discusses its role as a development strategy. We then make the case for the importance of place in economic development. Subsequently, we will discuss the methodology we employ in exploring the components of a system that integrates community and entrepreneur capacity building and share the results of our field studies. We conclude by offering a set of research and policy questions raised by this work.

Building the systemic frame

A significant body of research on the economic impact of entrepreneurship indicates a growing awareness of the importance of entrepreneur-focused economic development (Acs & Armington, 2004; Fritsch & Mueller, 2008; Hafer, 2013). From the perspective of community economic development practitioners and policy-makers, the question becomes one of identifying and implementing the most effective strategies to support entrepreneurs. Over the years, there have been several calls to pursue entrepreneur-focused economic development by taking a systems approach at the community or regional level (Emery & Flora, 2006; Feldman, 1994; Flora, Sharp, Flora, & Newlon, 1997; Korsching & Allen, 2004; Lichtenstein & Lyons, 2006, 2010; Lichtenstein, Lyons, & Kutzhanova, 2004; Lyons, 2002b). These prescriptions assert that successful enterprise development must take into account the entire community and build the necessary capacity to foster entrepreneurship across that community.

How such a systems approach to encouraging entrepreneurial activity should manifest itself is not entirely clear. There appears to be a bifurcation in approach, wherein some practitioners and scholars take a business development perspective, while others are community development focused. The approaches of Lichtenstein and Lyons (2001) and Macke, Markley, and Fulwider (2014) represent this split.

Lichtenstein and Lyons (2001) have effectively argued that entrepreneur-focused economic development requires creation of an entrepreneurial service system, or support ecosystem, which is systemic, focused on the needs of the entrepreneur not the business, and committed to transforming the entrepreneur and the community. This ecosystem, however, is place-based and rooted in a particular community's environment. Thus, the capacity of the community to engage in ecosystem building may prove to be a limiting factor in the effectiveness of such a strategy, particularly in more rural places where human, physical, and financial resources are fewer.

Macke et al. (2014) report on a decade of work focused on addressing the limiting factor of community capacity by working with communities to create the intellectual, social, cultural, and financial capital needed to support a robust system. This field-based learning documents the importance of leadership, collaborative networks, and financial and political support for entrepreneurship development. In light of this, Macke et al's framework and the entrepreneurial service system approach taken by Lichtenstein and Lyons (2001) have the potential to be mutually supportive and transformational for communities and the entrepreneurs they support.

This article will develop the conceptual underpinnings for an approach to creating entrepreneurial communities that builds (1) the capacity of the community to host and support an entrepreneurial ecosystem and (2) the capacity of entrepreneurs to grow themselves and their businesses in support of community economic development. Using action research conducted in rural Kansas and Australia, along with learning from larger, more metropolitan places, we will identify the key components of a community-based entrepreneurial development system (EDS) and describe both the strengths and challenges of taking a more holistic systems approach to entrepreneur-focused economic development.

Entrepreneurship as a development strategy

The term "entrepreneur" has been applied to a wide range of individuals, from small to large business owners who participate in a community's economy on both global and local scales (Aulet & Murray, 2013). Our definition encompasses a broad notion of entrepreneurs, and includes any person who applies an entrepreneurial mindset, tools, skills, and techniques to transform an idea into an enterprise that creates value for profit and/or social good.

The importance of entrepreneurs to the economic development of nations has been the subject of academic scholarship since economist Joseph Schumpeter published in the 1940s. In the last half century, Baumol (1990) has advanced understanding of the role of entrepreneurs in economic growth, challenging economists to recognize the entrepreneur's role in combining factors of production to achieve development. Eliasson and Henrekson (2003, pp. 8–9) summarize Baumol's argument in this way:

> The accumulation of factors of production per se – be they knowledge, physical or human capital – cannot alone explain economic development. They are necessary inputs in production, but they are not in themselves sufficient for economic growth to occur …
>
> Human creativity and productive entrepreneurship are needed to combine these inputs in profitable ways, and hence an institutional environment that encourages free entrepreneurship becomes the ultimate determinant of economic growth.

In addition to the entrepreneur, Baumol (1990) acknowledged the importance of the institutional environment as either supportive of or detrimental to the encouragement of entrepreneurship.

On a transnational level, the Global Entrepreneurship Monitor (GEM) project has provided detailed information on entrepreneurial activity since 1999 (www.gemconsortium.org). The project includes 100 country teams. Those countries cover most of the world's geography and account for most of the world's gross domestic product (GDP). GEM studies highlight differences in both the rate of entrepreneurial activity across countries and the character or quality of that activity. The 2012 report found that total entrepreneurial activity rates were higher in countries with low GDP per capita, but much of that activity was driven by necessity, such as the lack of other viable ways to earn a living. Rates were lower in high GDP per capita countries, but more of the activity was driven by the recognition and pursuit of an opportunity than by the necessity of earning a living (Xavier et al., 2012). More significantly for this article, the 2012 report (Xavier et al., 2012, p. 18) acknowledges the place-based and skill building dimensions of the entrepreneurial process:

> The entrepreneurship process is a complex endeavor carried out by people living in specific cultural and social conditions. Societies benefit from people who are able to recognise valuable business opportunities and who perceive they have the required skills to exploit them.

> If the economy in general has a positive attitude towards entrepreneurship, this can generate cultural and social support, financial and business assistance, and networking benefits that will encourage and facilitate potential and existing entrepreneurs.

More recently, the discussion about entrepreneurship as a development strategy has focused on the role of entrepreneurs as job creators, partially in response to the 2007–2009 Great Recession. Research advanced by the development of the Business Dynamics Series database offers useful insights into this role (http://www.census.gov/ces/dataproducts/bds/overview.html). Kane (2010) demonstrated the contribution that start-up firms make to job creation. Gross job creation associated with start-up firms from 1995 to 2005 was 3,000,000 jobs per year, as compared to 800,000 jobs created by firms in their first full year and 500,000 jobs created by firms in their third full year. This pattern was persistent over the years of this study. Kane concludes that "[E]ffective policy to promote employment growth must include a central consideration for startup firms" (Kane, 2010, p. 6). While not all of these start-ups are driven by entrepreneurs, they do define the pool from which entrepreneurial talent in a community or region may emerge.

Another recent study focused on the longer term trends related to job creation by new businesses and uncovered a new and discouraging trend. Using both US Census Bureau and Bureau of Economic Analysis data series, the authors found that employer firms, a subset of new firms that employ people beyond the owner/entrepreneur, are starting with fewer employees (an average of 7.5 jobs per new establishment in the 1990s vs. 4.9 jobs per new establishment in 2009). Additionally, businesses that survive beyond the first year are adding jobs at a historically slower rate (Reedy & Litan, 2011). These authors conclude that rising numbers of the self-employed, particularly those associated with an increase in contract employment, are not the most effective target for entrepreneurship strategies, since many of these enterprises may not grow and employ others. Rather, "the clear challenge for the US economy instead is to *start more employer businesses*, *ensure that they are starting larger*, and *nurture their growth*" (Reedy & Litan, 2011, p. 16). This research provides context for targeting entrepreneurs who are building growth or Stage 2 businesses as a core part of an entrepreneur-focused development strategy.[1]

While there is a research base documenting the role and importance of entrepreneurs in economic development, this research lacks clarity as a guide for practice and policy. Guidance for community practitioners and policy-makers comes from the implementation, assessment, and evolution, over the past two or more decades, of the interventions associated with entrepreneurship practice. These interventions have moved from the formation of specific programs to the creation of individual support organizations to a more intentional focus on ecosystem development. This evolutionary process is illustrated with specific examples below.

Entrepreneurship programs

The origins of many of today's entrepreneurial support programs can be traced to federal recognition of the important role that small businesses play in the economy, resulting in the creation of programs including SCORE (Service Corps of Retired Executives), the Minority Business Development Agency, the Small Business Development Center system, and Women's Business Centers. Concurrently, the incubation movement began in the late 1950s but increased in acceptance in the 1980s and 1990s, with the development of notable state (e.g. Pennsylvania, one of the first states to adopt a state-wide incubation policy) and private sector efforts (e.g. Control Data Corporation, operating several of the earliest business incubators that became models for others.) Another private sector actor, The Kauffman Foundation, played an important role in training (i.e. FastTRAC), research, advocacy, and policy development.

More recent advancements in program offerings provide more targeted assistance to entrepreneurs identified through a variety of means. Accelerators, most often based in urban places (e.g. TechStars in Boulder, Colorado), combine rigorous screening of entrepreneurs with intensive mentoring and assistance over a defined period of time to help entrepreneurs move through the start-up phase. Economic Gardening, an approach to economic development pioneered in Littleton, Colorado, provides an alternative "grow from within strategy" for regional development, focused on providing market intelligence and strategic information to existing entrepreneurial companies with the potential for growth.

Entrepreneurial support organizations

The evolution toward entrepreneurial support organizations is, in part, a product of what Feldman (2014, p. 17) describes as the shift in focus of economic development "from a preoccupation with lagging regions and eradication of poverty to a new focus on innovation and international competitiveness that is universally relevant to the full range of communities." Two of the earliest place-based entrepreneurial support organizations, Kentucky Highlands Investment Corporation (serving Appalachian Kentucky) and Coastal Enterprises Inc. (serving coastal Maine), were innovative Title VII community development corporations with a focus on job creation in areas of persistent poverty. These organizations, started in the late 1960s, evolved from a focus on creating jobs to supporting entrepreneurs by channeling technical assistance, capital access, and capacity building within their regions.

Other place-based organizations evolved from other movements or initiatives such as the federal Manufacturing Extension Partnership program. Northern Initiatives began in the mid-1980s in the Upper Peninsula of Michigan as a university-based Manufacturing Extension Partnership program. Over time, the organization has combined their technical assistance capacity with the tools of a Community Development Financial Institution to serve entrepreneurs in an ever-expanding region.

Ecosystem development

Both entrepreneurship programs and entrepreneurial support organizations focus on increasing the supply of technical assistance, other advisory services, and capital available to entrepreneurs. In 2001, Lichtenstein and Lyons argued that such an approach was not sufficient to create the scale of impact needed for regional economic development. "Entrepreneurs do not start businesses because services are available; services are demanded and used as the result of the existence of entrepreneurs. Although services are necessary, they are not sufficient to transform a region's economy into a dynamic force" (Lichtenstein & Lyons, 2001, p. 5). What is needed instead is a systems approach based on growing the pipeline of talent in a region and connecting that talent to an integrated, facilitated support network of service providers. The EDS (Lichtenstein & Lyons, 2001) described in more detail below is one approach to ecosystem development.

The evolution of entrepreneurship practice marks the beginning of a shift from a supply-side to a demand-side focus, from providing services to developing the pool of entrepreneurs. Lichtenstein and Lyons (2001, 2010) effectively argue that this pool of entrepreneurs can be expanded over time and present a model to do so and evidence of its effectiveness. However, enterprise development is essentially a place-based activity. In the short term, at least, entrepreneurs are rooted to a particular place. The capacity of the community or region to embrace and advance ecosystem development becomes a precursor to, a necessary condition for, developing entrepreneurial talent.

Importance of place in economic development

Increased globalization and technological innovations bring into question the place-based nature of economic development. In fact, one argument in favor of entrepreneurship as a development strategy particularly for rural places is the fact that, increasingly, one can start and grow a business from anywhere. Yet, at least in the USA, communities, counties, and to some extent regional development entities are responsible for economic development planning. Absent a strong and centrally determined industrial or economic policy, local jurisdictions are charged with designing and implementing economic development strategies to achieve growth and prosperity. And, for these local and regional entities, place does matter.

The importance of place derives from the need for asset-based economic development, what Kretzmann and McKnight (1993) describe as "capacity-focused development." There continues to be a strong rationale and theoretical basis for building on the assets of a place (Emery & Flora, 2006). In a time of constrained federal resources, local communities, rural and urban, determine their own economic futures by the decisions they make to support and build upon their assets, including their entrepreneurial talent.

For rural communities with more limited capacity to engage in effective economic development, the relationship between place and entrepreneurship is critical. Korsgaard, Müller, and Tanvig (2011, p. 7) argue that rural entrepreneurship involves a "dual and complementary dynamic." Entrepreneurs create economic value from the local assets they use and are more likely to combine rural assets in unique and innovative ways to pursue a market opportunity. The result is a more effective use of rural resources to drive economic activity that provides benefits to both the entrepreneurs and, through jobs, revenue, and tax payments, to the community. Entrepreneurs also impact the social structure and value of the place itself. For example, the presence of a vibrant community of entrepreneurs may create an atmosphere of innovation encouraging imagination and creativity in the next generation of entrepreneurs. Likewise, area entrepreneurs may nurture generosity and encourage philanthropy in the community. In turn, rural entrepreneurs are potentially more likely to remain in their rural locale if they are deriving value from both the economic and social/cultural assets of that place.

Korsgaard et al's thesis (2011) on the connection between place and rural entrepreneurs focuses on entrepreneurs as the primary actors in a place. However, the broader community, through its leadership and decision-making choices, also plays a role in determining the characteristics, resources, and capacity for economic development. Entrepreneurs operate within a particular economic and community environment. While they drive decision-making related to how they combine assets to respond to market opportunities, their ability to easily access the resources needed to build their own skills and further develop their business enterprise may be determined by the community's capacity and commitment to entrepreneur-focused economic development. According to Feldman (2014, p. 20), "entrepreneurial attachments and investment, government capacity building, and local communities of common interest define the character of a place. In my conceptualization, geography provides a platform to organize resources toward a specific purpose." In the context of this article, that purpose is the development of entrepreneurs.

Community capacity building for ecosystem development

Methods

In order to better understand the nature and composition of a holistic system for fostering entrepreneurship as a community economic development strategy, we engaged in action research in three rural regions – the state of Kansas in the USA and two sub-state regions in Victoria, Australia. Action research is a research method that engages directly with practitioners in their context for the purpose of finding solutions to problems and developing best practices (Argyris, Putnam, & Smith, 1985; Denscombe, 2010; Greenwood & Levin, 2007; Schein, 1999). At its essence, action research is a process of problem identification, field data gathering and analysis, sharing findings with participants, mutually acting on those results, and jointly reflecting on the outcomes of the action (Berg, 2008).

In Kansas, the local participants were community leaders, including those acting as community coaches, as well as the staff of regional and statewide organizations, such as NetWork Kansas, who were partners in ecosystem development. One of the authors of this paper provided remote and on-site research, community engagement and coaching support, strategy development, and sustainability planning with local and state partners beginning in 2008 and continuing into 2015.

In the Australian sites, the local participants were faculty and staff of the college administering the enterprise development program in question, on-site enterprise developers/coaches, local government officials, and entrepreneurs. One of the authors of this paper spent several months in 2013 and 2014 remotely working with college officials and the local enterprise developers to identify the problems to be addressed and to design and implement the program. In the summer of 2014, that author spent a month in Australia meeting with all the participants to better understand their needs, discuss the program's utility, and modify the program to meet the needs. This latter activity involved individual meetings, workshops, seminars, and bus tours of local entrepreneurial ventures.

The regions under study were selected because they are representative of the Macke et al. (Kansas) and the Lichtenstein and Lyons (Australia) approaches. They also permit examination across distinct communities in an international context. In this way, they serve as case studies for comparison and from which to cull common themes (Yin, 2003).

This methodology has its limitations. The results cannot be generalized to a larger population, nor are they conclusive (Hamilton, 1981). Baskerville (1999, p. 5) has argued that action research is more social inquiry than social science. However, we emphasize that the intention here is not to test theory but to build it.

The remainder of this section lays out the elements of a capacity-building framework for creating entrepreneurial communities, describes the elements of an entrepreneur development system, and identifies opportunities for accelerated outcomes through the intentional combination of these frameworks into an effective ecosystem.

Entrepreneurial communities framework

Communities need capacity to actively design, implement, and sustain an economic development strategy focused on entrepreneurs. Based on more than a decade of action research, the Center for Rural Entrepreneurship has developed a framework to help communities build the capacity to leverage their assets in support of entrepreneur-focused economic development (Macke et al., 2014). Each component of the framework serves to identify, build, or direct investment in the assets needed to support economic development. It is a framework that builds the capitals needed to create an entrepreneur development system, where those capitals are defined consistent with the Community Capitals framework. The components of this framework are outlined in more detail below and illustrated using action research in Kansas.

Readiness and organizing

Economic development, particularly when the goal is the transformation of a local or regional economy, must involve a long-term process and commitment. To generate economic development outcomes, communities must invest human and financial capital and have the political consensus to stay the course long enough to first build capacity and then achieve results. This course of action requires a degree of readiness on the part of the community, often associated with building the intellectual capital associated with seeing entrepreneurship as a development strategy and having the political capital to influence the community's preferred course of action related to economic development. Once that readiness is established, the community must create or strengthen the social capital needed to create an effective organizational structure to guide the process and commit the financial capital to support that organizing effort. The commitment to entrepreneurship and to building entrepreneurial communities in Kansas demonstrates this process (Markley & Binerer, 2014).

Public sector commitment to entrepreneurship development in Kansas began in 2001 with the launch of a pilot project focused on implementing Sirolli's Enterprise Facilitation® model (Sirolli, 1999) in several multi-county regions. Based on the lessons learned from this early initiative and strong collaborative support from key legislators, state agency staff, and business service providers, the Kansas Economic Growth Act of 2004 cemented support for entrepreneurship as a core development strategy through the creation of a center for rural entrepreneurship; NetWork Kansas was established as that central hub in 2005. Through this legislation, the state signaled a readiness to embrace entrepreneurship, provided an organizing structure for distinct partners to collaborate toward that end, and provided financial capital to support both the creation of this infrastructure and the aspirations of the state's entrepreneurs.

In Kansas, readiness and organizing at the state level also transferred to the community level. NetWork Kansas' entrepreneurial leaders recognized the need to create community capacity to connect more effectively to the state's infrastructure. The E-Community Partnership was created to build stronger community capacity for entrepreneur-focused economic development. Readiness and local organizing were influenced by the best practices of the more successful partners and codified over time into the application process. Concurrent with NetWork Kansas' community engagement process, other efforts across the state focused on building community capacity for entrepreneurship through community coaching and the application of elements of the HomeTown Competitiveness® model (Kansas Farm Bureau, 2011).

Assessment

Readiness and organizing create the foundation for launching an entrepreneurship strategy; assessment provides communities with a deeper understanding of their development assets and opportunities. The assessment process targets five focus areas tied to entrepreneurship:

(1) Development opportunities: understanding a community's current economic structure, its place in a broader regional and statewide economy, relevant emerging sectors, and demographic trends that might be supportive of or detracting from development efforts.
(2) Entrepreneurial talent: identifying and understanding entrepreneurs, the primary assets upon which an entrepreneur-focused economic development strategy is built.
(3) Relevant resources: mapping current local and other resources that, with appropriate connections, could make up the ecosystem infrastructure serving entrepreneurs.
(4) Development goals: identifying a community's development goals and aligning an entrepreneur development strategy to achieve desired outcomes.
(5) Stakeholders: engaging stakeholders in the community or region who have a self-interest in the development of entrepreneurs and the economic development outcomes that result.

Assessment provides the information needed to drive more effective strategy development. In Kansas, assessment is a key part of efforts being undertaken by multiple partners to build entrepreneurial communities, and the information from these assessments is used in communities to design relevant strategies to address their development goals (Macke, 2013).

Strategy development and implementation

An effective strategy confronts the constraints of human, financial, and political capital by targeting development efforts to achieve the greatest return on investment. In this case, the targeting relates to the entrepreneurs prioritized by the community. Organizations have limited staff time and budget capacity. Stakeholders (particularly elected officials responsive to election cycles) increasingly focus on return on investment, wanting to achieve the greatest outcomes for their investments, in the shortest period of time. An effectively designed and well-implemented strategy focused on entrepreneurs with the potential to achieve desired outcomes is one way to increase the return on investment.

An entrepreneurial talent assessment helps to identify the community's pipeline of entrepreneurs (Figure 1), including opportunity entrepreneurs, defined by GEM as those who are "pulled into entrepreneurship" because they recognize opportunities and choose to pursue them (Xavier et al., 2012, p. 28). An effective community-based strategy for entrepreneur development would focus on identifying and providing resources to opportunity entrepreneurs so they can accelerate economic development impacts they create.

A key part of the strategy put in place in Kansas communities has been to have an engaged community identify and connect entrepreneurs to a diverse yet coordinated set of resources needed to support the entrepreneurs' growth aspirations and potential. The result has been a stronger set of economic development activities and outcomes. Using

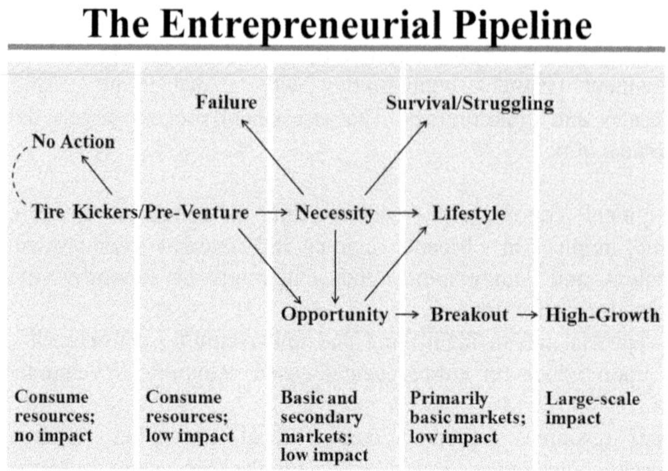

Figure 1. Conception of the entrepreneurial pipeline.
Source: Center for Rural Entrepreneurship, 2014.

data only from NetWork Kansas over the 2007 to 2013 period, the following outcomes were documented (Markley & Binerer, 2014, p. 22)[2]:

- Increased development impacts: nearly 400 business development deals associated with NetWork Kansas and E-Community partner efforts; $61 million in capital allocated and leveraged; 1060 full-time and 865 part-time jobs created.
- Increased access to resources for entrepreneurs and support providers: number of partners increased from 9 to more than 500; active contacts increased from 5 to 436 per month; total calls increased from 23 to 192 per month; website requests increased from 74 to 179 per month.
- Increased reach of community engagement efforts: 44 E-Community partners covering 39 counties (37% of the state's geography); 70% of E-Community partners have less than 10,000 population.

Scaling, impact, and transformation

A key question related to the entrepreneurial community-building efforts in Kansas is whether they are resulting in the transformation of community futures leading to widespread prosperity, particularly in more rural places. The research base to support an answer to this question is limited. However, there is anecdotal evidence of changing trends in a few communities with a longer history of building and strengthening community capacity for entrepreneurial development. While the state has benefited recently from a strong agricultural and energy-based economy, the impacts on rural communities have been uneven. Rawlins County, an ongoing participant in the evolving work in Kansas, has experienced several potentially transformational changes in long-established trends (Macke, 2013):

- After almost three decades of stable or declining income, personal income generated by nonfarm proprietors (a proxy for entrepreneurs) increased 133% from 2000 to 2010, a period coinciding with the community's focus on entrepreneurial development;

- County population increased from 2009 to 2010 for the first time since the 1930s; and
- elementary school enrollment, declining from 2000–2001 to 2006–2007, stabilized in 2006–2007 and grew in the 2009–2010 school year.

The outcomes achieved in this single community represent the results of intentional efforts to build community capacity for ecosystem development and the unique application of the community's assets to this challenge.

More evidence of the outcomes associated with the entrepreneurial communities framework comes from Emery and Flora (2006). This framework grew out of one component of HomeTown Competitiveness (HTC), a comprehensive approach to community development. Emery and Flora applied the Community Capitals Framework to one community's application of HTC, including entrepreneurship development, and found increases in multiple capitals and a spiraling up in the community as a result of these interactions. While the evidence from these communities is promising, further research is needed to understand how application of this framework can build a community's capacity to achieve similar results.

EDS framework

While the entrepreneurial communities framework described above focuses on the community as the critical actor, the heart of Lichtenstein and Lyons's (2001, 2010) EDS framework is the entrepreneur. They offer a new enterprise development paradigm based on a number of clear principles:

(1) The primary focus of enterprise development efforts must shift from providing services to developing entrepreneurs.
(2) Economies require different kinds of entrepreneurs and, therefore, the focus of development efforts must be to create a diverse mix of entrepreneurs rather than a specific focus on one type of talent. A corollary to this principle is that if a community is going to invest in Stage 2 entrepreneurs (firms with 10–99 employees) as an economic development strategy, it must also invest in the development of first stage entrepreneurs who will become the next generation of Stage 2 entrepreneurs.
(3) To achieve transformation of a local community, attention must be given to improving the network of relationships (social capital) that exists within the business community so that a shift in the performance of all entrepreneurs and their firms occurs.
(4) Entrepreneurs need a range of skills to start and grow an enterprise, and they typically start the entrepreneurial process without all the skills they need; those skills can be intentionally developed over time.

The operational model for this new enterprise development paradigm is the EDS. The central challenge of the EDS is how to "effectively, efficiently, equitably, and continuously develop entrepreneurial talent and build successful companies on a large scale" (Lichtenstein & Lyons, 2001, p. 11). The model includes two significant and interconnected systems: a system for developing the skills of entrepreneurs and a system for organizing and rationalizing support partners.

System for developing the skills of entrepreneurs

Drawing on research in a variety of disciplines, Lichtenstein and Lyons (2001) identify four categories of skills needed to create, operate, and grow a business:

- Technical: ability to perform key business operations;
- Managerial: ability to organize and manage business operations;
- Entrepreneurial: ability to identify and seize market opportunities; and
- Personal maturity: level of self-awareness, creativity, emotional development, and ability to shoulder responsibility.

Each entrepreneur begins the enterprise development process with a particular set of skills that can be assessed, and the entrepreneur can be assigned to a particular rung on the development ladder (Table 1).

The goal of this skill-building system is to create a stronger pipeline of entrepreneurs in a community or region. To illustrate the pipeline concept, Lichtenstein and Lyons (2006) add another dimension to the analysis: stage of business development. These stages encompass the life cycle of an enterprise:

- Stage 0 – Pre-venture: idea to product or service launch;
- Stage 1 – Existence or infancy: launch to break even from sales;
- Stage 2 – Early growth: from break even to sustainable, profitable business;
- Stage 3 – Expansion or sustained growth: from incurring debt or risking equity to pursue growth to emergence as a growth company;
- Stage 4 – Maturity: from market advantage to adapting and preserving entrepreneurial spirit and market advantage; and
- Stage 5 – Decline: from complacency to either shuttering or reinvention.

The two-dimensional pipeline (Table 2) demonstrates that a goal of the EDS is to move entrepreneurs through the pipeline in both directions: first by building the entrepreneur's skills and then applying those increased skills to the successful growth of the enterprise itself. It expands upon the opportunity entrepreneur category embedded in the pipeline concept described earlier in this article.[3]

Key components of the skill development system are accurate assessment of the starting point for each entrepreneur and then effective coaching to help the entrepreneurs move up the skills ladder, enabling them to make the structural changes in their businesses necessary to move from one life cycle stage to the next. Kutzhanova, Lyons, and Lichtenstein (2009) address the important role of coaching in creating the conditions under which individual entrepreneurs experience the transformations needed to move

Table 1. Entrepreneurship skill levels.

Skill dimension/skill level	Technical	Managerial	Entrepreneurial	Personal maturity
Level 5	Superior	Superior	Superior	Superior
Level 4	High	High	High	High
Level 3	Moderate	Moderate	Moderate	Moderate
Level 2	Low	Low	Low	Low
Level 1	Low to no	Low to no	Low to no	Low to no

Source: Adapted from Lichtenstein and Lyons (2001).

Table 2. Conception of the entrepreneurial pipeline.

Life Cycle/ Skill Level	Stage 0 Pre-venture	Stage 1 Existence	Stage 2 Early growth	Stage 3 Expansion	Stage 4 Maturity	Stage 5 Decline
Level 5						
Level 4						
Level 3						
Level 2						
Level 1						

Source: Adapted from Lichtenstein and Lyons (2006).

from one skill level to the next. Successful skill building hinges upon learning how to apply knowledge through strategically identified, intensive practice, with regular feedback. The coach helps the entrepreneur identify what needs to be practiced, focus on a regimen of practice, and understand what is and is not working as the entrepreneur builds her/his skills (Lichtenstein & Lyons, 2010). Action research in Australia provides insights into the skill assessment and building process.

EntruBIZ is a rural entrepreneurship development effort in Victoria, Australia, implemented by the Center for the Study of Rural Australia at Marcus Oldham College, a higher education institution located in Geelong, focused on business and agriculture, and funded by the William Buckland Foundation. This effort is applying the elements of the EDS to assess entrepreneur skills, identify opportunities to apply coaching and mentoring, and develop innovative businesses to increase community and regional prosperity. More specifically, EntruBiz has established offices in the regional centers of two rural regions in Victoria: Shepparton in the Goulburn-Murray Region (an agricultural region specializing in fruit, livestock, and wine production) and Bairnsdale in the Gippsland Region (an agricultural and tourism region). Each of these offices houses a coach, known as a Rural Enterprise Developer (RED). The REDs provide four key services to the entrepreneurs of their region: (1) an assessment of the entrepreneur's skills; (2) help with developing the business concept; (3) one-on-one coaching for skill development; and (4) referral to appropriate local service providers for specialized knowledge and/or technical and financial assistance.

At the heart of EntruBiz's entrepreneur-focused approach is the Readiness Inventory for Successful Entrepreneurship (RISE) tool, developed by Drs. Thomas S. Lyons and John S. Lyons. This tool employs the communimetric model of psychological assessment, which is clinical as opposed to psychometric, permitting a current diagnosis of the entrepreneur's strengths and weaknesses and the ability to make an informed intervention that can leverage the strengths and address the weaknesses (Lyons, 2009; Lyons & Lyons, 2002). The RISE builds on Lichtenstein and Lyons's (2001) research on entrepreneurship skills (noted above) by identifying four new dimensions of skill, or management skill categories: (1) Transformation Management Skills – the skills needed for creativity and innovation; (2) Relationship Management Skills – the skills required for building social capital; (3) Business Management Skills – the skills of day-to-day business administration; and (4) Organizational Process Management Skills – the skills needed to sustain an organization. The RISE is a web-based tool designed to identify an entrepreneur's skills at several levels, including an overall skills assessment that can be used by a coach to develop a support plan to grow the entrepreneur's skills over time. Given the importance of skill development to the success of the EDS, this type of field-based assessment offers the opportunity to better align an entrepreneur's need for skill development with the service providers best able to meet that need, improving the efficiency and the effectiveness of the EDS.

System for organizing and rationalizing support partners

Central to the skill building activities of the skill development system is access to the right type and level of support at the right time (Lyons, 2002a). The focus of the service provider system is not to create new resources, but rather to organize and coordinate existing resources into a more effectively operating system of support. This process provides benefits to service providers by improving efficiency and reducing wasted effort when entrepreneurs are better matched with service providers; improving outcomes when service providers are connected with entrepreneurs before the crisis stage; and offering economies of scale when services are offered to entrepreneurs at a similar skill level (Lichtenstein & Lyons, 2001).

In Australia, the EntruBiz program operates in rural regions where formal service providers of the type discussed earlier in this paper are few. Thus, the REDs cast a wider net on behalf of their client entrepreneurs, identifying individuals who can act as role models and mentors and nontraditional sources of technical and financial assistance. The RISE assessment is used as the guide for determining the intervention required, and then the REDs become highly innovative in scouring the context for sources of support. Subsequent RISE assessments can measure the entrepreneur's skill building progress and guide the RED in determining when a particular service provider is no longer appropriate and a new, more relevant, one must be found.

While EntruBiz was about one year old at this writing and still installing and refining its system, making meaningful measurement of its impact premature, the EDS model has proven effective in several pilot projects. In the Advantage Valley (an 11-county region spanning parts of Kentucky, Ohio, and West Virginia), for example, over a 38-month period, the following outcomes were achieved (Kutzhanova et al., 2009, p. 206):

- $33 of sales revenue generated by EDS clients for every dollar invested in the system;
- 13% of the total sales revenue increase was generated by sales outside the region;
- 49 new direct jobs were generated, sans a multiplier effect;
- a cost per job created of $34,344, which is substantially lower than that of the average business attraction strategy in the USA; and
- a strong correlation between sales revenue generated and the skill level of the entrepreneur, with each skill level generating multiples of the revenue produced by the skill level just below.

Connecting frameworks for ecosystem development

The entrepreneurial communities framework and the EDS approach recognize the inherent strengths in taking a more holistic approach to entrepreneur-focused economic development. They acknowledge the central role that the entrepreneur plays in driving enterprise development and the important role that coaching plays in building the skills of the entrepreneur. They recognize the value of coordination and collaboration among resource providers to create a more seamless and efficient system of support for entrepreneurs. They are ultimately focused on community transformation as the outcome of the entrepreneur development process.

The two frameworks also offer the potential to create a more powerful place-based entrepreneurial development ecosystem and, in turn, more sustainable development impacts if viewed as interlocking components of a single system. Figure 2 proposes a model for such an integrated system. The Entrepreneurial Communities framework lays the groundwork through its readiness, investment and assessment approach designed to build the community's capacity (capitals). When the community is ready, critical investments can be made to put into place a strategy for rural enterprise development, using the EDS's pipeline and support partner systems. The expected result is a community transformed – economically, socially, culturally, and politically. Such a connected approach would create advantages in several dimensions.

Advantages

First, the EDS requires an inflow of entrepreneurial talent into the pipeline in order to be transformational. An organized entrepreneurial community can provide that inflow by cultivating latent entrepreneurial talent, such as intentional efforts to expose youth to

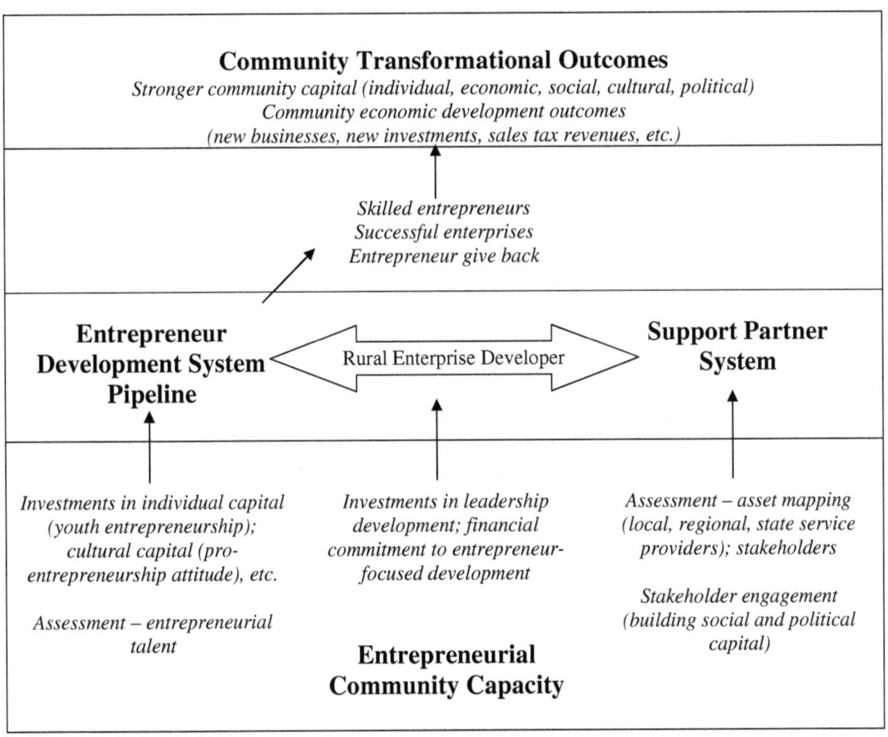

Figure 2. Place-based entrepreneurial development ecosystem.

entrepreneurship through educational programming, summer camps, job shadowing, and internships. Second, an organized entrepreneurial community can provide the foundation for and help to strengthen the system of support providers critical to the successful functioning of the EDS. The organizing and assessment processes that are part of the entrepreneurial communities framework identify key resources and stakeholders, including service providers. The social capital built through this process creates the type of system critically important to an effective EDS.

A third advantage relates to the need to demonstrate impacts quickly in order to build momentum and sustain efforts to achieve transformational change. Through its assessment of entrepreneurial skills, the EDS can help identify and target particular interventions to entrepreneurs with the potential to create greater economic development returns. However, the EDS also requires that the community commit to the development of new talent and not use targeting as a way to skim entrepreneurial talent (Lichtenstein & Lyons, 2010). The tools and structure provided by the EDS become powerful tools in the hands of a community's business coach. Fourth, the EDS provides a proven framework for developing entrepreneurs in sufficient numbers to create impacts, at scale, over time. When applied strategically by an entrepreneurial community, the EDS can create the kinds of development outcomes that lead to transformation and prosperity.

Two additional advantages of this more powerful connected ecosystem approach relate to sustainability. Ultimately, the sustainability of an entrepreneurial ecosystem in any community will depend upon continued investment. Financial investment is important, as well as investment of time and talent via mentoring and community leadership. Successful place-based entrepreneurs have an important role to play in giving back to the community. They may give back by supporting community-based philanthropy, mentoring young entrepreneurs, becoming angel investors, or supporting youth entrepreneurship education. Entrepreneurs, developed through an EDS, become a vital component of the entrepreneurial community going forward.

A sustainable entrepreneurial ecosystem depends on quality of place investments that attract and retain entrepreneurial talent and their ventures. If entrepreneurs can start and grow a business anywhere, entrepreneurial communities must invest to create a place that has the assets that entrepreneurs are seeking. While business climate is important, the willingness of entrepreneurs to cluster in high-cost locations (e.g. Silicon Valley, Boston) suggests that broader community amenities carry sway in the decision about where to start, grow, and sustain an entrepreneurial venture. An organized, committed entrepreneurial community can bring its social and political capital to bear on discussions about investing to create and maintain a quality of life that is attractive to a range of entrepreneurial talent.

Conditions and requirements for success

While there are clear advantages to the more holistic approach of bringing the entrepreneurial communities framework and the EDS approach into alignment, such an approach brings with it a set of conditions for success that must be addressed. First, systems building for transformational impact and community capacity building both require a long-term commitment. Key leaders and other stakeholders need to be dedicated to a long-term agenda. At the same time, building the capacity of the community to effectively engage in the process of entrepreneur-focused economic development in combination with the implementation of the key elements of an entrepreneur development system offers the opportunity to accelerate the impact and build continued support for entrepreneurship.

Second, these frameworks, alone or combined, require collaboration among partner organizations. While such collaboration is necessary and recognized as such, rarely is the cost of collaboration acknowledged or funded. Investment in building strong social capital may address this challenge, along with efforts to measure and communicate to key stakeholders the value that collaboration creates.

Third, entrepreneur development as described in this article requires a shift in focus from supporting the business to supporting the entrepreneur. This shift has been slow to come to conventional business support organizations and economic development entities. The EDS articulation of the need for skill building to drive enterprise development may add some additional evidence to encourage this shift in smaller communities and regions.

Fourth, there is a need to shift policy along with practice toward supporting and encouraging more holistic solutions, such as those articulated here, versus creating new, programmatic interventions. The latter tend to be categorical and lead to fragmentation of effort and an inability to meet the entrepreneurs' true needs.

Fifth, if the goal of a more holistic approach to entrepreneur development is community prosperity, these efforts must result in a scale of impact that is measurable and transformational. Measurable impacts are necessary to continue support and investment in a systems approach. Transformation will occur when the capacity of the community to support entrepreneurs and the entrepreneurs' skills in starting and growing enterprises become positively reinforcing.

Conclusion

The aim of this article is to offer new insights through the intentional juxtaposition of two complementary frameworks. While the entrepreneurial communities framework is focused on building the *capacity of communities* to organize and build on their assets in support of entrepreneur-focused development, the EDS is focused on building the *capacity of entrepreneurs* to start and grow their enterprises. Together these frameworks provide a more holistic approach to undertaking the long-term, often generational, work of creating community prosperity through entrepreneur development. This exercise raises several key research and policy questions that are worthy of future attention:

(1) How can we best organize and fund field experiments that allow for the testing of the holistic approach to creating entrepreneurial communities discussed herein?
(2) How can we better measure the impact of these systems approaches on development outcomes over time? To what extent can we attribute causality to these approaches?
(3) What policy changes are necessary to better support more holistic approaches to entrepreneur development? What similar models exist in other countries that might inform the development of effective policy in the USA?
(4) How must community economic development research adapt to document the impacts of long-term community change brought about through the application of frameworks such as those discussed in this article? What longitudinal research models would be most effective?

Disclosure statement

No potential conflict of interest was reported by the authors.

Notes

1. Stage 2 businesses are defined by the Edward Lowe Foundation as those businesses with 10–99 employees (www.youreconomy.org).
2. These outcomes were achieved through a comprehensive approach to entrepreneurial support, involving multiple partners in both the public and private sectors. The Center's framework both contributed to and benefited from the action research and learning afforded in Kansas.
3. This approach addresses the question of how communities can predict when a business reaches Stage 2 – they cannot. However, this is not necessary when you can assess where an entrepreneur's skill level currently lies and track her skill level advancement *and* trace the progression of her business through its life cycle stages.

References

Acs, Z. J., & Armington, C. (2004). Employment growth and entrepreneurial activity in cities. *Regional Studies, 38*, 911–927.

Argyris, C., Putnam, R., & Smith, D. (1985). *Action science: Concepts, methods, and skills for research and interventions*. San Francisco, CA: Jossey-Bass.

Aulet, B., & Murray, F. (2013). *A tale of two entrepreneurs: Understanding differences in the types of entrepreneurship in the economy.* The Kauffman Foundation. Retrieved July 28, 2014, from http://www.kauffman.org/~/media/kauffman_org/research%20reports%20and%20covers/2013/05/ataleoftwoentrepreneurs.pdf

Baskerville, R. L. (1999). Investigating information systems with action research. *Communications of the Association for Information Systems, 2*(1), 1–31. Article 19.

Baumol, W. (1990). Entrepreneurship: Productive, unproductive, and destructive. *The Journal of Political Economy, 98*, 893–921.

Berg, B. (2008). *Qualitative research methods for the social sciences*. Boston, MA: Allyn & Bacon.

Denscombe, M. (2010). *Good research guide: For small-scale social research projects* (4th ed.). Berkshire: Open University Press.

Eliasson, G., & Henrekson, M. (2003). *William J. Baumol: An entrepreneurial economist on the economics of entrepreneurship* (SSE/EFI Working Paper Series in Economics and Finance, No. 532). Retrieved July 22, 2014, from http://swopec.hhs.se/hastef/papers/hastef0532.pdf

Emery, M., & Flora, C. (2006). Spiraling-up: Mapping community transformation with community capitals framework. *Journal of the Community Development Society, 37*, 19–35.

Feldman, M. P. (1994). The university and economic development: The case of Johns Hopkins University and Baltimore. *Economic Development Quarterly, 8*, 67–76.

Feldman, M. P. (2014). The character of innovative places: Entrepreneurial strategy, economic development, and prosperity. *Small Business Economics, 43*, 9–20. Retrieved July 30, 2014, from http://link.springer.com/article/10.1007%2Fs11187-014-9574-4

Flora, J. L., Sharp, J., Flora, C., & Newlon, B. (1997). Entrepreneurial social infrastructure and locally initiated economic development in the nonmetropolitan United States. *The Sociological Quarterly, 38*, 623–645.

Fritsch, M., & Mueller, P. (2008). The effects of new business formation on regional development over time: The case of Germany. *Small Business Economics, 30*, 15–29.

Granovetter, M. (1985). Economic action and social structure: The problem of embeddedness. *American Journal of Sociology, 91*, 481–510.

Greenwood, D. J., & Levin, M. (2007). *Introduction to action research* (2nd ed.). Thousand Oaks, CA: Sage.

Hafer, R. W. (2013). Entrepreneurship and state economic growth. *Journal of Entrepreneurship and Public Policy, 2*, 67–79.

Hamilton, D. (1981). Educational research in the educational sciences: Problems and purposes. In T. S. Popkewitz & B. R. Tabachnick (Eds.), *The study of schooling: Field methodologies in educational research and evaluation* (pp. 227–241). New York, NY: Praeger.

Kane, T. (2010). *The importance of startups in job creation and job destruction.* The Kauffman Foundation. Retrieved July 29, 2014, from http://www.kauffman.org/~/media/kauffman_org/research%20reports%20and%20covers/2012/07/firm_formation_importance_of_startups.pdf

Kansas Farm Bureau. (2011). *Search for solutions: The future of rural Kansas* (Kansas Hometown Prosperity Initiative Report). Retrieved July 28, 2014, from https://energizingentrepreneursorg.presencehost.net/file_download/b53129ab-ddbd-4097-afd0-7a23ff5b9384

Korsching, P. F., & Allen, J. C. (2004). Local entrepreneurship: A development model based on community interaction field theory. *Journal of the Community Development Society, 35*, 25–43.

Korsgaard, S., Müller, S., & Tanvig, H. (2011, June 15–18). *Rural entrepreneurship: Between place and space.* Paper presented at the 56th Annual International Council for Small Business (ICSB) Conference, Stockholm, Sweden.

Kretzmann, J. P., & McKnight, J. L. (1993). *Building communities from the inside out: A path toward finding and mobilizing a community's assets.* Evanston, IL: Institute for Policy Research.

Kutzhanova, N., Lyons, T. S., & Lichtenstein, G. A. (2009). Skill-based development of entrepreneurs and the role of personal and peer group coaching in enterprise development. *Economic Development Quarterly, 23*, 193–210.

Lichtenstein, G. A., & Lyons, T. S. (2001). The entrepreneurial development system: Transforming business talent and community economies. *Economic Development Quarterly, 15*, 3–20.

Lichtenstein, G. A., & Lyons, T. S. (2006). Managing the community's pipeline of entrepreneurs and enterprises: A new way of thinking about business assets. *Economic Development Quarterly, 20*, 377–386.

Lichtenstein, G. A., & Lyons, T. S. (2010). *Investing in entrepreneurs: A strategic approach for strengthening your regional and community economy.* Santa Barbara, CA: Praeger/ABC-CLIO.

Lichtenstein, G. A., Lyons, T. S., & Kutzhanova, N. (2004). Building entrepreneurial communities: The appropriate role of enterprise development activities. *Journal of the Community Development Society, 35*(1), 1–20.

Lyons, T. S. (2002a). *The Entrepreneurial League System®: Transforming your community's economy through enterprise development.* Washington, DC: The Appalachian Regional Commission.

Lyons, T. S. (2002b). Building social capital for rural enterprise development: Three case studies in the United States. *Journal of Developmental Entrepreneurship, 7*, 193–216.

Lyons, J. S. (2009). *Communimetrics.* New York, NY: Springer.

Lyons, T. S., & Lyons, J. S. (2002, November 24). *Assessing entrepreneurship skills: The key to effective enterprise development planning?* Association of Collegiate Schools of Planning 2002 Conference, Baltimore, MD.

Macke, D. (2013). *Atwood and Rawlins County Kansas: A development success story.* The Center for Rural Entrepreneurship. Retrieved July 23, 2014, from https://energizingentrepreneursorg.presencehost.net/file_download/2df38a82-0627-44dc-a938-aa61eaaf9910

Macke, D., Markley, D., & Fulwider, J. (2014). *Energizing entrepreneurial communities: A pathway to prosperity.* Lincoln, NE: Center for Rural Entrepreneurship.

Markley, D., & Binerer, A. (2014). *Creating entrepreneurial communities in Kansas: Listening... learning...adapting.* The Center for Rural Entrepreneurship. Retrieved July 22, from http://www.energizingentrepreneurs.org/file_download/c2d3d20f-c9e6-4f1d-bdd2-6997a39b02e2

Reedy, E. J., & Litan, R. E. (2011). *Starting smaller; staying smaller: America's slow leak in job creation.* The Kauffman Foundation. Retrieved July 20, 2014, from http://www.kauffman.org/~/media/kauffman_org/research%20reports%20and%20covers/2011/07/job_leaks_starting_smaller_study.pdf

Schein, E. (1999). *Process consultation revisited.* Reading, MA: Addison-Wesley.

Sirolli, E. (1999). *Ripples from the Zambesi: Passion, entrepreneurship and the rebirth of local economies.* Garbiola Island: New Society Publishers.

Xavier, S. R., Kelley, D., Kew, J., Herrington, M., Vordewülbecke, A., & the Global Entrepreneurship Research Association. (2012). *Global Entrepreneurship Monitor 2012 global report.* Retrieved July 30, 2014, from http://gemconsortium.org/docs/download/2645

Yin, R. K. (2003). *Case study research: Design and methods* (3rd ed.). Thousand Oaks, CA: Sage.

Index

Note: **Bold face** page numbers refer to figures and tables. Page numbers followed with "n" refer to endnotes.

For Product Safety Concerns and Information please contact our EU representative GPSR@taylorandfrancis.com
Taylor & Francis Verlag GmbH, Kaufingerstraße 24, 80331 München, Germany

www.ingramcontent.com/pod-product-compliance
Ingram Content Group UK Ltd.
Pitfield, Milton Keynes, MK11 3LW, UK
UKHW050754180926
475701UK00007B/1033
* 9 7 8 0 3 6 7 5 9 4 7 5 6 *